Mathilde Bourrier · Corinne Bieder
Editors

Risk Communication for the Future

Towards Smart Risk Governance and Safety Management

Editors
Mathilde Bourrier
Geneva School of Social Sciences
University of Geneva
Geneva
Switzerland

Corinne Bieder
Ecole Nationale de l'Aviation Civile
Toulouse
France

Preface

Risk communication is considered an essential pillar in safety and risk science. However, it has too often been reduced to a set of practices and how-to guidelines (Do's and Don'ts) that have prevented this essential part of any safety and risk mitigation strategy from getting the attention that it requires.

Offering a richer perspective on the topic, through a reflection on the underlying assumptions and intentions that are behind any attempt at "communicating" about risks and safety matters, was the ambition of a 3-day workshop held in April 2016 in the spectacular Abbaye of Sorèze, near Toulouse, France. The contributors, international researchers, and professionals in many disciplines and domains were brought together by the NeTWork[1] think tank. It is a tradition of NeTWork to foster relationships and understanding between academics and practitioners. This book is yet another example of the benefit that such dialogue can bring to the public arena. The conversation is just started and we wish to continue to wrestle with risk communication challenges and safety management requirements in the future.

The co-editors, Mathilde Bourrier and Corinne Bieder, are deeply grateful to the FonCSI (Foundation for an Industrial Safety Culture)[2] for the support and funding of this research initiative.

Geneva, Switzerland
Toulouse, France
November 2017

Mathilde Bourrier
Corinne Bieder

---

[1] NeTWork: http://www.network-network.org/.

[2] FonCSI: https://www.foncsi.org/.

Contents

Risk Communication 101: A Few Benchmarks

Mathilde Bourrier

Abstract Risk and crisis communication constitutes a rich field of expertise and practices. For a long time, it has been mainly viewed and still is, as a practical rather than a theory-based approach. Numerous manuals and "how-to" books have been published over the last decades. It is often believed that they provide more recipes, refined over the years, than solid scientific literature upon which an evidence-based risk and crisis communication strategy can be developed and fostered. This review is based partially on a surprise: contrary to what was expected, there is an abundant stock of theories and approaches, albeit very diverse. The intention of this chapter is to guide the reader through some of them, considered, maybe over hastily, as the most prominent. The objective is not to produce an exhaustive review, but rather to provide an orientation in a field, whose popularity is growing throughout industries, companies, public health institutions, and public services.

Keywords Risk communication · Crisis communication · Emerging crises
Risk and safety management

Introduction

Risk and crisis communication constitutes a rich field of expertise and practices. It has long been (and still is) mainly viewed as a practical rather than a theory-based approach. Numerous manuals and "how-to" books have been published over the last decades (Lundgren and McMakin 2009; Heath and O'Hair 2010; Sellnow et al. 2009 to name only a few). It is often believed that they provide more recipes, refined over the years, than solid scientific literature upon which an evidenced-based risk and crisis communication strategy can be developed and fostered (McComas 2006). This review is based partially on a surprise: contrary to

M. Bourrier (✉)
Department of Sociology, Institut de recherches sociologiques, University of Geneva, Geneva, Switzerland
e-mail: Mathilde.bourrier@unige.ch

M. Bourrier and C. Bieder (eds.), *Risk Communication for the Future*, SpringerBriefs in Safety Management, https://doi.org/10.1007/978-3-319-74098-0_1

what was expected, there is an abundant stock of theories and approaches, albeit very diverse. The intention of this chapter is to guide the reader through some of them, considered, maybe too hastily, as the most prominent. The objective is not to produce an exhaustive review, but rather to provide an orientation in a field, whose popularity is growing throughout industries, companies, public health institutions, and public services.

The profile of risk and crisis communication was elevated to a major topic in the aftermath of 9/11 as scenarios of massive terrorist attacks, large-scale natural disaster and the threat of reemerging diseases attracted resources, scholarships, funding, and new concepts (Bastide 2017). Indeed, nowadays it is deemed to be integral to any public policy intervention. However, repeated examples of fiascos and less than adequate campaigns and responses have naturally shed light on complex and often controversial issues that risk and crisis communication involves. The risk communication fiasco concerning anthrax in the United States in the aftermath of the 9/11 attacks is one famous example (Glik 2007). During Hurricane Katrina (2004), it is believed that people died in greater numbers than predicted as a result of internal communication and coordination failures at the State and Federal levels (Gheytanchi et al. 2007; Perrow 2007). The terrible mistakes made in West Africa during the Ebola crisis aggravated relationships with populations already in despair, leading them into hiding (Faye 2015; Calain and Poncin 2015; Le Marcis 2015).

Nevertheless, attempts at promoting breakthroughs in risk and crisis communication in order to promote evidence-based campaigns are on the agenda of numerous powerful organizations. For example, it should be recalled that the topic of risk communication has already been identified as one of the eight core capacities of International Health Regulations (2005) (Malley et al. 2009). Lately, in 2015, World Health Organization, in the aftermath of Ebola Virus Disease Crisis, has set up a working group in charge of drafting "guidelines on building national capacity for communicating health risks during public health emergencies".

Research in the field of risk and crisis communication is at a crossroads: it can both enhance and sophisticate its current tools, or it can look for alternatives to its current work practices and develop new thinking. Indeed, the emergent crises of our times are putting pressure on various types of authorities to develop communication tools and preparedness as well as capacities to deal with unpredictable outcomes and lasting uncertainties. The general philosophy for risk and crisis communication is rather straightforward: planning in advance, announcing early, being transparent, respecting public concerns, and building trust (Abraham 2009): "Be first, be right, be credible" is the slogan of the famous Centers for Disease Control and Prevention (US CDC). But, is it enough?

Risk and crisis communication now has a history of over three decades. It is often associated with technological disasters, natural disasters, floods, bio-terrorism, and sanitary crises (including infectious disease epidemics). But this sort of communication is also associated with a wide range of public health priorities and concerns, such as the hazards of smoking, obesity, air quality, VIH detection, to name only a few. Its profile has been raised, when powerful organizations such as the CDC in the United States issued, in 2002, their Crisis and Risk Emergency Communication (CERC) manual, followed in 2005 by World Health Organization's own guidelines for outbreak communication.

There is a historic distinction between "care communication", "consensus communication", and "crisis communication" (Lundgren and McMakin 2009). Risk and crisis communication differs in definition and scope, however they are also interconnected. As Bennington explains (2014, p. 32): "Risk communication addresses probabilities and potential situations of harm and danger, while crisis communication focuses on a specific event or action that has already occurred or will almost certainly occur in the near future (…). Risk communication messages almost always address likely (future) consequences, are based on some form of persuasive and compelling evidence and are intended to prevent or modify specific behaviors and practices" (…) "crisis communication is an on-going process that occurs during the actual crisis" (…). "It addresses both what is known and not known about a situation".

Interestingly, in today's practice of risk communication at CDC, the two concepts have been merged and are combined in a same model called "Crisis and Emergency Risk Communication" (CERC model).

Disciplines and fields such as psychology, social-psychology, economic psychology, behavioral sciences, sociology, media studies, information technology and political science have greatly contributed to the clarification of what is risk and crisis communication (Glik 2007). One can only stress in this brief overview that "good" risk or crisis communication can do little in the face of massive governance problems, where controversies and conflicts naturally arising inside first-line institutions dealing with complex crises will inevitably also be visible on the outside. Suppressing controversies over uncertainties is not possible. Therefore, crisis management is increasingly becoming a question of (risk) governance (Renn 2008; Haferkorn, *this volume*) rather than being confined only to a question of communication technics.

Risk and crisis communication is a part of risk management, which can be understood as a technical field applying probabilities to articulate and recommend prevention and mitigation strategies—at the technical, organizational, and individual level. Yet, it has long been demonstrated that recommendations based on the balance of risks and benefits, made by experts, are not sufficient. Anthropologist Mary Douglas with political scientist Aaron Wildavsky (1983) pioneered studies, aiming at emphasizing the gap existing between different segments of society on what an acceptable future might look like. Slovic's (2000) numerous studies confirmed that social actors hold different risk perceptions, depending on their position in society. In this book, several chapters touch upon these various issues, and examples of risk communication strategies belonging to different perspectives, and even mixing some of them are presented, reflecting on the tensions that the field is currently experiencing.

In the remainder of the chapter, a brief overview of the main theories in use and their respective merits will introduce the reader to a more complex field. We choose a somewhat chronological presentation for practical reasons. However, the reader should not be lured by an apparent evolutionary trend. In fact, these successive attempts at enriching the field continue to coexist largely in the academic literature and within organizations. Fischhoff cautioned us with this false evolutionary promise already and gave this humorous synthesis reproduced below (1995, p. 138).

- All we have to do is get the numbers right
- All we have to do is tell them the numbers
- All we have to do is explain what we mean by the numbers
- All we have to do is show them that they've accepted similar risks in the past
- All we have to do is show them it's a good deal for them
- All we have to do is treat them nice
- All we have to do is make them partners
- All of the above.

The Crisis, the Experts and the Public

Baseline

Historically, risk and crisis communication has been considered as a subset of technical communication (Ogrizek and Guillery 2000). Mainly, it has been viewed as the communication of some risk to affected parties by experts. The emblematic model of such conception is the classical crisis communication approach, which is mainly instrumental and rests only within risk communication professionals. The idea is to only give the audience the information they need to protect themselves, usually radically (like accepting an evacuation). This crisis communication can be referred to as the firefighters type, where threats are tangible and protection vital. During time of crisis, as Bennington (2014) explains, decision-makers need to "construct a crisis response narrative that (1) meets the organization's goals of informing, reassuring, and protecting the public and (2) instills sufficient confidence in the organization to insure the public will be influenced to take the actions deemed necessary to manage the threat." (p. 8).

The dominant paradigm is to persuade the general public of the sound basis of expert's judgments. Irrationality, misperception, misconception, misinformation, inaccurate reporting, and rumors (Bennington 2014, p. 10) are the main obstacles to be suppressed by "effective" risk and crisis communication strategies.

This rather one-sided view has not disappeared and when it comes to crisis communication, public officials or industry representatives often refer to irrational public fears, or unfounded doubts, that they have to fight. Rumors, myths, urban legends, inaccurate information, fake stories, or conspiracy theories are often targeted as the main limitations of successful campaigns. They have always existed, especially during epidemics (Berce 1993). Nowadays, they have the potential to reach millions of people in an instant through the internet and via social media. Some studies show that rumors and conspiracy theories are now part of mainstream political opinion (Hargrove and Stempel III 2007). As academic research has highlighted since the 1930s, rumors develop and amplify where uncertainties and lack of leadership are apparent (Prasad 1935; Allport and Postman 1947). Rumors help to make sense of what is happening and reduce the level of anxiety. They provide narratives and attribute clear responsibilities. Other scholars also explained that groups with less access to "legitimate" sources of information are more subject to rumors and more prone to disseminate them in their communities (Mirowsky and Ross 1983; Knight 2003).

In this perspective, "educating" and "persuading" the public are the main drivers of any risk communication strategy. Using psychological and behavioral research to establish adequate and efficient messages, and identify proper vehicles (community and/or religious leaders; trustworthy institutions; and now social media) are the main focus of risk communicators, wanting to modify behaviors and reducing what they call "knowledge gaps". Bringing more knowledge in better formats are key to these activities.

First Cracks in the Conventional Wisdom

The "Mental Models approach" grounded in cognitive psychology and artificial intelligence, developed at Carnegie-Mellon by researchers like Baruch Fischhoff and Granger Morgan (Morgan 2002) looks like a first attempt to enrich the perspective. Based on the Radon information program, located at the U.S. EPA (Environmental Protection Agency), researchers established that it is of crucial importance to understand what the audience already knows about the risk, and for crisis communication purposes what is the culture of the audience, to be able to discuss ways to mitigate a crisis. In their publications, they strongly advocate for in-depth qualitative interviews prior to developing risk communication programs of any kind: "Communications can be crafted to fill gaps, reinforce correct beliefs, and correct misconceptions—with some assurance that the messages are to the point and be comprehended by recipients" (Fischhoff 1995, p. 140).

With the "hazard + outrage" approach, later popularized by Sandman (2003), it is argued that the audience's view of risk (as opposed to that of the expert assessing the risk) reflects not only the danger of the action (hazard) but also how people feel about the action, and even more important, what emotions they feel about the action (their outrage).

Later Covello (2010) developed the "Mental Noise approach" which stipulates that when people perceive themselves as being at risk, their ability to hear and process information decreases dramatically. They are preoccupied with a great deal of "internal mental noise" and are less able to attend to externally generated information. His various studies show that the ability to pay attention and to retain information is estimated to be 80% less than normal. This is especially true in sudden and unexpected crises. Unfortunately, this line of research distilled for a long time the idea that emotions are only on the public's side.

Contemporary to these lines of research, Everett Rogers and colleagues (Rogers and Lincaid 1981) developed an approach called the "Convergence Communication approach". For these researchers, communication is an "iterative long-term process" in which the values (culture, experiences, and background) of the risk communication organization and the audience affect the process of communication. In their view, this iterative process will naturally push the two groups (the organization and the audience) to converge on common ground, while exchanging information back and forth. In their theory, exchanging information modifies the outcome, bringing the two sides closer.

Unsurprisingly, these studies contributed to build a long-lasting consensus on the intrinsic qualities of a professional risk and crisis communication campaign (Covello et al. 1988): (i) Audiences tend to simplify messages and reduce their complexity; therefore, it is important to communicate with this principle in mind; (ii) Credibility and believability go hand in hand; therefore, experts really need to be independent; (iii) Risk messages should include some efficacious action that individuals can take to alleviate risk; (iv) Messages should be matched to audience needs and values, and their particular economic, political, and sociological backgrounds; (v) Candor, openness, and transparency are the cornerstones of risk and crisis communication.

From these principles, Covello and Allen (1988) derived seven cardinal rules of risk communication: (i) Accept and involve the public as a partner; (ii) Plan carefully and evaluate your effort; (iii) Listen to the public's specific concerns; (iv) Be honest, frank and open; (v) Work with other credible sources; (vi) Meet the needs of the media; (vii) Speak clearly and with compassion.

For years, these cornerstones of best practices have been the alpha and omega of any serious risk and crisis communicator. Major companies and institutions have largely integrated these principles, at least officially. Yet, they sometimes failed to completely embrace them in practice.

Disputing Experts' Central Position: The Dialogic Turn

Since these pioneered studies, the risk communication field has known different tipping points. One of the main issues of the 1990s has been to revise and recast the central position of experts in the communication process. From all-too-powerful, and central in the production of knowledge and guidance, the tendency is now to encourage experts to engage in genuine listening exercises. These are not only "nice-to-do" but crucial in terms of knowledge production and ultimately key for designing the risk mitigation strategies.

The origin of this new line of research is often described as an early comprehensive effort led by the US. National Research Council (NRC) in 1989 to improve risk communication. Its definition of risk communication is the following: "Risk communication is an interactive process of exchange of information and opinions among individuals, groups, and institutions concerning a risk or potential risk to human health or the environment (…) social context of the risk should start from the very beginning" and must incorporate "exchange of information and opinions" (NRC 1989).

In this vein, Waddell (1995) opposed the view that during a risk communication campaign and assessment, the scientific community provides technical knowledge while the audience or stakeholders manifest values, beliefs, and emotions through feedback on the risk communication effort. His approach holds that in fact inputs come from both sides. There are no "hard facts" on one side and "soft facts" on the other, *expertise* on one side and *emotions* on the other. Experts get emotional on risk matters as well.

Finally, risk communication based on an understanding of the public as an active participant in the process of apprehending and controlling risk, based on its own rational understanding of risk, implies a different dialogic communication between so-called "experts" and so-called "lay publics" (Abrahams 2009).

Entering the Twenty-First Century: Facing Social Networks and Governance Issues

At the turn of the twenty-first century, observers and experts of the field tend to all agree that risk and crisis communication had to move away from the now classical and state-of-the-art public relations campaigns toward strong anticipatory and elaborate strategies (Berger and Journé, *this volume*; Baram and Lindoe, *this volume*). It appears to many that the "seven cardinal rules of risk communication", recalled above, are insufficient when confronted with massive crises, capable of challenging preestablished plans and preconceptions.

Recent examples might include: The management of A (H1N1) pandemic in 2009–2010 (mostly in Europe); The *Deepwater Horizon* drilling rig explosion in 2010 and its environmental consequences in the Gulf of Mexico; The Great East Japan Earthquake, Tsunami, and *Fukushima Daiichi* Nuclear Power Plant Accident in March 2011 and its lasting impact on the population (Nishizawa, *this volume;* see also Baumont, *this volume*); The 2014 Ebola Virus Disease epidemic in West Africa and its burden in Guinea, Liberia, Sierra Leone (Bastide, *this volume*). These book chapters are precisely looking back at the complex challenges that risk communicators have had to face during these dramatic crises. They highlight the daunting tasks that communicators had to fulfill, when disorganization was so complete and fears so overwhelming.

Some experts believe that current crises are very different from older ones: "The accidental, compartmentalized crises of the twenty-first century have mutated into systemic dislocations calling for new intelligence" (Granatt et al. 2009, p. 1). Furthermore, scholars call for more elaborate strategic thinking that deliberately moves away from the "planning" culture. Plans give false comfort to managers and leaders. Plans may be counterproductive in the face of rapidly evolving crises (Clarke 1999; Lagadec 2009). To move away from a "planning culture" means allowing actors in charge to develop ad hoc strategies, according to local situations and needs. This cautious note should not be understood as a plea against predetermined scenario, nor against the scenario planning philosophy (Bieder and Bourrier 2013). They remain important tools to develop and rehearse. However, they should be enriched and augmented with the development of resilient, agile, self-designing risk communication strategies, aiming at facing the unexpected (Weick and Sutcliffe 2011). These strategies cannot be developed in a vacuum. They need to be supported by organizational practices that encourage this mindfulness, reliability, and high performance.

Recent examples of massive crises, like *Fukushima Daiichi* disaster or Ebola Virus Disease, still give steam to the "social amplification of risk" approach, developed in the late 1980s by Roger Kasperson and colleagues (among them were Jeanne Kasperson, Paul Slovic, Ortwin Renn) at Clark University (Kasperson et al. 1988; Kasperson and Kasperson 1996). The most fundamental argument of Kasperson and his colleagues is that social activities will magnify the consequences of a risk event, often in unexpected ways. Potential "social amplification stations" (Wiig et al. *this volume*) might include mass media and journalists, groups of scientists, governmental agencies, and politicians. Stigmatization is a primary concern. Later, Leiss and Powell (1997) theorized that a risk information "vacuum" is most likely to blame for the social amplification of risks. When experts refuse to provide information, or when they are seen as untrustworthy, a hungry public will fill the void, often with rumors, suppositions, easy to blame targets and fakes.

Following the social trust argument, Earle and Cvetkovich argue that "social trust, understood in everyday terms, is the process by which individuals assign to other persons, groups, agencies, or institutions, the responsibility to work on certain tasks" (1995, p. 4). They further explain that "within the realm of risk management, most tasks are too big and complex for individuals, regardless of technical training, to successfully complete alone" (p. 4). This situation leads to a necessary measure of trust allocated to institutions, or agencies in charge of communicating mitigation strategies. They further argue that if people do not trust an organization, negative information associated with that organization reinforces their distrust, whereas positive information is discounted. In essence, no matter how well thought through and well packaged an information might be, it will not communicate risk effectively if trust and credibility are not established first.

Other scholars have also contributed to the renewal of the research agenda, by importing concepts from other subfields. Taking seriously the network paradigm and the "network society" we live in (Castells 2011) could rejuvenate a risk communication's perspective and imply revision of the principles under which risk communication campaigns and activities are devised. Organization studies (Bovasso 1996; Burt 1987), for example, have demonstrated that social networks influence behavior and attitudes in the workplace, as well as within the family and among friends: "A majority of these network studies, particularly those exploring the idea of social contagion through cohesive network ties, have been conducted in organizational settings. In addition, thousands of studies have examined community networks from a diffusion of innovation perspective (Rogers 1995). These studies suggest that interpersonal networks influence the adoption of ideas, innovations, and behaviors" (Scherer and Cho 2003, p. 262). This strongly suggests that who we spend time with affects our worldview and our risk perception. Looking beyond individuals to their communities, networks, neighborhoods, including social ties built on social media might be promising venues to learn more on publics' and audiences' knowledge, adaptations, and prejudices toward risks.

The development of new social media and electronic networks (blogs, Facebook, Twitter, chats, forums, etc.) poses new challenges to risk communicators (Veil et al. 2011; Liu et al. 2016). Risk communication campaigns must now be tailored to a variety of audiences that do not read the same news media outlets, nor inform themselves in the same ways. Campaigns must be devised in many more subcategories and must reach out to many more different communities and stakeholders. This is true both for routine risk communication and ad hoc crisis communication.

Following this perspective, another venue has gained momentum (Renn 2008). More recently, some scholars (Lofstedt et al. 2011) have suggested that risk communication should be envisaged as two-way communication, and that each segment brings knowledge and expertise to the problem. When confronted with risks and threats, recurrent or sudden, affected communities and multiple stakeholders have generally developed mitigation strategies worth investigating. Prior knowledge exists and should not be ignored or too easily labeled as false preconceptions.

Issues of transparency, participation, and democracy are central to this agenda. Building trust, understanding and establishing symmetrical relationships are essential to these developments. In this view, risk communication is a long-term strategy that cannot only be deployed in case of emergencies. Nowadays, for many experts in this field, and beyond, a mature risk communication strategy shall include and articulate different perspectives, held by affected professionals, communities, segments of the population, from experts to lay persons, in order to adequately engage with the risks considered. The coproduction of risk communication strategies is considered as an optimal goal, not yet achieved in many arenas (Guérard *in this volume*). This is especially the case when concerned members of the public or nonofficial experts are tweeting and using the blogosphere to post their own analysis of the situation.

This new philosophy also implies moving away from dogma such as "educating the public", or "educating the media". Major public health emergencies and alerts will instantly engage the media, who should be seen as major stakeholders in all the processes of communication. The media are not an adjunct to public emergency response. They have their own obligations to the public (see Wiig et al. *this volume*). Public health emergency planners now acknowledge the media's role in a crisis and plan to meet reasonable media requirements during an outbreak. The idea is to use public perceptions, resources (cognitive, social, symbolic, etc.), opinions, knowledge, rationales, beliefs, assumptions, as well as the opinions and perceptions of experts, stakeholders, and political appointees to build a reasonable communication strategy capable of dealing with uncertainties.

After 2010: The Narrative Turn

An interesting development has recently taken place and concerns more directly the format of information transmission. Central to this discussion is the following question: How to design an effective message in risk communication, capable of bringing about changes and altering behaviors? This is not a novel theme in risk communication research, nor is it new when looking back at numerous handbooks. Constructing guidelines, using adequate language, materials, graphs, and iconography is the subject of entire sections in handbooks (see for example, Lundgren and McMakin 2009, pp. 145–157).

Didactic, expository, nonnarrative forms are often opposed to narrative forms. "The (narrative style) consists of presenting the risk information in the form of a personal story instead of, or in addition to, presenting exposure calculations or other data. The story structure helps the audience understand the risk by simplifying it and focusing on cause and effect" (Lundgren and McMakin 2009, p. 150). For a long time, medical, public policy and scientific organizations have regarded narrative forms as being less rigorous: "Non-narrative forms were viewed as objective, and therefore more credible than narratives, which were seen as anecdotal and subjective, and consequently unscientific" (Barbour et al. 2016, p. 813). Yet, evidence gathered so far is in favor of narrative forms, when dissemination of information is key. It is reported that narrative formats fare better on social media and will be shared more often and disseminate more easily than nonnarratives (Green and Sestir 2008; Hinyard and Kreuter 2007; Kreuter et al. 2007).

Nowadays, storytelling is considered to be integral to any business strategy and a key feature of organizational management (Brown et al. 2004). Organizations and institutions are increasingly using stories to reach out to their audiences (donors, patients, advocates, employees, communities, etc.) to communicate on their programs, products, and services, and on their worldviews (Krause 2014). For example, during the Ebola Virus Disease, *Médecins sans frontières*, along with *World Health Organization,* and *Centers for Disease Control and Prevention*, displayed numerous stories on their websites to explain the situation, document their activities, and promote certain types of messages, and avoid others. These organizations also promoted "their" own narratives about the crisis and used their deployees' stories to present facts in line with their baseline (Casaer 2015).

As Barbour et al. (2016) noted, having recourse to narratives does not please every group inside these complex organizations, often afraid to lose their scientific reputation. The narrative turn is not always embraced by all constituencies inside an organization. This exposes yet another feature of the narrative turn. It affects the power dynamics and asymmetries inside the organization, and should not be treated only as a communication tool toward the public. The same can be said on the outside: narratives can also be understood as defensive and active propaganda. They could look like poor transparency exercises, lacking candor in the end.

It remains to be seen whether the narrative turn we are witnessing will be more beneficial than detrimental to risk and crisis communication: Beneficial because of its power to disseminate key messages to wider audiences and tailored to their needs; or detrimental because of the potential dangerous slippery road to detestable institutional propaganda?

Conclusion

Big data and citizen science, combined, might well open a new era to embrace two crucial elements for risk and crisis communication success: (1) Getting precise, accurate, reliable feedback from the field; (2) Allowing affected populations to develop some efficacious action to alleviate risk. However, it remains to be seen whether this can lead to the promise of empowerment that many hope for with this new stage in risk and crisis communication development.

In conclusion, we might be willing to add a few stages to Fischhoff's scale in line with the developments one sees coming, as some of the chapters in this book exemplify. First, we could start by adding "All we have to do is show them they are part of it" to break through the "insider view" that still threaten risk and crisis communication strategies and alienate many publics, who feel estranged by what they frequently perceived as opaque organizational logics. Second, we might add this twist: "All we have to do is show them they are the experts" which signals that knowledge and cognition are distributed. Inhabitants of contaminated areas near *Fukushima-Daïchi* are indeed the experts of their land's contamination and its monitoring. But the true leap forward will probably happen when it will be possible to abandon "we" and propose "All that has to be done is to make them part of "we"".

- All we have to do is get the numbers right
- All we have to do is tell them the numbers
- All we have to do is explain what we mean by the numbers
- All we have to do is show them that they've accepted similar risks in the past
- All we have to do is show them it's a good deal for them
- All we have to do is treat them nice
- All we have to do is make them partners
- All we have to do is show them they are part of it
- All we have to do is show them they are the experts
- All that has to be done is to make them part of "we".

Adapted from Fischhoff, supplements by Bourrier.

References

Abraham, T. (2009). Risk and outbreak communication revisited: The search for a broader paradigm. *Bull World Health Organ, 87*(8) (Geneva Aug).

Allport, G. W., & Postman, L. (1947). *The psychology of rumor*. Oxford, England: Henry Holt.

Barbour, J. B., Doshi, M., & Hernandez, L. (2016). Telling global public health stories: Narrative message design for issues management. *Communication Research, 43,* 810–843.

Bastide, L. (2017). Future now. *IRS Working Paper Series*. Geneva: University of Geneva.

Bennington, B. (2014). Crisis communication: Sensemaking and decision-making by the CDC under conditions of uncertainty and ambiguity during the 2009–2010 H1N1 pandemic. Doctoral dissertation, University of South Florida.

Berce, Y. M. (1993). Les semeurs de peste. *La vie, la foi, la mort, le temps: Mélanges offerts à Pierre Chaunu* (pp. 85–94). Paris: Presses Universitaires de France.

Bieder, C., & Bourrier, M. (2013). *Trapping safety into rules: How desirable or avoidable is proceduralization?* Ashgate-CRC Press.

Bovasso, G. (1996). A network analysis of social contagion processes in an organizational intervention. *Human Relations, 49*(11), 1419–1435.

Brown, J. S., Denning, S., Groh, K., & Prusak, L. (2004). *Storytelling in organizations: Why storytelling is transforming 21st century organizations and management*. Boston: Butterworth Heinemann.

Burt, R. S. (1987). Social contagion and innovation: Cohesion versus structural equivalence. *American Journal of Sociology, 92*(6), 1287–1335.

Calain, P., & Poncin, M. (2015). Reaching out to Ebola victims: Coercion, persuasion or an appeal for self-sacrifice? *Social Science and Medicine, 147,* 126–133.

Casaer, P. (2015). Film *Affliction*. MSF.

Castells, M. (2011). *The rise of the network society: The information age: Economy, society, and culture* (Vol. 1). NJ: Wiley.

Clarke, L. (1999). *Mission improbable: Using fantasy documents to tame disaster*. Chicago: University of Chicago Press.

Covello, V. T. (2010). Strategies for overcoming challenges to effective risk communication. In *Handbook of risk and crisis communication* (pp. 143–167).

Covello, V., & Allen, F. (1988). *Seven cardinal rules of risk communication*. Washington, DC: US Environmental Protection Agency, Office of Policy Analysis (OPA-87-020).

Covello, V. T., Sandman, P. M., & Slovic, P. (1988). *Risk communication, risk statistics, and risk comparisons: A manual for plant managers* (pp. 1–57). Washington, DC: Chemical Manufacturers Association.

Douglas, M., & Wildavsky, A. (1983). *Risk and culture: An essay on the selection of technological and environmental dangers*. Univ of California Press.

Earle, T. C., & Cvetkovich, G. (1995). *Social trust: Toward a cosmopolitan society*. Greenwood Publishing Group.

Faye, S. L. (2015). L' « exceptionnalité » d'Ebola et les « réticences » populaires en Guinée-Conakry. Réflexions à partir d'une approche d'anthropologie symétrique. Anthropologie & Santé. *Revue internationale francophone d'anthropologie de la santé*, (11).

Fischhoff, B. (1995). Risk perception and communication unplugged: twenty years of process. *Risk Analysis, 15*(2), 137–145.

Gheytanchi, A., Joseph, L., Gierlach, E., Kimpara, S., Housley, J., Franco, Z., et al. (2007). The dirty dozen, twelve failures of the Hurricane Katrina response and how psychology can help. *American Psychologist, 62*(2), 118–130.

Glik, D. C. (2007). Risk communication for public health emergencies. *Annual Review of Public Health, 28,* 33–54.

Granatt, M., Young, J., & Lagadec, P. (2009). The Magellan Initiative. *Crisis Response Journal, 5* (2), 10–11.

Green, M. C., & Sestir, M. (2008). *Transportation theory*. The International Encyclopedia of Media Effects.

Hargrove, T., & Stempel, G. H., III. (2007). Use of blogs as a source of news presents little threat to mainline news media. *Newspaper Research Journal, 28*(1), 99–102.

Heath, R. L., & O'Hair, H. D. (Eds.). (2010). *Handbook of risk and crisis communication*. London: Routledge.

Hinyard, L. J., & Kreuter, M. W. (2007). Using narrative communication as a tool for health behavior change: A conceptual, theoretical, and empirical overview. *Health Education & Behavior, 34*(5), 777–792.

Kasperson, R. E., & Kasperson, J. X. (1996). The social amplification and attenuation of risk. *The Annals of the American Academy of Political and Social Science* (pp. 95–105).

Kasperson, R. E., Renn, O., Slovic, P., Brown, H. S., Emel, J., Goble, R., … & Ratick, S. (1988). The social amplification of risk: A conceptual framework. *Risk analysis, 8*(2), 177–187.

Knight, P. (Ed.). (2003). *Conspiracy theories in American history: An encyclopedia*. Abc-clio.

Krause, M. (2014). *The good project: Humanitarian relief NGOs and the fragmentation of reason*. University of Chicago Press.

Kreuter, M. W., Green, M. C., Cappella, J. N., Slater, M. D., Wise, M. E., Storey, D., … & Hinyard, L. J. (2007). Narrative communication in cancer prevention and control: A framework to guide research and application. *Annals of behavioral medicine, 33*(3), 221–235.

Lagadec, P. (2009). *La question des Plans: Entre points d'appui et pièges stratégiques*.

Le Marcis, F. (2015). « Traiter les corps comme des fagots » Production sociale de l'indifférence en contexte Ebola (Guinée). *Anthropologie & Santé. Revue internationale francophone d'anthropologie de la santé*, 11.

Leiss, W. & Powell, D. (1997). *Mad cows and mothers milk*. Montreal: McGill–Queen's Press.

Liu, B. F., Fraustino, J. D., & Jin, Y. (2016). Social media use during disasters how information form and source influence intended behavioral responses. *Communication Research, 43*(5), 626–646.

Lofstedt, R., Bouder, F., Wardman, J., & Chakraborty, S. (2011). The changing nature of communication and regulation of risk in Europe. *Journal of Risk Research, 14*(4), 409–429.

Lundgren, R. E., & McMakin, A. H. (2009). *Risk communication: A handbook for communicating environmental, safety, and health risks*. Wiley, NJ.

Malley, P. O., Rainford, J., & Thompson, A. (2009). Transparency during public health emergencies: From rhetoric to reality. *Bulletin of the World Health Organization, 87,* 614–618.

McComas, K. A. (2006). Defining moments in risk communication research: 1996–2005. *Journal of Health Communication, 11*(1), 75–91.

Mirowsky, J., & Ross, C. E. (1983). Paranoia and the structure of powerlessness. *American Sociological Review*, 228–239.

Morgan, M. G. (2002). *Risk communication: A mental models approach*. Cambridge, MA: Cambridge University Press.

National Research Council, (1989). *Improving risk communication*. National Academies Press.

Ogrizek, M., & Guillery, J. M. (2000). *La communication de crise*. Paris: Presses universitaires de France.

Perrow, C. (2007). *The next catastrophe: Reducing our vulnerabilities to natural, industrial, and terrorist disasters*. Princeton University Press.

Prasad, J. (1935). The psychology of rumor: A study relating to the great Indian earthquake of 1934. *British Journal of Psychology, 26*(1), 1–15.

Renn, O. (2008). *Risk governance coping with uncertainty in a complex world*. London: Earthscan.

Rogers, E. M. (1995). *Diffusion of innovations* (4th ed.) New York: Free Press.

Rogers, E. M., & Lincaid, D. L. (1981). *Communication networks: Toward a new paradigm for research*. New York: The Free Press.

Sandman P. M. (2003). Four kinds of risk communication. http://www.petersandman.com.

Scherer, C. W., & Cho, H. (2003). A social contagion theory of risk perception. *Risk Analysis, 23* (2), 261–267.

Sellnow, T. L., Ulmer, R. R., Seeger, M. W., & Littlefield, R. S. (2009). *Effective risk communication: A message centered approach*. New York: Springer.

Veil, S. R., Buehner, T., & Palenchar, M. J. (2011). A work-in-process literature review: Incorporating social media in risk and crisis communication. *Journal of Contingencies and Crisis Management, 19*(2), 110–122.

Waddell, C. (1995). Defining sustainable development: A case study in environmental communication. *Technical Communication Quarterly, 4*(2), 201–216.

Weick, K. E., & Sutcliffe, K. M. (2011). *Managing the unexpected: Resilient performance in an age of uncertainty*. New York: Wiley, Free Press.

Part I
Persuading in Peace Time: A Long Lasting Story

Public Participation in the Debate on Industrial Risk in France: A Success Story?

Caroline Kamaté

Abstract This chapter addresses the participation of civil society in the debate on industrial risk in France. The body of research regarding citizen participation, notably in environmental issues, is substantial, as is the literature on industrial risk perception. However, given the multitude of participatory systems and experiments, the dialogue between hazardous companies and their local host communities merits further analysis. The findings summarized here are mainly based on French case studies in the major industrial zones of the Rhône Valley, Dunkirk, Le Havre and Marseille. [In addition, FonCSI supported international works, notably a study in Norway and the US by M. Baram and P. Lindøe (Cf. Chapter "Risk Communication Between Companies and Local Stakeholders for Improving Accident Prevention and Emergency Response", *this volume*).] These studies focused on the topic of 'living together with hazardous industry', examined the Technological Risk Prevention Plan (PPRT), the functioning of institutional communication/consultation bodies and local initiatives to encourage participation in industrial risk. The results showed that the opportunity not only to be informed on industrial risk but also to participate in the debate was sometimes underused by the public. These studies help us understand the factors that can undermine communication and participation processes with respect to industrial risk in France.

Keywords Public participation · Industrial risk · Decision-making Territory

This research was supported by the Foundation and the Institute for an Industrial Safety Culture (FonCSI and ICSI), created as a result of the significant societal and legislative shift that followed the disaster at the AZF factory in Toulouse in 2001.

C. Kamaté (✉)
FonCSI, Toulouse, France
e-mail: caroline.kamate@foncsi.org

M. Bourrier and C. Bieder (eds.), *Risk Communication for the Future*, SpringerBriefs in Safety Management, https://doi.org/10.1007/978-3-319-74098-0_2

Introduction: The Growth of Public Participation

In many domains, and particularly in the field of environment and sustainable development, decision-making practices are moving towards greater public participation (Brodie et al. 2009). This change finds its origins in the civic action and urban struggles observed around the world notably since the last third of the twentieth century (Bernfeld 1983; Bresson 2014). As early as the 1950s, citizen participation programmes were launched, based on the assumption that an engaged citizenry was better than a passive citizenry, and that the involvement of citizens would lead to more democratic and effective governance (Irvin and Stansbury 2004). Another driver was increasing mistrust and questioning of the links between political powers and scientific experts, who played a central role in several controversies (Nelkin 2016). While citizens demanded greater involvement in decision-making processes, participation also became an object for researchers working in many of the social sciences (Blondiaux and Sintomer 2009). The theoretical foundations of participatory democracy were established (Pateman 1970). The literature on participation integrates the significant contribution of studies on deliberation, particularly rich in the Anglophone world (Sintomer 2011). While public deliberation theorists have diverse backgrounds, they all consider it as a cornerstone of participatory democracy (Dewey 1954; Fishkin 1991; Habermas 1996). Despite their criticism of existing representative institutions, they acknowledge that deliberative democracy is an expansion of, rather than an alternative to, representative democracy, and highlight the benefits of the public discourse on citizen engagement (Delli Carpini et al. 2004). Scholars not only study the concepts and theories of participation, they also are very active in designing operational participatory devices and working to define criteria for their evaluation (Blondiaux and Fourniau 2011; Piriou and Lénel 2010a).

Although the term 'participation' has multiple interpretations, it is typically used in the scientific and legal literature to refer to a kind of democratic ideal based on the 'empowerment' of 'ordinary people' (Glucker et al. 2013; Bresson 2014). Arnstein (1969) proposed a typology of participation ranging from 'manipulation' to 'citizen control' as a function of the extent of citizen power. Based on this framework, we assume that between 'informing' the public (where citizens simply receive data), and 'co-decision' (where decision-making is shared), there are multiple modes of citizen involvement, notably 'consultation', which consists in obtaining the public's feedback on different alternatives (Brodie et al. 2009; Kamaté 2016).

The 'participatory market' has given rise to many deliberative models, methods and tools: the twenty-first-century town meeting, the consensus conference, the citizen advisory board, the citizen panel, deliberative polling, the Charrette procedure, participatory budgeting, the Delphi method, etc. (FRB 2006). And while the participatory movement is global, citizen participation is perceived, understood and therefore 'practiced' differently depending on the historical, institutional, social and political context (IDLC 2016). The public debate *à la française* can be contrasted with Switzerland's tradition of semi-direct democracy (Bevort 2011; ALNabhani et al. 2016), or a post-Apartheid democracy such as South Africa (Leonard 2014), reflecting the diversity of the participatory landscape (although a comparative study is beyond the scope of this chapter). Clearly, the level of deliberative and participatory democracy is closely linked to the so-called culture of participation of a country or even an area, and the modalities of participation will vary with its goals. By 'participation', we mean all of the ways of contributing to the preparation of a project, by offering opinions and viewpoints that will be taken into account at different levels in a decision-making process.

By highlighting the difficulties in the dialogue between hazardous companies and residents, whether they be related to participation in general, or more specifically to the topic of industrial risk or the French context, we aim to identify some of the levers that can improve public participation and the organization of the debate on industrial risks.

Public Participation on Industrial Risk: The French Context

French participatory democracy originates in decentralization and regionalization policies that were initiated in the mid-twentieth century. Growing interest is also linked to a 'crisis' in the representative democracy model that has manifested, beginning in the 1960s, in falling voter turnout (Rosanvallon 2006; Piriou and Lénel 2012b). Traditionally, the French have a high degree of trust in their governmental institutions and the scientific elite (ALNabhani et al. 2016). This partly explains why the large, centrally managed nuclear programme that started in the 70s after the oil shock and aimed to achieve energy independence, was largely accepted. However, this great confidence in technocratic elites has been shaken by major industrial accidents and a series of health scandals. As early as the 1970s, new mechanisms that involved a plurality of actors began to emerge.

Citizen participation is regulated by law. The Bouchardeau law of 12 July 1983 relates to the democratization of the public inquiry, while the Barnier law of 2 February 1995 created the National Public Debate Commission (CNDP[1]). At the international level, the Earth Summit in Rio in 1992 reinforced the concept of sustainable development and put citizen participation in its core. At the European level, the Aarhus Convention, signed by the European Community and its Member States in 1998, made public participation a fundamental principle of environmental law. It ensures the integration of civil society in decision-making related to environmental policy. Similarly, in France, the Environmental Pact[2] (2007–2012) provides for environmental governance measures that involve all stakeholders in a

[1] *Commission nationale du débat public* in French.

[2] The *Grenelle de l'environnement* in French.

consultation process in order to arrive at decisions that are more democratic and better understood (Décider Ensemble 2011; FNE 2009).

On the specific topic of industrial risks, the 1982 Seveso I Directive and the European Council Directive of 7 June 1990 introduced European regulations related to the public's right to information. In France, the 2003 Bachelot-Narquin law was promulgated following the accident at the AZF factory in 2001 (Bonnaud and Martinais 2007). It implemented Technological Risk Prevention Plans (PPRT)[3] and created mandatory consultation bodies known as Site Monitoring Committees (CSS[4]) at high-threshold Seveso sites. The CSS explicitly solicited citizen participation and marked a turning point in the communication of industrial risk to the public (Suraud et al. 2009). Furthermore, operators and project leaders started to become willing to go beyond their legal obligations, and voluntary participation systems and experiments emerged.

Clear Progress and Significant Benefits

In practice, whatever form it takes, public participation is seen as leading to better decisions and greater benefits for all stakeholders (Beierle 1999).

The public has a growing need for better knowledge and control of their environment (Orée 2004), and is increasingly willing to become involved in the development of their local area. The CSS that was implemented in 2003 has the great merit of bringing all stakeholders to the table and, to some extent, opening industrial facilities to the public, which represents considerable democratic progress (Suraud 2012; Grembo et al. 2013). While pollution and chronic risks have been long-standing subjects and remain on the agenda in many consultation bodies like the SPPPI[5], the CSS is a body dedicated to the topic of the hazard posed by a major accident. If these official structures do not meet all of the public's expectations, notably in terms of the weight given to their views, developments linked to the emergence of new external actors have disrupted the technocratic model of industrial risk management that has historically prevailed. It is interesting, therefore, to examine their scope, in terms of their positive or negative effects on negotiations between decision-makers (Bonnaud and Martinais 2010; Suraud 2012).

Moreover, participatory processes help to increase the confidence of the public in the political–industrial sphere and thus reinforce the legitimacy of the latter (FRB 2006). On the one hand, it is in a company's interests to supplement mandatory

[3]*Plan de prévention des risques technologiques* in French, that regulates urban planning around Seveso high-threshold industrial sites.

[4]*Commission de suivi de site* in French, formerly named the *Comité local d'information et de concertation* (CLIC, the Local Committee for Information and Consultation).

[5]Permanent Secretariat for Industrial Pollution Prevention (*Secrétariat permanent pour la prevention des pollutions industrielles* in French). The first SPPPI was created in the 1970s in the area of Marseille.

consultation processes with voluntary actions that aim to take better account of the expectations of residents. It can become a lever to improve relations between industrial facilities and local residents. On the other hand, a lack of trust and suspicion make local communities less inclined to accept, or—even more so—to support, an industrial project. In the case of an unwanted event, such as a near miss or an accident, an upstream participatory approach can mean the continuation of a dialogue that has already begun, rather than a knee-jerk response in the form of litigation.

Finally, 'alternative' local consultative bodies appear to be better suited to handling local problems related to the presence of the hazardous industry and could serve as a counterpoint to the extension of centralized, mandatory standards and regulations. For local governments, citizen participation at the municipal level offers a way to reappropriate the issue of industrial risk. It places the region at the heart of the tensions that exist between hazardous industry, residents and the French administration (Suraud 2012, 2013).

Why Is the Public Unenthusiastic?

Despite the benefits, the lack of citizen participation in public inquiries or other consultation initiatives is regularly deplored. Residents continue to suffer from a lack of information; notably, they are sometimes poorly informed about PPRT and mandatory consultation bodies (Zwarterook 2010; Martinais 2015). Why, despite the efforts of industrial operators and authorities, are communication campaigns, official bodies and outreach initiatives failing to reach their intended public?

Just the Latest Hot Topic?

The cohabitation of local communities and hazardous industry is a very sensitive topic as it impacts society at different levels. Industrial risk, whether or not it is linked to a major accident, is characterized by its complexity. Therefore, the debate must take into account the many dimensions of a region, including urban planning, human health, economy and biodiversity (FNE 2009). In addition, despite the constant extension of regulations (e.g. the 'duty to inform' that applies to industrial facilities falling under the Seveso Directive) issues of industrial confidentiality have regularly clashed with the requirement for transparency and the involvement of civil society (Suraud et al. 2009). The public's legal right of inspection distinguishes industrial risk from other types of risks, rendering the issue even more sensitive, as questioning an industry's choices can impact its internal operations (Suraud 2012).

Industrial Risk: A Motivating Theme?

There is no way around it: despite the high stakes, major accident risk is just not that 'interesting'. This can be partly explained by actors' perceptions. Until there is an accident, the danger remains abstract (Zwarterook 2010). Furthermore, the naturalization and euphemization of risk, which are both likely to be linked to psychological protection mechanisms, have important consequences for the public's relationship to risk (Zonabend 1989; Coanus et al. 2007; Peretti-Watel 2010). The naturalization of risk is consistent with the naturalization of the plant (i.e. its integration into the landscape): risk becomes a familiar element, just another part of daily life (Leborgne 2014). Euphemization can be defined as the tendency to mitigate risk the closer you are to it; residents who are 'objectively' more exposed to industrial hazards feel less exposed than those who are in the second line (Zwarterook 2010). Moreover, industrial risk is usually assessed in relation to other issues, including economics, and consequently may not carry much weight. The Dunkirk case study clearly showed that despite differences of opinion, local actors agreed on one point: the need to defend socio-economic interests, which may compete with industrial safety issues (Grembo et al. 2013).

The studies also highlight that a useful entry point for involving the public in the debate is to link it to daily activities and quality of life: chronic risks, nuisance, etc. Unlike the risk of a major accident—an explosion, for example—these risks are much more palpable as they take the form of smoke, noise, smells, etc. Residents are also quick to become involved when they are aware of a potential impact on their property as observed with implementation of the PPRT.

> "I remember my parents saying: the property will be condemned, what are we going to bequeath to our children? (…). Then I said: we'll create an association. The Conference,[6] for me, is a result of this association" *a resident*. (Piriou and Lénel 2012a)

Thus, getting people interested in industrial risk necessarily requires broadening the discussion. Notably, it implies a move away from the conventional definition of risk as something that is determined by industrial experts, towards an examination of how risk is understood by residents (Castel et al. 2010) and the local media (Auboussier et al. 2015).

A Potentially Brutal Introduction

The risk of an industrial accident does not inspire the public to take action unless and until it affects their daily life. Regarding the tensions related to the PPRT in France, even in the absence of an accident, the public's first encounter with the

---

[6]The *Conférence riveraine*, which can be translated as the Residents' Conference, is a dialogue structure set up in Feyzin (close to Lyon, France) on the initiative of its refinery and its Mayor.

topic can be very sudden and painful. For example, some residents learned from one day to the next that their home was located in a hazardous area, only then to quickly mobilize themselves around a confrontation (Martinais 2015). Notwithstanding the lack of public participation, this latter example again highlights that basic information does not always reach its intended audience. How can the public become involved when they may not even be aware that they live in a hazardous area?

An Expensive Process

Participation is not free. Residents and non-governmental organizations (NGOs) in particular must voluntarily invest their time and energy, and can incur the financial expense. As the number of consultation structures multiplies, resources become increasingly limited (GEc CSN 2011). Two factors that work against participation are the fear of redundancy and the weariness effect (Gibout 2006), although it should be noted that both of these factors affect public participation in general and are not specific to industrial risks (Grembo et al. 2013). For their part, industrial and political decision-makers are legally bound to involve the public in industrial risk consultation processes. Beyond their legal obligations, the decision to voluntarily adopt a participative approach represents an additional investment that varies as a function of the project's characteristics and, notably, its timescale.

Organizing the Debate: What Is at Stake

Trust and Transparency

While there may be a certain level of trust between some industrial risk stakeholders, the picture is more mixed for others. The survey in Dunkirk shows that the public has a high level of trust in firefighters, the police and mayors (Zwarterook 2010). The latter are seen as particularly close to the local community. These key players form the interface between national authorities, industry and citizens, and they have seen a dramatic improvement in their risk management skills following the changes introduced by the Bachelot-Narquin law (Martinais 2014). They have the difficult task of reconciling the protection of populations with, on the one hand, urban development and, on the other hand, economic activities.

Zwarterook's (2010) study reveals a lack of confidence in industrial actors' ability to prevent industrial risks: 68% of residents said they did not trust them, while 54% considered that preventive measures were insufficient. Paradoxically, in another study, respondents expressed confidence in industrial operators, who were seen as professionals that knew their process and its risks, and had a direct interest in protecting their employees and production facilities (Piriou and Lénel 2010b).

Trust, understood as 'to rely on someone', is not a prerequisite for a successful participatory process. It could even appear contradictory, as participative democracy is born, in part, from a lack of confidence in policymakers to defend the public interest (ALNabhani et al. 2016), and from the will of the public to reappropriate decisions that affect their lives. But the more convinced they are of decision-makers' commitment to make the process as transparent as possible, the more they may be willing to participate.

We now turn to the issue of whether the way the debate on public risk is organized strengthens or weakens its credibility. The public has been known to denounce official bodies as simply offering a 'mock' debate. In France, decisions can appear to be made upstream—suggesting collusion between hazardous industries and a state administration that has a long tradition of co-management (Suraud et al. 2009; Bonnaud and Martinais 2010; Le Blanc and Zwarterook 2012). This lack of transparency, together with poor communication, does not help to build confidence (Grembo et al. 2013). Credibility can be dramatically weakened, or even destroyed, if decision-makers abandon the process, while the public expects their opinions to be taken into account. They can feel that they have been misled and become reluctant to participate in future debates, creating a serious deadlock.

Moreover, mistrust extends to both sides. Politico-industrial actors can be suspicious of the newcomers: residents and employees' representatives. It appears that it remains difficult for industrial risk managers to open the door to civil society, given their long history of relative isolation and co-management. The difficulty of implementing a (mandatory or voluntary) public participation process should therefore not be underestimated. Institutional mistrust often translates into strategies that attempt to maintain control over risk management (Grembo et al. 2013).

On the other hand, voluntary initiatives are both appreciated and seen as a token of mutual understanding. For example, the experimental participatory device implemented in Feyzin known as the *Conférence riveraine* (see footnote 6) is the result of a clear political and industrial will, and is a practical demonstration of how the process can be made to work (Piriou and Lénel 2012a).

Asymmetry Between Participants

Members of the residents' panel frequently criticize official bodies for limiting themselves to their primary role of informing the public:

> If, as time goes on, the culture of a 'debate for the public' develops, the development of a genuine 'debate with the public' is less obvious. (Grembo et al. 2013)

In some sense, this reflects the influence of the public education model on the public debate model (Callon 1998).

Differences between actors in participatory bodies may also hinder understanding. The complexity of scientific and technical data makes it difficult for non-expert actors to accurately assess the situation (Frère et al. 2012). Moreover, differences in education and experience mean that some actors are better at the game than others; it is easier for them to be heard and listened to. These verbal skills generally go hand in hand with technical and scientific skills. This creates an asymmetry between those that are in some sense doubly skilled and others who lack the necessary technical and verbal competences. In order to overcome the gap, some actors undertake training or on-the-job learning; others prefer to use their lack of knowledge as a lever to exert pressure on the opposing party (Grembo et al. 2013).

Furthermore, value systems, potentially due to cultural differences, vary from one group of actors to another. This reality is reflected in the widespread finding that the actors involved do not speak the same language, and that there is a juxtaposition of viewpoints, rather than a genuine democratic debate (Zwarterook 2010).

Legitimacy of Participants

Participatory bodies often include the same 'regulars', such as retirees, and lack young people and representatives of the working population. The legal composition of the residents' panel of the CSS is vague; consequently, it varies from one region to another. 'Residents' can be extended to include NGOs, the so-called 'lambda individuals' or even, in certain cases, local officials (Nonjon et al. 2007). In practice, the panel is often composed of environmental protection associations with extensive experience of both industrial risks and participation, and whose interests do not necessarily coincide with those of residents.

> "Between environmental associations and local residents, let's say that the issues are not the same. (…) Residents associations think of their walls and property, and they stop there", *a local official*. (Suraud 2013)

Formal and Informal Discussion Spaces

The CSS has been particularly criticized for its rigidity (Suraud 2012). Meetings are usually chaired by the government's representative,[7] formal communications are presented in sequence and not all participants are given the same opportunity to contribute. Nevertheless, this rigid format can be overcome, and the procedure

[7]The prefect (*préfet* in French) or their representative.

adapted to better suit the local context (Grembo et al. 2013). The importance of informal discussions and negotiations that take place outside the formal structure, often in smaller committees, is also highlighted, reflecting a culture of negotiation that remains very present between traditional risk managers. Although these practices can lead to criticism from other participants, if these parallel discussions end in consensus, they can eventually be accepted (Grembo et al. 2013). Finally, the concept of participation integrates many dynamics and interactions that are implemented in the debate and confrontation spaces, and negotiations also need to be taken into account.

The binding framework of legal devices is often contrasted with more flexible, open structures such as the SPPPI. The CLIé[8] or the *Conférence riveraine* are popular precisely because of their informality (Espina 2012). The processes of dialogue and mediation that they can provide in the event of a crisis greatly improve the relationship between hazardous industry, local residents and environmental NGOs. It is nevertheless important to highlight that they are not a substitute for official bodies, as they have different roles and powers—notably administrative authority is absent from informal bodies—and must rather be seen as complementary.

Who Makes the Decisions?

As Ballard (2008) asks, where do the scales of participation and decision-making intersect? The first point to note is that the decisions of politico-industrial actors predominate in mandatory participation devices. It is clear that participation and decision-making are two different things. Participation relates to making a contribution to the development of a project, by putting forward a viewpoint that is taken into account at different levels, during a more or less collective decision process. The weight of public opinion is closely related to the selected approach and, crucially, when citizens are invited to intervene. This varies and, in any case, must be clarified and formalized upstream.

Conclusion: A Passing Trend? Be Aware of Limitations and Avoid Pitfalls

There is increasing interest in placing citizens at the heart of the debate in many domains. This leads to the following injunction:

> Nothing is decided without citizens being consulted. (Castel et al. 2010)

[8]An informal body created at the initiative of industrial operators.

However, public participation follows trends: it is therefore of overriding importance to pay attention to the pitfalls. On the one hand, participation must not be an end in itself, an empty shell or an illusory debate to rubber-stamp a project that has already been decided. The risk of the instrumentalization of citizen participation, or the 'domestication' of civil society groups for political purposes, is real (Ballard 2008). On the other hand, too much credit should not be given to opposing arguments, which claim that participation is useless as citizens do not, ultimately, take decisions. Involving more stakeholders, sharing multiple viewpoints—whether mandated by law or stemming from a voluntary initiative—lead to collective decisions that are more inclusive, fairer and better reflect the common good (Lukensmeyer 2014). Such efforts contribute to achieving the same aim: to make decision-making more democratic. Logically, these issues raise the complex question of the evaluation of participatory approaches. How do we measure, beyond the 'democratic demonstration', the impact of the introduction of citizens' expertise on the quality of public action (Lacroix 2008)? Nevertheless, in addition to this inherent goal, each project has specific objectives that must be formalized upstream and whose achievement might be assessed. Furthermore, the participation process is at least as important as its result and may generate numerous by-products: it can counterbalance stereotypes and preconceived ideas about others; rather than denying them, it can help to make conflicts explicit; it can be educational for all stakeholders making them less prone to amplifying and distorting risk evaluations; and it can foster mutual understanding, social learning and cooperation (Kasperson and Kasperson 1996; Di Mauro et al. 2012; Kamaté 2016). Such benefits can be assessed using indicators, which can help to (at least partially) solve the problem of evaluation. The issue of participation is challenging, but also rewarding, as much for civil society as for policymakers and project leaders (Brodie et al. 2009).

References

ALNabhani, K., Khan, F., & Yang, M. (2016). The importance of public participation in legislation of TENORM risk management in the oil and gas industry. *Process Safety and Environmental Protection, 102*, 606–614.

Arnstein, S. (1969). A ladder of citizen participation. *Journal of the American Institute of Planners, 35*(4).

Auboussier, J., Gœpfert, E.-M., & Garcin-Marrou, I. (2015). Le risque industriel dans la presse écrite de 1970 à 2010. In FONCSI (Ed.), *Les Cahiers de la sécurité industrielle* (2015-06).

Ballard, R. (2008). Between the community hall and the city hall: Five research questions on participation. *Transformation: Critical Perspectives on Southern Africa, 66*(1), 168–188.

Beierle, T. C. (1999). Using social goals to evaluate public participation in environmental decisions. *Policy Studies Review, 16*(3/4), 75–103.

Bernfeld, D. (1983). *Un nouvel enjeu: La participation. Aspects du mouvement participatif en Afrique, en Asie, aux Etats-Unis d'Amérique et en Europe.* Paris, France: Unesco.

Bevort, A. (2011). Démocratie, le laboratoire suisse. *Revue du MAUSS, 2011/1*(37), 447–475. https://doi.org/10.3917/rdm.037.0447.

Blondiaux, L., & Fourniau, J.-M. (2011). Un bilan des recherches sur la participation du public en démocratie: Beaucoup de bruit pour rien? *Participations, 1/2011*(1), 8–35. https://doi.org/10.3917/parti.001.0008.

Blondiaux, L., & Sintomer, Y. (2009). L'impératif délibératif. *Rue Descartes, 1,* 28–38.

Bonnaud, L., & Martinais, E. (2007). *Écrire la loi. Socio-genèse de la loi Bachelot du 30 juillet 2003.* Paris: Ministère de l'Ecologie et du Développement Durable.

Bonnaud, L., & Martinais, E. (2010). Expertise d'État et risques industriels. La persistance d'un modèle technocratique depuis les années 1970. In Y. Bérard & R. Crespin (Eds.), *Aux frontières de l'expertise. Dialogues entre savoirs et pouvoirs* (pp. 161–175). Rennes: PUR.

Bresson, M. (2014). La participation: Un concept constamment réinventé. Analyse sociologique des enjeux de son usage et de ses variations. *Socio-logos. Revue de l'association française de sociologie* (9).

Brodie, E., Cowling, E., & Nissen, N. (2009). *Understanding participation-a literature review.* NCVO: Institute for Volunteering Research.

Callon, M. (1998). Des différentes formes de démocratie technique. *Annales des Mines, 9,* 63–73.

Castel, S., Cézanne-Bert, P., & Leborgne, M. (2010). Le partage social du risque comme impératif de gestion? Le cas de l'industrie du risque aux portes de Marseille. In FONCSI (Ed.), *Les Cahiers de la sécurité industrielle* (2010-03).

Coanus, T., Duchêne, F., & Martinais, E. (2007). L'industrie chimique et ses riverains: Une relation ambivalente. *Responsabilité et Environnement, 48,* 68–76.

Décider Ensemble. (2011). *Analyse des pratiques de la concertation en France.* Paris: Décider Ensemble.

Delli Carpini, M. X., Lomax Cook, F., & Jacobs, L. R. (2004). Public deliberation, discursive participation, and citizen engagement: A review of the empirical literature. *Annual Review of Political Science, 7,* 315–334. https://doi.org/10.1146/annurev.polisci.7.121003.091630.

Dewey, J. (1954). *The public and its problems* (Première édition 1927 ed.). Athens, Ohio: Swallow Press.

Di Mauro, C., Bouchon, S., & Torretta, V. (2012). Industrial Risk in the Lombardy Region (Italy): what People perceive and what are the gaps to improve the Risk Communication and the Participatory Processes. *Chemical Engineering Transactions, 26.*

Espina, C. (2012). Les CLIÉ ont créé un climat de confiance. *Ouest Provence Journal.*

Fishkin, J. (1991). *Democracy and deliberation: New direction for democratic reforms.* New Haven: Yale University Press.

FNE. (2009). *Evaluation du fonctionnement des comités locaux d'information et de concertation.* France Nature Environnement. Retrieved from http://www.fne.asso.fr/.

FRB. (2006). *Méthodes participatives: Un guide pour l'utilisateur.* Bruxelles: Fondation Roi Baudouin.

Frère, S., Gibout, C., & Zwarterook, I. (2012). *De la formation à l'incertitude à la gouvernance par l'incertitude.* Ministère de l'Environnement, Programme CDE. Paris: Ministère de l'Environnement. Retrieved from http://concertation-environnement.fr/.

GEc CSN. (2011). Industries à risques technologiques: Un enjeu de société à négocier?, *In ICSI (Ed.), Les Cahiers de la sécurité industrielle* (2011-05).

Gibout, C. (2006). *Sociologie et espace public.* Strasbourg: HDR, Université Marc Bloch.

Glucker, A. N., Driessen, P. P., Kolhoff, A., & Runhaar, H. A. (2013). Public participation in environmental impact assessment: Why, who. *Environmental Impact Assessment Review, 43,* 104–111.

Grembo, N., Le Blanc, A., Gibout, C., & Zwarterook, I. (2013). Les PPRT dans le Dunkerquois: Des artifices d'une concertation obligée à la construction de compromis. In FONCSI (Ed.), *Les Cahiers de la sécurité industrielle* (2013-08).

Habermas, J. (1996). Three normative models of democracy. In S. Benhabib (Ed.), *Democracy and difference: Contesting the boundaries of the political.* Princeton: Princeton University Press.

IDLC. (2016). Brief conference review. *Democratic Participation in a Citizen's Europe: What Next for the EU?* Liverpool.

Irvin, R. A., & Stansbury, J. (2004). Citizen participation in decision making: Is it worth the effort? *Public Administration Review, 64*(1), 55–65.

Kamaté, C. (2016). Participation citoyenne et risques industriels: Quelques pistes pour engager une démarche. FONCSI (Ed.), *Les Cahiers de la sécurité industrielle* (2016-03).

Kasperson, R. E., & Kasperson, J. X. (1996). The social amplification and attenuation of risk. *The Annals of the American Academy of Political and Social Science, 545,* 95–105.

Lacroix, F. (2008). *Le concernement des habitants dans les dispositifs de participation du public a des échelles territoriales atypiques.* Master thesis, Université Paris XII.

Le Blanc, A., & Zwarterook, I. (2012). *Industrial risks, resilience and participatory processes.* New York: Association of American Geographers Annual Meeting.

Leborgne, M. (2014). Concertation et réalités territoriales: Les leçons de Salaise sur Sanne. In ICSI (Ed.), *Les Cahiers de la sécurité industrielle* (2014-05).

Leonard, L. (2014). Participatory democracy against industrial risks: Environmental justice in Durban, South Africa. *Politikon South African Journal of Political Studies, 41*(2). https://doi.org/10.1080/02589346.2014.905263.

Lukensmeyer, C. J. (2014). Key challenges facing the field of deliberative democracy. *Journal of Public Deliberation, 10*(1).

Martinais, E. (2014). Les collectivités locales à l'épreuve du PPRT: Une redéfinition du rôle pour des décisions plus concertées. In FONCSI (Ed.), *Les Cahiers de la sécurité industrielle* (2014-09).

Martinais, E. (2015). Citoyens en danger contre riverains responsables. La mobilisation habitante engendrée par l'élaboration des PPRT. In FONCSI (Ed.), *Les Cahiers de la sécurité industrielle* (2015-05).

Nelkin, D. (2016). Savoir scientifique, politiques gouvernementales et démocratie: Survol des perspectives. *Lien social et Politiques, 75*, 46–56. https://doi.org/10.7202/1036290ar.

Nonjon, M., Duchêne, F., Lafaye, F., & Martinais, E. (2007). *Ouvrir la concertation sur les risques industriels. La constitution du CLIC de Feyzin* (Vol. 69). Programme RDT. Paris: Ministère de l'Environnement.

Orée. (2004). *Vade-mecum de la concertation locale.* Paris: Association Orée.

Pateman, C. (1970). *Participation and democratic theory.* Cambridge University Press.

Peretti-Watel, P. (2010). *La société du risque*. Paris: La Découverte.

Piriou, O., & Lénel, P. (2010a). La Conférence Riveraine de Feyzin: Conception et mise en place. In ICSI (Ed.), *Les Cahiers de la sécurité industrielle* (2010-04).

Piriou, O., & Lénel, P. (2010b). La Conférence Riveraine de Feyzin: Un modèle pratique de démocratie participative. In ICSI (Ed.), *Les Cahiers de la sécurité industrielle* (2010-08).

Piriou, O., & Lénel, P. (2012a). La Conférence Riveraine de Feyzin: Évaluation d'un dispositif original de concertation sur les risques industriels. In ICSI (Ed.), *Les Cahiers de la sécurité industrielle* (2012-01).

Piriou, O., & Lénel, P. (2012b). La démocratie pratique raisonnable, nouveau dispositif de concertation: Guide d'aide à la mise en œuvre. In ICSI (Ed.), *Les Cahiers de la sécurité industrielle* (2012-02).

Rosanvallon, P. (2006). *La contre-démocratie, la politique à l'âge de la défiance*. Paris: Seuil.

Sintomer, Y. (2011). Délibération et participation: Affinité élective ou concepts en tension? *Participations, 1*, 239–276.

Suraud, M.-G. (2012). La concertation sur les risques industriels: 10 questions. In ICSI (Ed.), *Les Cahiers de la sécurité industrielle* (2012-09).

Suraud, M.-G. (2013). La thématisation des risques industriels majeurs en France: La concurrence « participative » comme enjeu. *VertigO-la revue électronique en sciences de l'environnement, 13*(3). https://doi.org/10.4000/vertigo.14390.

Suraud, M.-G., Lafaye, F., & Leborgne, M. (2009). La concertation: Changements et questions. FONCSI (Ed.), *Les Cahiers de la sécurité industrielle* (2009-03).

Zonabend, F. (1989). *La presqu'île au nucléaire*. Paris: Odile Jacob.

Zwarterook, I. (2010). Les risques et pollutions industriels sur le territoire dunkerquois: Des perceptions à la « concertation ». In FONCSI (Ed.), *Les Cahiers de la sécurité industrielle* (2010-07).

Organizing Risk Communication for Effective Preparedness: Using Plans as a Catalyst for Risk Communication

Amandine Berger-Sabbatel and Benoit Journé

Abstract Crisis response preparedness is a problematic issue for local governments. It is a responsibility with high stakes, but at the same time it is very distant from the daily management of the community. In France, local governments engage to a limited extent with preparedness by designing crisis response plans, which very often lack operationality. This paper examines the contribution of risk communication to effective crisis response preparedness. Indeed, technical and organizational issues are at the core of preparedness concerns, but we argue that political and cognitive dimensions are equally important, although often overlooked. The use of risk communication thus plays a critical role in the construction of reliable organizational response capabilities in order to face the unexpected, across all these dimensions. To understand this process, we examined the activity of a French risk manager whose objective is to support a group of municipalities in the organization of their respective organizational crisis responses. We found that to help the municipalities go beyond the limits of strictly organizational responses and engage in resilience, this manager uses the formal and technical character of the plan to generate rich cross-sectional communication that produces the conditions for resilience.

Keywords Crisis response plans · Preparedness · Resilience · Organizational reliability

Introduction: The Xynthia Disaster, a Failure of Risk Communication?

In 2014 in France, heavy prison sentences were handed down to the mayor and deputy mayor of La Faute-sur-Mer, a small coastal town, following the deaths of 29 inhabitants in the 2010 storm named Xynthia. Among other charges, they were

A. Berger-Sabbatel (✉) · B. Journé
Université de Nantes, Nantes, France
e-mail: abergersabbatel@gmail.com

M. Bourrier and C. Bieder (eds.), *Risk Communication for the Future*, SpringerBriefs in Safety Management, https://doi.org/10.1007/978-3-319-74098-0_3

accused of failing to inform the population and of failing to prepare a crisis response plan. They were also accused of having deliberately ignored the risks at the expense of the population's safety to favour economic interests. In his defence arguments, the mayor described himself as a '*small-town mayor*' with a poor understanding of crisis situations and little communal resources.

> How can you expect a small-town mayor, who does not always have the prior information needed, to plan [for the level of water reached during Storm Xynthia].
>
> I do not personally have the culture or the knowledge required to assess and anticipate such a disaster.
>
> I will not stop apologising, but at the time, I did not appreciate the situation, I could never have imagined such a catastrophe.[1]

However, government officials had alerted the mayor on several occasions about flooding risks. Detailed information on crisis response plans is also available specifically to mayors in order to help them prepare their own. The sentences were reduced on appeal after a long and painful trial that would go down in history as the first trial to convict elected municipal officials for '*involuntary manslaughter*'.

In this highly complex case, failures in risk communication were specifically highlighted by the court for their contribution to the drama. These failures are mainly attributed to the elected municipal officials. Externally, the lack of information for the population is to blame. Internally, there was no organizational risk communication within the municipality, so an organizational response to the crisis could not be put in place. But it seems fair to us to also mention a failure in risk communication at inter-organizational level. Although State officials (which represent expertise) had alerted the mayor many times over the years about the flooding risks, they clearly failed to raise sufficient risk awareness with the elected representatives of La Faute-sur-Mer to induce actual cognitive commitment into preparedness. They were aware of the attitude of denial of the mayor, but limited themselves to written warnings or oral warnings during meetings. '*What more could the government have done to make you aware of this major risk of a natural disaster?*' the President of the Court asked the mayor.

This is a central question for us. Administrative directives, information leaflets and oral warnings seem to have failed to reach their target, but this did not lead State officials to reconsider their risk communication methods. Indeed, we consider that effective risk communication should include much more than technical or organizational information transfers. This case shows us that cognitive and political dimensions must be taken into account in any risk communication strategy.

[1]2016, October 6. Court session. Mayor of La Faute-sur-Mer. Retrieved from http://www.charentelibre.fr/2014/10/06/proces-xynthia-l-ancien-maire-assure-avoir-tout-fait-pour-securiser-la-population,1918240.amp.html.

Communication as a Critical Element in Crisis Response Preparedness

Local governments are key players in risk management. The territories under their administration face numerous and various hazards, and they are responsible for the protection of the population. Regardless of the extent of the prevention measures they take, these organizations must be prepared to cope with a potential crisis. As the first level of crisis response, they are morally and legally responsible for organizing the safety of the population and leading civil defence operations. For example, they evacuate people, organize the water supply or rehouse stricken populations. This is a critical step to manage. Because of the seriousness of the threats, they cannot fail. Yet, unlike firefighters or emergency services, local governments are not 'crisis professionals', and managing the unexpected is not part of their daily work. Consequently, crisis response preparedness is all the more crucial to these actors.

Yet, despite their accountability, crisis management is not a core competency of local governments and preparedness is hardly ever a priority as it always competes with more pressing and more predictable issues (Boin and 't Hart 2003; Perry and Lindell 2003). Dramatic events like Hurricane Katrina in the United States (2005) or the Xynthia storm in France (2010) attest to the poor level of preparedness of public organizations. In both examples, the authorities were unprepared to face the events and proved themselves unable to make decisions that could have saved lives. Despite the seriousness of the issue, barely one-third of French municipalities have set up a formal crisis organization. Even where one exists, the preparedness process is often reduced to a written document with limited outreach and poor efficiency. Why do public administrations find it so difficult to organize the crisis response? In the United States, the House of Representatives raised a similar question after the Katrina disaster in 2005: '*Why do we continually seem one disaster behind?*' (Lagadec 2009b).

The traditional explanations of 'lack of resources or skills' are no longer enough. We argue that the level of resilience of a community is not directly linked to its size or the amount of resources invested in risk management (Berger-Sabbatel 2016). However, we analyse risk communication as a critical process in preparedness issues. Poor use of risk communication can seriously impact the effectiveness of crisis response, but this process remains underexplored and suffers from a general lack of understanding. In most cases, risk communication is reduced to formal information transfer to a limited audience, between those who design crisis response plans (very often, non-specialist civil servants) and those who implement them (the responders, particularly elected representatives). It excludes large parts of the organization and the external environment and does not require effective commitment from the responders in the preparedness process.

This restrictive approach to risk communication seems to have failed in its task of developing risk awareness and making crisis response preparedness a priority within local administrations. This approach focuses on the technical/organizational dimension of risk communication at the expense of political or cognitive considerations, which are also critical, as shown at La Faute-sur-Mer. Moreover, we argue that this approach to risk communication limits the capacity of municipalities to manage unexpected events. A purely technical approach to risk communication might lead actors to consider crisis response plans only as 'written documents', as a set of formal procedures and directives. It locks the organization into a crisis response strategy strictly based on anticipation, with no room for resilience (Wildavsky 1988).

Thus, our key research question is: how can we rethink the use of risk communication in order to improve the level of preparedness within organizations? Effective community preparedness requires a global risk communication strategy, including both the internal (the local public administration) and external audiences (citizens and other stakeholders). In this paper, we will focus more particularly on the internal aspect of risk communication that takes place within the organization regarding preparedness. We present a different perspective on risk communication that is often overlooked by field actors and little developed in preparedness theories. We propose to analyse risk communication as a key element in the construction of organizational response capabilities in order to face the unexpected. Communication can be a powerful linchpin between the two opposite organizational logics of anticipation and resilience (Weick 1987). From this perspective, risk communication significantly contributes to producing the political, organizational and cognitive conditions required for organizational reliability.

In this chapter, we will address this question through the use of crisis response plans, which are the principal tools available to municipalities in order to organize and manage their crisis response. Our results are based on a field study exploring the managerial work of a French risk manager. The main findings show that plans can be creatively used to develop intensive communication activity. Thus, the communication initiated during the planning process goes far beyond fostering the technical organization of crisis response. As it produces substantial social interactions and actual/effective cognitive commitment (Keller et al. 2012), it enables sensemaking and self-reflection, which are necessary requirements for better resilience and reliability in crisis response.

The Stakes of Anticipation and Resilience for Preparedness

In post-2001 United States, the priority in terms of risk management was given to homeland security at the expense of prevention of natural disasters, which partly explains the poor management of Hurricane Katrina. Nevertheless, management of the next major hurricane, hurricane Gustav, that occured in 2008 was also unsatisfactory, despite the efforts initiated in this area since the Katrina disaster. '*Five days before the expected arrival of Hurricane Gustav, Governor Jindal declared a state of emergency and the population of New Orleans was evacuated before the storm reached the coast*' (Steiger 2007). However, the various shelters that had been prepared proved to be inadequate to house the displaced populations. Baton Rouge was considered to be a shelter town for those fleeing New Orleans and the authorities even located the crisis management operations centre there. In fact, the consequences of Gustav were quite different from those of Katrina. The authorities had prepared a response to a Katrina-like situation: they focused on a massive flooding scenario and on the New Orleans area. Instead, they faced a wind event that seriously damaged the Baton Rouge area: Hurricane Gustav caused a massive power outage (Boin 2009) that totally paralysed Baton Rouge, with severe consequences on shelters, hospitals, transports, water and food supply networks.

Like Xynthia, these examples from Hurricanes Katrina and Gustav both illustrate that preparedness is simultaneously a political, an organizational and a cognitive issue. Indeed, the initiation of preparedness actions results from political decisions and initially requires effective awareness and involvement from senior management (Boin and t'Hart 2003). But the process of preparedness itself is equally important in order to ensure the effectiveness of preparedness actions. Indeed, this example proves the inherent limits of strictly planned crisis responses. In this way, effective preparedness cannot solely depend on the anticipative logic conveyed by plans. We argue that effective preparedness requires more flexibility and the ability to analyse and to make sense of the crisis situation before making decisions. It is a call for more resilience, according to Wildavsky's definition (1988). Thus, the need for both anticipation and resilience presents us with an organizational dilemma, because these two organizational models have opposing features (Journé 2009).

Crisis Response Plans in the French Preparedness Framework

We selected the French preparedness framework to support our argument. Indeed, France is also confronted with the twofold problem described above: the general lack of preparedness coupled with a lack of efficiency in existing preparedness actions. Of the 36,000 French municipalities, barely one-third of them have set up a formal crisis organization, 10 years after the enactment of a binding law.[2] This often takes the form of a written plan, the PCS (for Plan Communal de Sauvegarde, or Crisis Response Plan). There are no mandatory rules for designing the PCS—each municipality is free to design a model that fulfils its needs—but a template is proposed by the French Ministry of the Interior to guide municipalities.[3] As the

[2]Loi n° 2004-811 du 13 août 2004 de modernisation de la sécurité civile.

[3]A PCS template (guidelines provided by an institutional actor, Le Mémento du maire, IRMa) includes sections on the definition of major hazards; A territorial risk analysis; Information to the population; Alert: Strategy and resources for dissemination; Safety instructions; Hazard mapping; Potential shelter areas; Recommended routes; Housing capacity; Available technical, material and human resources; Specific requirements for the involvement of a pool of volunteers from civil society (if any); On-call duty procedures; Crisis management centre: location, actors; Phonebook; Summary documents with the basic procedures; Pre-prepared administrative documents; Instructions for training, crisis simulations and PCS tests; Recovery process.

PCS is the only compulsory element of crisis response organization at local level, the preparedness process is often reduced to a written document with limited outreach. Very few municipalities have a dedicated risk department or officer. Generally, plans are designed internally, by a non-specialist employee, a trainee, or by an external consultant. Many times, the responders are not included in the planning process, and they are informed of their role in crisis response at the end of the process. As a result, people do not buy into the plan, and it lacks operationality (Blanc 2015).

Using Crisis Response Plans as Living Documents: The Limits of Anticipation

Although preparedness cannot be limited to the written plan, the latter centralizes all the elements of the process; it is the visible part of crisis response organization. Because of its formal character, for many organizations, the plan is mainly seen as an administrative document, as a legal obligation to fulfil, instead of as a living document.

However, there is an intangible part of planning that is essential but that cannot be documented directly on paper, such as '*the development of managers' knowledge of the resources of governmental and private organizations, the sharpening of their conceptual skills in anticipating emergency demands and balancing these against available resources, and the establishment of linkages across organizational boundaries between emergency planners and operations personnel*' (Perry and Lindell 2003, pp. 346–347). This intangible part of planning can be developed through frequent crisis simulations and the provision of feedback that helps to transform the written plan into a living document, as preparedness handbooks rightly recommend. In this way, we should distinguish the 'Plan' (as a document) from 'planning' (as a process). But we also argue that preparedness is even more than an organizational planning process and must involve cognitive and political considerations. To this end, we believe that preparedness strategies must go beyond the pure organizational logic of anticipation conveyed by the plans and simultaneously commit to a logic of resilience.

The Organizational Logic of Resilience as Opposed to the Anticipatory Logic Conveyed by Plans

The written, documented and formal part of the Plan is important as a first set of guidelines in the unstable environment of the crisis (Lagadec 2009a). However, there is a danger of blindly following the written procedures. According to Weick (1987), crisis management requires both anticipation and adaptation in order to cope with the unexpected. For decision-makers, this is a delicate situation in which communication processes are strategic. Social and time pressures often hasten decision-making. Instead, Weick argues that in unstable environments, decisions do not need to be made first but that it is important to understand the situation before making decisions, '*in order to see what, if anything, there is to decide*' (Weick 1987, p. 123). This ability to stand back and assess the situation, to see the big picture, is a core competency for organizations that seek to manage the unexpected. Sensemaking requires the association of reflection and action, through an intensive communication process that allows constant adjustments of procedures according to the specific features of the situation, whereas a crisis response strategy strictly based on anticipation does not allow for management of the unexpected. Anticipation intends to eliminate ambiguity and uncertainty by dissociating reflection from action, in order to reduce action to the mere implementation of endorsed procedures and plans (Journé 2009). This clear division between those who design plans and those who implement them raises the question of buy-in (Wildavsky 1973). Thus, it is not just a communication matter, but also a political one, a question of power and legitimacy for those who design the plan. We note the antagonism that appears between the logic of anticipation, which mainly relies on plans, rigid decision-making process and top-down communication, and the logic of resilience (as defined by Wildavsky 1988), which relies on adaptation, decentralization of decision-making and ongoing communication.

The articulation of these two opposing logics results in a rare organizational ability that we place at the core of effective preparedness. The development of this ability challenges the management of preparedness processes, as it is theoretically impossible for all but a very limited category of organizations[4] (LaPorte and Consolini 1991). Our study points out some particular forms of communication that, if wisely managed, can support the articulation of anticipation and resilience within organizations engaged in preparedness processes.

Communication Processes as a Way to Combine Anticipation and Resilience

The use of 'storytelling' as described by Weick (1987) is a good example of communication used as a tool for the combination of anticipation and resilience. According to the author, '*stories are important, not just because they coordinate, but also because they register, summarize, and allow reconstruction of scenarios that are too complex for logical linear summaries to preserve (…) Models are*

[4]These organizations are qualified as 'High Reliable Organizations' by organizational literature. These are a group of very specific organizations capable of maintaining very high levels of safety in high-risk environments on a daily basis, such as nuclear power plants or aircraft carriers. This literature inspired our research.

unable to connect as many facts as stories, they preserve fewer interactions, and they are unable to put these interactions in motion so that outcomes can be anticipated' (Weick 1987, p. 125). In this way, the use of stories during the anticipation phase effectively fills the breaches of the plans. It enables sensemaking during the resolution of crises.

Godé-Sanchez (2011) highlights another particular form of communication: the practice of feedback is a collective method for sensemaking, which is a critical process during the management of unexpected events (Weick 1993), especially for coordination. Godé describes the particular form of feedback used by an aerobatic crew of pilots for the French air force. This particular form of feedback—tending to be rather direct and informal—significantly differs from more classic forms of feedback, because it focuses on the '*experiential nature of the knowledge*' transferred. During these feedback sessions, '*we don't talk about theoretic knowledge. We talk about perceptions*' says a pilot. '*Knowledge is mainly transferred through discussions and informal dialogues*' (Godé-Sanchez 2011, p. 424). The direct and informal character of the feedback encourages frequent self and group reflection. Besides, doubt is singled out as an essential cognitive process for the management of the unexpected (Weick 2009). Godé insists on the verbal tradition of this feedback and highlights the importance of the existence of areas that encourage it (we will compare this area with the '*discussion spaces*' described by Detchessahar 2003). In this case, the restroom is a place where pilots, mechanics and office staff can discuss recent but also older experiences over a coffee. These informal practices of socialization favour the cohesion of a collective of various profiles (pilots, mechanics and office staff); they allow better knowledge and trust between the actors. They contribute to the development of a '*collective mind*' that is essential for the development of sensemaking capacities (Weick and Roberts 1993). Indeed, the authors insist on the importance of the collective for the development of personal and organizational capabilities to manage the unexpected.

Empirical Settings

The case we present in this chapter comes from a longitudinal case study,[5] designed on the principles of action and intervention research (Allard-Poesi and Perret 2003, 2004; David 2012). We studied the case of a group of French municipalities[6] confronted with the double difficulty of a general lack of preparedness throughout

[5]The case study comes from our doctoral research: Berger-Sabbatel (2016). 'Organiser la montée en fiabilité d'un collectif d'organisations. Acteurs, outils et modes de management. Le cas des collectivités territoriales face à la crise'. Ph.D. thesis, Université de Nantes.

[6]In France, the municipalities are the level of local administration. They are given the opportunity to work together (an assembly of several municipalities constitutes an intercommunality) in order to pool some resources. Regarding risk issues, the management of any crisis remains a municipal attribution; the intercommunality cannot supersede the municipality in this area.

the intercommunal area and the limited efficiency of the few existing emergency preparedness plans. In that sense, this case is significant regarding the overall French preparedness situation. What is specific and interesting in this case was the existence of a risk manager, from the intercommunal organization, whose mission was to provide support to the various municipalities regarding preparedness, in the absence of relevant expertise within most of the municipalities in this area.

Indeed, according to French law, each municipality is responsible for implementing its own PCS, but very few of them have the organizational skills to do so. For example, in the group we studied, only 3 out of 24 municipalities have a dedicated risk department (or at least a dedicated risk manager). Most of the time, the PCS is designed by a municipal officer,[7] whose main job is not related to risk, in addition to their daily tasks. The municipalities explain that their limited resources mean they cannot dedicate more organizational capacity to risk management. Nevertheless, as we mentioned earlier, the level of preparedness of an organization is also the result of political arbitrations.

The very existence of an intercommunal expert position regarding risk and crisis management makes this case specific, as it is the first French intercommunal organization to offer such a resource to its members. Through a close follow-up of the managerial activity of this intercommunal expert, we observed the evolution of preparedness over the intercommunal area in the different municipalities, using shadowing and observation techniques (Czarniawska 2007, 2008). We balanced this intercommunal perspective by conducting interviews in different municipalities. Our result highlights the original way the intercommunal risk manager uses the PCS, as the linchpin of a combination of three organizational resources that support risk communication towards municipalities: an actor (the risk manager), a management tool (the PCS) and a discussion space (the GT PCS).

The Organizational Resources that Support Risk Communication

As expertise (intercommunal level) and decision-making (municipal level) depend on distinct organizational entities, communication between these entities is a decisive process. The intercommunal risk manager mainly channels his expertise to the municipalities through the intermediary of municipal officers in charge of the PCS who try, in turn, to pass on their new knowledge throughout their respective organizations. At different levels, the intercommunal risk manager and the PCS officers both act as communication intermediaries. The communication process between the experts from the intercommunal risk manager and the PCS officers is

[7]For example, in the group of municipalities we studied, we identified an elected councilor, a technical employee, an employee from the civil defence or legal department and even a municipal policeman as PCS officers.

intense, regular and structured. It takes the form of regular meetings (the GT PCS, discussed in the next section), data collection and information sharing (e.g. hazard mappings, crisis management feedback, etc.), training sessions (e.g. crisis simulations), individual support when necessary and one-off events (e.g. meetings with risk experts).

What is particularly interesting is that the communication initiated by the intercommunal risk manager is not limited to top-down knowledge transfer. Above all, they act as an intermediary between the different PCS officers so that they can meet and exchange about risk issues in their respective areas (particularly during the GT PCS meetings), and as an intermediary between the municipalities and other organizations involved in risk management (police, firefighters, state administrations, industries, etc.). In this way, this stakeholder has a very central position in the preparedness strategy of the intercommunal area. While officially providing technical assistance for planning, they simultaneously build a collective of other stakeholders and develop the organizational capacities to articulate anticipation and resilience within that collective. We discovered that the intercommunal risk manager uses the PCS as a real gateway to legitimize preparedness and implement an extensive preparedness strategy that goes far beyond mere planning. Legal, technical dimensions of the plan and the overall planning process are a pretext for in-depth (inter)organizational and cognitive work: the anticipation logic supports the development of a resilience logic. This is the purpose of the GT PCS working group, which we identified as the central communication space built around the PCS. The aim of the intercommunal manager is not to replace the municipalities in designing the plan, but to create the conditions for sensemaking, to enable social interactions and cognitive commitment.

GT PCS: The PCS Working Group as a '*Discussion Space*'

Every 6 weeks or so, the intercommunal risk manager (or project manager) leads a working group named 'GT PCS' to help the municipalities produce a living document. The group members are mainly the PCS officers from each municipality, but the group also includes some senior managers and elected officials. During the GT PCS sessions, the intercommunal risk manager leads the meeting with the following themes:

- Basic and specific knowledge on crisis management (legal developments, benchmark on crisis management, etc.),
- Methodological help for planning the crisis response (PCS and other specific procedures),
- Articulation of the municipal plans with the intercommunal crisis procedures,
- Feedback on crisis resolutions and on crisis simulations,
- External network and general risk knowledge: introduction of partners for crisis resolution (e.g. firefighter or prefectural services), visits to industrial sites, etc.

These GT PCS meetings constitute a specific and exceptionally rich communication channel that structures the action of the intercommunal risk manager towards municipalities and the relationships between the different entities. The project manager's objective is for the working party to fulfil the needs of the municipalities. Although the meeting is led by the project manager, the goal is for the municipal representatives to become proactive in these meetings: to propose which themes they want to discuss, to share feedback on crises, to take the lead and drive the organization of the next GT PCS session, etc. In this way, the PCS as a document is a communication medium for all risk- and crisis-related issues; it is a support for discussing operational matters and describing what crisis management really means in the field, with the added strength of details and anecdotes which do not always appear in written feedback. Crisis management is not always what you imagine, nor does it always require sticking to the plan.

> When there is something to say, I say it. Sometimes it's even a bit…not gory but I do go into the details. It never happens as we think it would, because we can't identify the victim, can't find the family, there isn't a doctor available because it's Sunday night, and because it's a Sunday night the main police force isn't available, only the weekend auxiliaries (Mayor of a small town).

> We had the case of someone who killed themselves by jumping under a train. As it was very early in the morning, around 7:30 am, (…) the elected official went directly to the site before going to work. He saw the firemen, the close family (…) and then at 9 am, journalists appeared in the Town Hall saying 'so, tell us more about this suicide' and everyone just stared, no one knew what they were talking about. The communication department was not happy at all, and the Mayor discovered there had been a suicide in his town… (PCS officer of a medium-sized town)

> I was an hour away from [my town] when [my manager] called one Sunday afternoon to tell me there was a huge fire in the city centre and he couldn't get in touch with anyone. Ok, so he couldn't get in touch with anyone. He'd called all the work mobiles and no one had answered except me. (…) So, I went back to the city. And, to make matters worse, it was carnival, so it took me ages to reach [the site of the fire]. And then I asked him to get me the file with the list of people on call in it…Because it hadn't occurred to him to look at this file and ring those on call at home for example. (Senior manager of a big city).

> When there was this [major fire in the city centre] we put in place a communal meeting place, a hub of assistance for the population. (…) But, this hub did not get structured the way it had been planned (in our emergency plan) because what we had written did not actually correspond to the reality. (Risk manager of a big city).

Mutual trust is important for sharing this informal feedback, that is why forming and managing this group is a critical ability.

As the intercommunal risk manager (which represents the intercommunal organization) has expertise but no authority in crisis management, it uses the anticipative culture of municipalities combined with the mandatory character of the PCS to establish its legitimacy, to take action within a municipal area of decision and responsibility. Hence, the PCS is first used by the intercommunal risk manager as a gateway to initiating communication between the actor with the expertise and the actor with the authority concerning crisis management. Nevertheless, the action of the intercommunal risk manager goes far beyond providing technical assistance to produce a formal document. Our study shows that the more the time passes, the more the agenda of the GT PCS sessions moves away from organizational and technical topics towards more political and cognitive issues: social networking, argumentative PCS reviews and collective lectures of crisis management feedback by the PCS officers. We even noticed a tendency for the municipal PCS officer to use these meetings to discuss unrelated risk issues in the absence of any other collective areas to openly discuss inter-organizational matters (like problems of coordination between the municipal and intermunicipal services for daily management, about equipment or bills, for example).

As the 'GT PCS' is a regular meeting, it creates a solid network based on deep relationships (participants know and trust each other) and enriched by a variety of profiles and competencies (see the concept of 'requisite variety', Weick 1987). Thanks to these regular meetings, the PCS officers from different municipalities exchange information about their problems and methods to achieve and implement the PCS. For example, there is frequent feedback on crisis management. Every time a crisis occurs in a municipality, the PCS officer explains what happened and how the crisis was managed, emphasizing the strengths but also the weaknesses of the crisis management experience. This narrative exercise, with the force of real examples and anecdotes, has a strong impact on the group, close to the storytelling effect (Weick 1987). Using the plan as a starting point, the action of the intercommunal risk manager enhances both the anticipative abilities of the municipalities and their resilience capacities: experience sharing raises general risk awareness that initiates preventive actions but also confronts the actors with their own practices and induces doubt and self-reflection, which are essentials characters for a better combination of anticipation and resilience. Sharing experiences also contributes to progressively developing a 'collective mind' (Weick and Roberts 1993) that helps to face the complexity of crisis situations. Communication during the GT PCS favours open discussions rather than a top-down transfer of the best practices. These discussions are based on experience sharing and the expression of doubts. However, we stress the important managerial work necessary to maintain group cohesion and to create the positive and confident atmosphere that facilitates those discussions.

Conclusion

We have analysed the GT PCS sessions as 'discussion spaces' that enable the organization of crisis management to be questioned (Detchessahar 2003). Without the existence of such a dedicated area (with an official role), it would be extremely difficult for the PCS officers to engage in deep self-reflection about their practices and to go beyond the anticipative logic of planning. The plan, which is initially a document, transforms into a reflexive tool through the intermediation of a discussion area, the GT PCS, which organizes intensive communication activity around the plan, and through the managerial work of an actor, the intercommunal risk manager. Thus, our work calls for a more communicational approach of preparedness.

References

Allard-Poesi, F., & Perret, V. (2003). La recherche-action. In Y. Giordano (Ed.), *Conduire un projet de recherche. Une perspective qualitative* (pp. 85–132). Caen: Editions EMS.

Allard-Poesi, F., & Perret, V. (2004). La construction collective du problème dans la recherche-action: difficultés, ressorts et enjeux. *Finance Contrôle Stratégie, 7*(4), 5–36.

Berger-Sabbatel, A. (2016). *Organiser la montée en fiabilité d'un collectif d'organisations. Acteurs, outils et modes de management. Le cas des collectivités territoriales face à la crise.* Ph.D. thesis, Université de Nantes.

Blanc, P. (2015). Les PCS 10 ans après, point de vue du Ministère de l'Intérieur. *Risques infos 34.*

Boin, A. (2009). The new world of crises and crisis management: Implications for policymaking and research. *Review of Policy Research, 26*(4), 367–377.

Boin, A., & 't Hart, P. (2003). Public leadership in times of crisis: Mission impossible? *Public Administration Review, 63*(5), 544–553.

Czarniawska, B. (2007). *Shadowing: And other techniques for doing fieldwork in modern societies.* Copenhagen Business School Press DK.

Czarniawska, B. (2008). Organizing: How to study it and how to write about it. *Qualitative Research in Organizations and Management: An International Journal, 3*(1), 4–20.

David, A. (2012). La recherche-intervention, cadre général pour la recherche en management? In A. David, A. Hatchuel, & R. Laufer (Eds.), *Les nouvelles fondations des sciences de gestion* (pp. 241–264). Presses des Mines.

Detchessahar, M. (2003). L'avènement de l'entreprise communicationnelle? Outils, problèmes et politique d'accompagnement. *Revue française de gestion, 142,* 6584.

Godé-Sanchez, C. (2011). Construire le sens par le retour d'expérience: le cas de l'Equipe de Voltige de l'Armée de l'air. *Management & Avenir, 41,* 416–434.

Journé, B. (2009). Les organisations de haute fiabilité. In X. Michel & P. Cavaillé (Eds.), *Le management des risques pour un développement durable. Qualité, santé sécurité et environnement,* (pp. 367–384), Dunod.

Keller, A. C., Ansell, C. K., Reingold, A. L., Bourrier, M., Hunter, M. D., Burrowes, S., et al. (2012). Improving pandemic response: A sensemaking perspective on the spring 2009 H1N1 pandemic. *Risk, Hazards & Crisis in Public Policy, 3*(2), 1–37.

Lagadec, P. (2009a). La question des plans. Entre points d'appui et pièges stratégiques. *Cahiers de recherche de l'Ecole Polytechnique, Département d'économie, 40.*

Lagadec, P. (2009b). A new cosmology of risks and crises: Time for a radical shift in paradigm and practice. *Review of Policy Research, 26*(4), 475–488.

LaPorte, T. R., & Consolini, P. M. (1991). Working in practice but not in theory: Theoretical challenges of "high reliability organizations". *Journal of Public Administration Research and Theory: J-Part, 1*(1), 19–48.

Perry, R. W., & Lindell, M. K. (2003). Preparedness for emergency response: guidelines for the emergency planning process. *Disasters, 27*(4), 336–350.

Steiger, E. (2007). *L'ouragan Katrina: les leçons d'un échec. Les faiblesses du dispositif de sécurité intérieure des Etats-Unis.* Mémoire. Collège interarmées de défense—Diploweb, janvier 2008.

Weick, K. E. (1987). Organizational culture as a source of high reliability. *California Management Review, 29*(2), 112–127.

Weick, K. E. (1993). The collapse of sensemaking in organizations: The Mann Gulch disaster. *Administrative Science Quarterly, 38*(4), 628–652.

Weick, K. E. (2009). *Leadership as the legitimation of doubt. making sense of the organization: The impermanent organization*. Chichester, UK: Wiley.

Weick, K. E., & Roberts, K. H. (1993). Collective mind in organizations. Heedful interrelating on flight decks. *Administrative Science Quarterly, 38,* 357–381.

Wildavsky, A. (1973). If Planning is Everything, Maybe it's Nothing. *Policy Science, 4,* 127–153.

Wildavsky, A. (1988). *Searching for safety*. New Brunswick: Transaction Books.

Nuclear Crisis Preparedness Lessons Learned from Fukushima Daiichi

Geneviève Baumont

Abstract Before the Fukushima Daiichi accident in 2011, the French Institute of Radiological Protection and Nuclear Safety, IRSN, was little-known to the French public. On the whole, French nuclear safety procedures are complex and the public is largely unaware of them. Moreover, communication was difficult because IRSN had to gain public trust as a result of the negative memory associated with the communication approach taken by the government in 1986 when managing the Chernobyl fallout. This communication approach led to a loss of public trust in official bodies in general. During the Fukushima Daiichi crisis, the importance of communication in such a period was largely emphasized, although France was absolutely not at risk. IRSN operations were adapted in order to explain the risks linked to this disaster to the media, companies, and French citizens. Two hundred IRSN staff members answered queries non-stop for 6 weeks, exploring the new ways of communication and interaction offered by social networks. In the years after the disaster, experts from institutions such as IRSN examined all the post-accident situations where Japanese citizens and expatriates turned to buying Geiger counters, developing new sensors to make measurements and becoming addicted to the internet to find information of all kinds, in an attempt to forge their own opinion about the importance of nuclear risks. This is the reason why IRSN developed a strategy not only to inform people with the basic useful knowledge in such situations but also to try to "empower people" by helping them to measure and share their data. The goal is to multiply the number of people aware of what radioactivity is and its associated risks, capable of measuring the level of radioactivity and interpreting it. This strategy requires communication tools and partners. IRSN is associated with IFFO RME, the French Institute of trainers on Major risks and the environment, a body with close links to the national education ministry.

G. Baumont (✉)
Institut de Radioprotection et de Sûreté Nucléaire (IRSN), Fontenay-Aux-Roses, France
e-mail: baumont.g@orange.fr

M. Bourrier and C. Bieder (eds.), *Risk Communication for the Future*, SpringerBriefs in Safety Management, https://doi.org/10.1007/978-3-319-74098-0_4

Keywords Fukushima · Crisis · Communication · Ionizing radiation
Contamination · Citizen science · Public information · Media · "Safecast"

Communication Challenges Before the Fukushima Accident

Created in 2002, IRSN is a public body with industrial and commercial activities, operating under the joint supervision of the Ministers in charge of Energy, Environment, Health, Defence, and Research. The main missions of the Institute are Research, Assessment, and Public service missions including Public Information. The fields of activity are broad, covering nuclear safety, radioprotection of workers, radioprotection of the population and the environment, radiation protection of workers and the public in nuclear medicine, emergency preparedness and post-accident operational support, security and control of nuclear sensitive materials, and security of nuclear facilities.

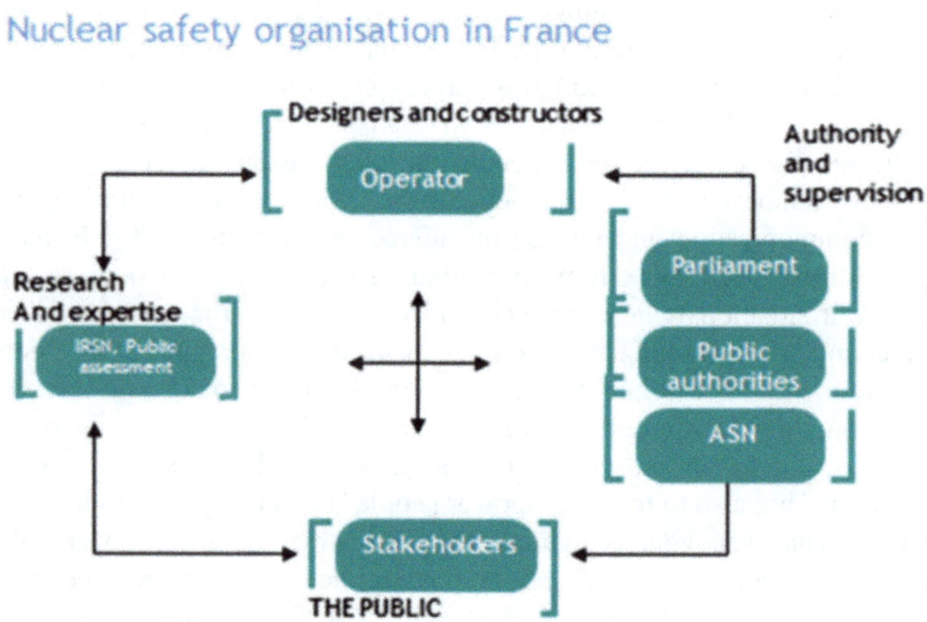

For IRSN, before the Fukushima crisis, communication was a challenge, because in April 1986, government communication when managing the Chernobyl fallout led to a loss of public trust in official bodies (even today more than 63% of French people still do not trust the Nuclear Safety Authority (IRSN 2011a, 2012a)). The general public believe that "the government lied," with the most symbolic sentence used in France to resume the communication at this period being "The fallout cloud stopped at the border."

The strategy of IRSN's communication department before the accident was to develop an independence of judgment inside the Institute and at the same time to increase IRSN's visibility and confidence in it from the media and the general public. All IRSN experts and researchers were involved to reach this objective through, for example, media training to better understand the ins and outs and the constraints of the media.

For the above reasons, in 2010, IRSN also developed specific actions to inform the public with the basic useful knowledge for crisis situations. The main thrust of this strategy is to reinforce background knowledge in high schools and among the general public encountered during science fairs. IRSN and its experts regularly provide interactive lectures for high schools based on a presentation freely distributed to teachers who integrate nuclear science into their program.

How Did IRSN Experience the Fukushima Daiichi Crisis?

During the Fukushima Daiichi crisis, the Institute provided accurate real-time information to local authorities, the media, the public and civil society, mobilizing experts and the communication unit (IRSN 2012a). Institutions such as IRSN were facing an unprecedented situation. With requests coming from all sides, the institute prepared daily electronic bulletins, summarizing our analysis of the state of Japanese nuclear plants and the consequences for the population and the environment. Nearly, all of the ministerial offices subscribed to these bulletins. IRSN also participated, each morning, in meetings of the French inter-ministerial emergency response group, led by the Secretary of the Defence and National Security, reporting to the Prime Minister. The Institute was called upon by the Parliamentary office of scientific and technological evaluation, which provides information to Parliament and guides its decisions. The simulation of the radioactive plume from Fukushima made available online shortly after the accident was followed all over the world, as were the reports on the contamination and environmental effects on land and in the sea (Video IRSN 2012). Consequently, for 6 weeks, 200 IRSN staff members answered questions non-stop from companies and French citizens to explain the risks linked to this disaster.

The health impact and environmental impact units quickly proved to be essential. The health impact unit set up base in an IRSN conference room. Eight full-time experts, assisted by 16 experts working in rotation, responded to 1300 requests received in just 4 weeks from physicians and Occupational Health Physicians, the press, and the general public. They were especially busy when the contaminated air masses reached France. The unit also scanned 250 people returning from Japan (journalists, expatriates, airline pilots, etc.) with a whole-body counter to check them for contamination and provided 300 passive dosimeters to people headed for Japan. The importance of communication in such a period was largely highlighted, even if France was absolutely not at risk.

Social Media and Media Pressure During the Crisis

From March 11 to March 31, 2011, social media demonstrated its incredible power. On Twitter, for example, the hashtag #Fukushima was used over 500 million times between March 11 and April 11, 2011. Already on March 11, the day of the accident, an increase of 33 million tweets per day was recorded, and the creation of 572,000 new accounts was seen from March 12, 2011 on. 1840 people subscribed to the IRSN Twitter account @suretenucleaire (on April 15, 2011). In France, the Fukushima nuclear accident entirely occupied the attention of all key players in the nuclear industry, politicians, and the media for more than 5 weeks.

The communication team organized press conferences and interviews with experts in response to some 1365 media requests. This meant responding to more than 100 interview requests per day, with mandatory deadlines, and using language that was easily understandable. For example, the French newspaper *Le Monde* wraps up at 10:30 am: they needed an expert by 9 am at the latest. Radio stations needed regular information bulletins, and television stations needed content for the 1 pm and 8 pm news programs. So, three representatives were quickly named for different fields: facility safety, environment, and health. Their greatest difficulty was to provide information in real time. The following data published by the agency Kantar Media, a French media analyst, proves the extreme media hype even in France due to the Fukushima accident: this event was mentioned more than 14,000 times in French press, radio, and television. IRSN was mentioned more than 5000 times.

Main Facts of the Crisis Management Strategy

11 March: 7:00 am Earthquake in Japan. At 11 h, the IRSN Technical Emergency and Response Center is activated, and at 5 pm a paper on the earthquake is published on the IRSN website.
12 March: 8:50 am reactor 1 exploded. At 8 pm, a paper on the situation is published on the IRSN website.
14 March: 3:30 am reactor 3 exploded. At 4 pm, the Japanese measurement results from the environment are available on the IRSN website.
15 March: 0:05 am reactor 3 exploded, reactor 4 is burning, first media conference in IRSN, first FAQ publication.
16 March: the Prime Minister, F. Fillon, announced in the National Assembly that data on the level of contamination in the environment are available on the IRSN website.
17 March: the first modeling of the fallout cloud in Japan is published on the IRSN website.
19 March: the modeling of the fallout cloud across the world is published on the IRSN website.
22 March: the cloud with very few radioactive particles reached France; consequently, the number of visits to the IRSN website reached a significant peak.

The IRSN documents in French and English used during this period are published on the IRSN web pages, FAQ and Earthquake and nuclear crisis in Japan in 2011 (IRSN 2011a).

The Website Success

The chart below shows the increase in the number of website visits during Fukushima crisis. From March 13–17, more than 50 technical suggestions proposed by the public to solve the situation were posted to the IRSN contact box. IRSN's website infrastructure was modified several times, from 2 to 20 servers, to address the increasing number of visits. The webmaster was on duty day and night and slept only a few hours a day, because there was no one to take over from him. Today, two webmasters will be able to replace each other in case of an emergency situation.

The IRSN (2011b) contact box received 1054 requests, not only from French public but also worldwide. More than 1000 questions were asked by the public. The following graph shows which topics were of most concern for the public, over time.

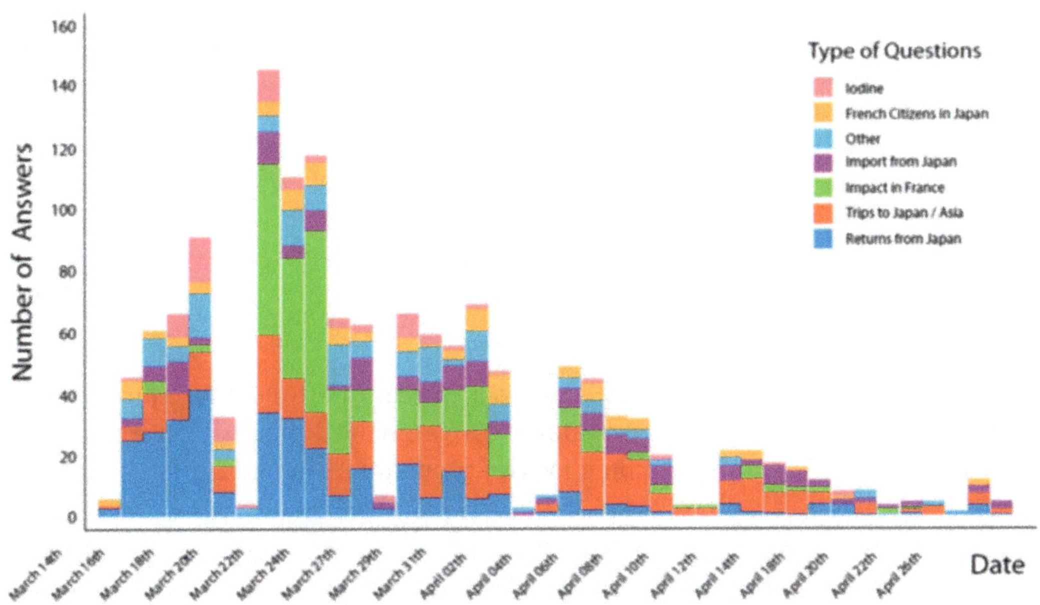

Why Was Communication "Successful"?

With a disaster such as the Fukushima nuclear accident, it is of course awkward to speak of "successful" communication by IRSN, but it was recognized that, for the first time, IRSN had increasing media attention, confidence, and website engagement. Naturally, the priority of Japanese experts was emergency response management to recover the situation and to deal with the safety of the population and workers of the plant affected.

As the IRSN experts were not directly involved in emergency response management, the experts were able to concentrate only on the scientific and technical assessments by closely following the daily situation of the NPP. The assessments, based on 30 years of research and experience feedback in the nuclear field, served to advise the French public authorities and to inform the public.

The technical and scientific competencies of IRSN staff (200 people during more than 5 weeks) were therefore available simply for communication purposes in the form of a 24 h information service. Five spokespersons were continuously available for the media. And from the beginning of the nuclear crisis, the IRSN experts never minimized the Fukushima accident. This was also the result of a long-term strategy of communication implemented by IRSN over more than 10 years, based on a strong relationship and understanding between scientific experts and the communication team.

Despite the clear and trustworthy information given by IRSN and despite the fact that there were no direct casualties in Japan due to the nuclear accident, public surveys showed that this did not stop French citizens losing confidence in nuclear power.[1]

How the Fukushima Accident Influenced the Communication Approach Worldwide

The shock of the earthquake, followed by a tsunami and the subsequent nuclear disaster, made the communication situation extremely difficult. Further difficulty was caused by the local population's lack of preparation and education concerning

[1]The proportion of respondents to IRSN's annual risk perception survey answering "no" to the question "Do you trust the French authorities concerning the risk mitigation actions for citizens" rose from 39 to 42% concerning nuclear power plants, and from 63 to 64% for radioactive fallout from the Chernobyl accident between 2011 and 2015 (IRSN 2011a, 2012a).

nuclear risks. A lot of the extra stress and trauma experienced by this population, as well as their dramatic stigmatization by certain parts of Japanese society but also by the rest of the world, could have been avoided by better public education.

In their article, Yamashita and Takamura (2015) draw attention to "*a lack of or inadequate knowledge and education on radiation protection and radiation health risk management has evoked a serious confusion and adverse reaction on information from the different communication tools such as social media that low-dose radiation effects still contain uncertainty, thus complicating risk perception of the general public.*"

The great difference between the communication during the Chernobyl nuclear accident and that of the Fukushima accident demonstrates how important it is to query and review the information and communication approaches not only at European level but also worldwide, in particular at IAEA OECD.

The experience feedback of the communication behavior during/in the aftermath of such an accident from the nuclear regulatory bodies and the different agencies were discussed in workshops with the aim of drafting guidelines in order to try and harmonize practices, taking into account the New Information Technologies (NIT) used by the public, in particular social media and new smartphone applications.

These reviews underline the influence of social media in the context of a nuclear accident. One IAEA document mentions the following:

> More casually, social media is described as a landscape of internet platforms where users can interact easily and share ideas, opinions and information. With social media, information dissemination – be it personal, commercial, or official government information – has become easier, faster, cheaper, and accessible to more people. One can target the audience in ways that weren't possible before. (Sköld and Feldman 2014)

Notably, the same document notes that: "*Statistics suggest that about 100 h of video are uploaded to YouTube every minute, 500 million tweets are sent daily, 1.6 million public photos are uploaded to Flickr per day and 30 billion pieces of content are shared on Facebook every month.*"

Most reports state that the main challenge in using social media is assuring not only data quality but also evaluating the credibility of sources, dealing with the transitory and voluminous nature of social media information, data management, and ethics.

In 2014, the IAEA published in their proceedings papers this analysis: the Efficacy of Social Media as a Research Tool and Information Source for Safeguards Verification (Sköld and Feldman 2014). It gives guidelines on communication with the public in a nuclear or radiological emergency (IAEA 2012). Later, in 2015, they published reference document which provides a method for developing a communication strategy dedicated to a nuclear or radiological emergency (IAEA 2015).

From Communication to Public Empowerment

Lessons learned from the Fukushima Daiichi NPP crisis and its aftermath have confirmed that lack of knowledge and understanding during emergencies is extraordinarily stressful and will have negative psychological consequences, not only for people directly affected but also for those witnessing it from a distance. For an individual, improved understanding changes their perspective, transforming them from feeling like a helpless victim into an actor who has some degree of power over the situation. One of the challenges of a nuclear accident is to prepare for the post-accident phase, and to be adequately aware of the wider consequences that can be produced by the accident. The population most affected by nuclear fallout may be obliged to evacuate or to live in contaminated areas with many constraints. Because citizens in this situation will likely need to carefully follow the recommendations of authorities in order to limit their individual exposure, it is very important that they trust decision-makers. Taking their own readings [of radiation] helps citizens become knowledgeable active participants in the safety dialogue. Other local citizens as well as consumers worldwide who might be considered less directly affected by radioactive contamination nevertheless have a valid stake in accurate information. Lack of knowledge, mistrust of authorities, and receptivity to misinformation can lead many to erroneously consider a country which in fact has suffered hazardous contamination in only a limited zone to be contaminated in its entirety. As has been seen after the Fukushima disaster, this can lead to product boycotts and lengthy embargos, particularly for foodstuffs, but also against travel and tourism (IRSN 2012b). The nuclear accident in Japan showed that these boycotts and embargos can have a significant economic impact and can lead to an entire country facing unexpected reputational challenges, leading to a deterioration of the living conditions for the whole country. This economic impact has been developed by IRSN in "Methodology of IRSN accident cost estimates" and in Pascucci-Cahen and Momal (2012).

In the wake of the Fukushima Daiichi NPP disaster, citizen-science-based radiation data collection efforts have proven very important in filling information gaps for the public. The technical abilities and organization of citizen groups have been increasingly recognized by governmental institutions, first responders, and international bodies, many of whom have expressed interest in integrating citizen efforts into disaster response plans (Brown et al. 2016a, b).

The best description of this challenge from a communication perspective was given by the Canadian health ministry's document called "The Health Canada Policy Toolkit for Public Involvement in Decision Making" (Health Canada 2000). The document is an excellent guideline on how to reach a satisfactory degree of public involvement in decision-making.

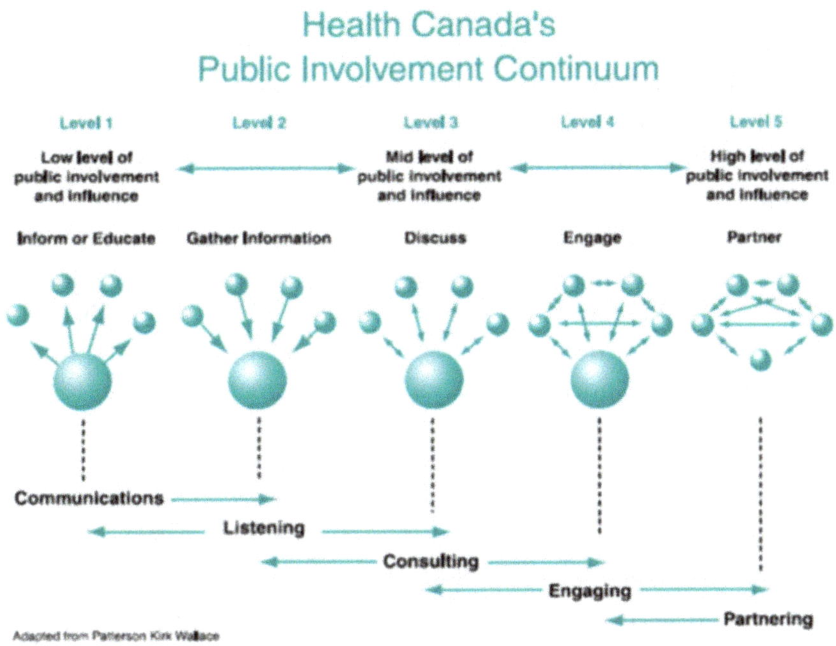

The different kinds of public participation and the different positions which could be adopted by a government communication team with the general public are clearly summarized in the above diagram. During the Fukushima crisis, IRSN mostly informed (level 1, communication) and listened to people (level 2, contact box, dialogue with journalists, expatriates, airline pilots, and health experts).

The review of new communication practices that appeared after the Fukushima accident shows not only the influence of NITs but also the active participation of Japanese citizens in data collection and sharing. Slowly but surely, this trend is becoming global and citizens may also be considered as partners of institutions when they begin to measure radiation by themselves (level 5).

This is well expressed in the paper by Macfarlane "*The nuclear reactor accident … led to a loss of trust in nuclear power around the globe and acutely in Japan. The reactions of the public in Japan and other countries, such as the United States, and the governmental reactions to the accident offer an opportunity to learn ways to improve safety and communication during and after a nuclear accident*" (Macfarlane 2016).

Since the Fukushima crisis, many ordinary citizens, organized in different groups or associations have engaged in radiation measuring with new devices they designed themselves, and have shared their data over the Internet. "Radiation watch" sensor or "Radioactivity counter" applications can be bought by citizens to measure radioactivity in their environment.

The project "Safecast" is a prime example of citizen mobilization (Brown et al. 2016a, b). Safecast is an international, volunteer-based organization devoted to monitoring and openly sharing information on environmental radiation and other pollutants. It was formed on March 12, 2011, one day after the start of the Fukushima Daiichi NPP accident, in response to what several official reports on the disaster have criticized as the chaotic nature of TEPCO, inter-agency, and inter-governmental communication. Since 2011, Safecast has implemented participatory, open-source, citizen-science-centered radiation mapping solutions developed through a process of collaborative open innovation. Safecast develops sensors and a variety of other innovative hardware and software for visualizing environmental measurement data. The group seeks to provide people who are concerned about environmental and nuclear issues with tools they can use to build alternative open means of measurement and communication, which can be easily shared and built upon by others. Five years after the start of the Fukushima disaster, Safecast volunteers have built and deployed hundreds of radiation sensors worldwide and have amassed the largest open data set of radiation measurements to date.

As it is clearly explained on their website, they are neither pro- nor anti-nuclear: "*Safecast is pro-data*". "Radiation *and its environmental and health effects are issues which are fraught with deep-seated controversy. Unfortunately, it has been difficult until now to find radiation data which truly has been free of bias, or of the perception of bias in favor of one ideological position or another. From the outset, Safecast has not sided with either the pro or anti-nuclear camps, and has striven to demonstrate the advantages to science and to the public of having an independent organization devoted solely to providing the most accurate and credible data possible. Safecast is "pro-data." Independence, transparency, and openness are essential for us and the key to our credibility. Safecast was quickly recognized in Japan and abroad as a reliable and unbiased source of environmental information which citizens can use when making decisions*" (SAFECAST 2017).

Their tool and their mapping (more than 35 million pieces of data, mostly in Japan) are the result of the engagement of the Safecast members as simple but engaged citizens.

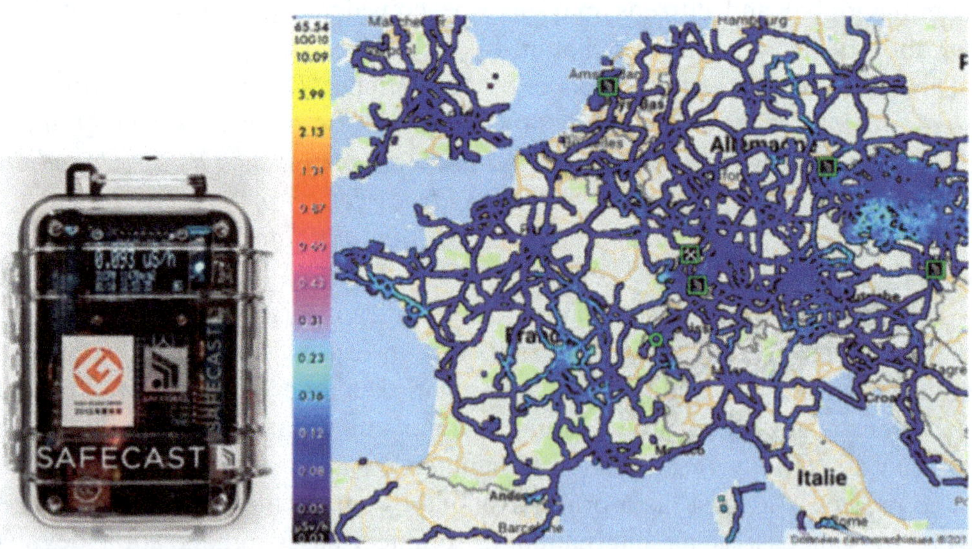

In Japan, these new competences were recognized by Abe Yasuhito: "*Since the Fukushima nuclear accident, many ordinary citizens have engaged in DIY (do-it-yourself) radiation measuring, and have circulated the data over the Internet. Considerable effort has been invested in studying citizen science movements in previous manmade environmental disasters. But as has been often emphasized in the case of 3.11 2011, a great variety of groups of people have generated all sorts of information on nuclear risks, using the Internet and social media. This is the first "known" major nuclear disaster since the advent of the Internet and social media. Whereas citizens engaged in generating information about nuclear risks after nuclear disasters such as Chernobyl, 3.11 opened the door for an alternative kind of collective production and circulation of nuclear risk information* via *the Internet and social media*" (Yasuhito 2014).

This is described by the sociologist Daniel Aldrich as a "*citizen reaction and the evolution of communication in a bottom up process: "Beyond economic concerns from the business community, several new initiatives show how Japan's civil society has been energized by this tremendous tragedy. The Safecast project … embodies a new focus on "citizen science"—that is the participation of everyday residents as volunteers in data collection, technical measurement, and analysis in fields as ecology, biodiversity and astronomy. Participants in such collaborative projects work together often using web based platforms and affordable instrumentation, to achieve results that lone researchers in highly funded laboratories would not be able to accomplish*" (Aldrich 2012).

It is interesting to note that the people behind Safecast worked in technical and scientific fields not even closely related to the radiation protection field before March 2011, but they were recently able to write a scientific publication in the peer-reviewed *Journal of Radioprotection* to present their approach and experience (Brown et al. 2016a, b).

In the Czech Republic, this new opportunity for participation based on these new tools and on citizen engagement was well-received by the Ministry of the Interior. Within the framework of security research, a program has been established which aims to improve public safety by introducing radiation monitoring systems at several levels, including institutions, schools, and citizens, in accordance with current international trends. The program is entitled "Radiation Monitoring Network for Institutions and Schools to Assure Early Awareness and Enhancing Safety of Citizens (RAMESIS)".

Through this program, tools for measurements plus the applications for receipt, storage, administration, and publication of radiation monitoring results are analyzed, projected, developed, and procured. The system is implemented at selected institutions and schools, with the provision of training and informational materials for improving overall understanding of radiation issues.

The project is running from 2015 to 2019, under the guidance of the National Radiation Protection Institute (SURO). The Safecast bGeigie Nano was chosen for mobile monitoring. SURO purchased approximately 30 units and distributed them to selected schools and institutions. SURO also prepared manuals and user guides for performing mobile monitoring and for sending the data to the central workplace.

It developed user-oriented, open-source based software modules to enable users to display their bGeigie nano-measurement results directly on online and offline maps. SURO collects the results of field measurements from all the users participating in this project and supervises their submission to the safecast.org database for visualization.

A New Perspective for the IRSN Communication Department

As already mentioned, these new challenges for increasing citizen participation and education could easily be incorporated into IRSN's existing practices as this was already partially implemented in the regulatory context.

Indeed, the following laws and European conventions promote the development of a transparent communication strategy for the general public and the active participation of citizens:

In the French law N 2004-811 of August 13, 2004, the Civil Protection Modernization Act aims to make the citizen a major player in civil security by spreading the risk culture among younger generations, in crisis situations, and recognizing the role and missions of associations.

This act, largely inspired by the European Aarhus Convention on Public Information (June, 25 1998) based on the following three pillars: right to know, right to participate, and right to justice, has been further adapted to French law.

This has been even better formulated in the Act on Transparency and Security in the Nuclear Field (2006) stipulating that transparency in the nuclear field consists of the set of provisions adopted to ensure the public's right to reliable and accessible information on nuclear safety and security.

For an individual, understanding the situation and seeing the perspectives makes this person an actor of the situation. Communication needs to give meaning during the nuclear crisis phenomenon because every person is entitled to be informed of the risks related to nuclear activities and their impact on personal health and security as well as on the environment, and to be aware of discharges from nuclear installations and their consequences. That is why, it is important that communication during a nuclear crisis situation seeks to increase the individual and collective understanding of the development of the accident, to maintain the trust of the population throughout the incident.

For France, the other challenge is to prepare the post-accident phase, to be aware of the stakes related to the accident and to try to minimize the cost of the direct and indirect consequences. This cost depends greatly on the societal response and the resilience factors strengthened inside the society before the accident: providing long-term information, partnering, and empowerment of citizens is essential for that objective. One way to reduce this kind of consequence would be to give citizens the tools to measure by themselves the level of radiation in their own environment although, of course, IRSN's experts and communication team could play a useful role in promoting understanding of these measurements.

Transparent communication also avoids fear and panic reactions from outsiders and reduces erratic mass behavior like boycotts of local products, boycotts of traveling to the country concerned, etc., and will consequently help to mitigate the economic and social costs of the accident on the food supply, the loss of image, etc.

After the Fukushima crisis, the French authorities and their technical support organization, IRSN, were well aware of the necessity to work toward citizen participation and were a nuclear crisis to happen in France, and they decided that the way to build public confidence was to improve the communication strategy by regular and transparent communication, educational programs for elementary schools, high schools, and universities, public events such as open days and exhibitions, public consultations at the local and national level via well-structured systems. An exhibition was specially designed by IRSN and ASN to inform the general public about radioactivity and covers several nuclear topics such as Radiation Basics, Nuclear Power Plants, Nuclear Accidents, Health Effects of Ionizing Radiation, Nuclear Medicine, Fuel Cycle, and Waste Management. The target audience is the population living in the vicinity of nuclear installations, the population living in areas where radon is likely to be found, professionals likely to be exposed to radioactivity, secondary school, and university students. For example, high schools can choose from 80 available stand-up posters to illustrate every possible question about radiation, and different tools for measuring radon and natural radioactivity are put at the disposal of the schools. In 2016, 17 high schools presented an exhibition, using these freely provided support materials.

But as a complementary action, they also seek to "empower the French public" by measuring and by sharing their data on a common map. The goal is to multiply the number of people aware about what radioactivity is and the associated risks, capable to measure the level of radioactivity and interpret this correctly.

In addition, IRSN suggests using different tools for measuring radon (Canary) or natural radioactivity (Safecast tools) on their territories in order to become more aware about the level of natural background of radioactivity, and on the radioactivity units (the previously unknown units Becquerel (bq), "Sievert" and "Gray" unfortunately became very familiar to Japanese people). IRSN experts monitor the studies carried out by students. For example, the blog shows the kind of results achieved by three high school students in Vichy (Sauvage et al. 2015).

In addition, to reinforce citizen empowerment, IRSN is adding a new element to its strategy. IRSN decided to partner with universities, with IFFO RME, the French Institute of trainers on Major risks and environment working adequately and in close collaboration with the national education ministry and with the association Planet Sciences. This partnership is called "Open Radiation". The idea is to have all citizen measurements, regardless of the sensor used, shared on a map and commented on a specially designed website. This website is currently under development.

Conclusion

The Fukushima accident gave fresh impetus to the thinking related to crisis management and particularly to the issues of communication and relations with citizens in such a period. Today more than ever, we live in a knowledge-based society and we are no longer able to ignore the growing desire from the public to have access to information.

The existence of social media means that information is available anywhere and everywhere and news travels fast. Social media have therefore taken on a growing importance for the nuclear agencies and imposed on them their speed, their multiple sources, and modes of treatments. Other competences, such as community managers, have appeared. The widened range of information channels imposes new modes of information besides the traditional reports on websites: Facebook page, Twitter accounts, a dedicated web page, videos on YouTube, etc.

In order to maintain trust, communication should be clear, timely, regular, and efficient. However, communication alone is not sufficient anymore. The new communication strategy on risk-related matters involves nurturing the ability of citizens to measure radioactivity themselves and become experts. So, a stronger partnership with this kind of citizens can help to increase confidence and trust.

A citizen data and information-sharing network offers a great opportunity to foster confidence today and to be a valuable aid for crisis management tomorrow. The project "Safecast" is proof of this and promotes the concept of a new form of citizen involvement by measuring and, together with the nuclear agencies concerned, building up a statistical base, thanks to the large number of measurements. In an emergency, governments or power companies will not have the manpower to provide the kind of radiation measurement information the public wants, not only around the accident site but from anywhere else, including abroad. In this case, a worldwide citizen network can be a great support.

At IRSN, faced with this new situation concerning the project "Safecast" or other similar citizens' networks, some experts immediately had a very positive reaction right away; others questioned the reliability and quality of measurements by non-professionals and expressed a certain criticism with the "radiation measurement priesthood" as one of the "Safecast" members described them. However, after discussions about the pros and cons, most crisis managers become increasingly interested, as these measurements could provide a huge set of data at very early stages after a nuclear accident. Of course, it will still take time to convince the entire nuclear scientific community!

Nevertheless, helping citizens and in particular the younger generation gather baseline data to show what is "normal", and engaging them in an ongoing educational process has become a very important part of the IRSN communication strategy. IRSN may be considered one of the trendsetters by combining hard sciences and soft sciences for communication and citizen empowerment purposes, and this trend is starting to spread worldwide, helping to build a better relationship between citizen groups and emergency responders in nuclear agencies.

Acknowledgements The author would like to thank Marie Pierre Bigot, director of the Communication Department of IRSN, who managed the crisis communication when Fukushima Daiichi accident occurred. This paper describes the challenges she faced.

References

Aldrich, D. (2012). Post-crisis Japanese nuclear policy: From top down directives to bottom-up activism…Analysis from the East West center. N°103, Jan 2012. Retrieved from www.eastwestcenter.org/sites/default/files/…/api103.p.

Brown, A., Franken, P., Bonner, S., Dolezal, N., & Moross, J. (2016a). Safecast: Successful citizen-science for radiation measurement and communication after Fukushima. *Journal of Radiological Protection, 36*(2), S82.

Brown, A. Baumont, G. Kuča, P., & Helebrant, J. (2016b). Citizen-based radiation measurement in Europe: Supporting informed decisions regarding radiation exposure for emergencies as well as in daily life. In *RICOMET Conference Poster*. Retrieved from http://ricomet2016.sckcen.be/~/mdia/Files/Ricomet2016/Day1/PP110%20Brown.pdf?la=en.

Health Canada. (2000). *Health Canada policy toolkit for public involvement in decision making*. Retrieved from http://www.hc-sc.gc.ca/ahc-asc/alt_formats/pacrb-dgapcr/pdf/public-consult/2000decision-eng.pdf.

IRSN. (2011a). *Baromètre Irsn 2011*. Retrieved from http://www.irsn.fr/FR/IRSN/Publications/barometre/Documents/IRSN_barometre_2011.pdf.

IRSN. (2011b). *FAQ during Fukushima accident*. Retrieved from http://www.irsn.fr/FR/connaissances/Installations_nucleaires/Les-accidents-nucleaires/accident-fukushima-2011/crise-2011/faq/Pages/sommaire-faq.aspx.

IRSN. (2012a). *Baromètre Irsn 2012*. Retrieved from http://www.irsn.fr/FR/IRSN/Publications/barometre/Documents/IRSN_barometre_2012.pdf.

IRSN. (2012b). *Repères 12 special report Fukushima, first lessons learnt*. Retrieved from http://www.irsn.fr/EN/publications/thematic/fukushima/Documents/IRSN_Reperes12_Fukushima_EN.pdf.

IAEA. (2012). *Communication with the public in a nuclear or radiological emergency*. Retrieved from http://www-pub.iaea.org/MTCD/Publications/PDF/EPR-Communcation_web.pdf.

IAEA. (2015). *Method for developing a communication strategy and plan for a nuclear or radiological emergency*. Retrieved from http://www-pub.iaea.org/MTCD/Publications/PDF/EPR-CommPlan2015_web.pdf.

Macfarlane, A. (2016). Radiation and regulation in a post-Fukushima World. *Health Physics, 110* (2), 118–122.

Pascucci-Cahen, L., & Momal, P. (2012). Methodology of IRSN accident cost estimates. In *Eurosafe, 2012*. USA: Mimeo.

SAFECAST. (2017). http://blog.safecast.org/.

Sauvage, A., Alkan, G, & Vaupres, G. (2015). *Quand les citoyens s'emparent de la mesure*. Retrieved from http://radioactivite-auvergne.blogspot.fr/.

Sköld T, & Feldman Y. (2014). *The efficacy of social media as a research tool and information source for safeguards verification*. Retrieved from https://www.iaea.org/safeguards/symposium/2014/home/eproceedings/sg2014-papers/000082.pdf.

Yasuhito, A. (2014). Safecast or the production of collective intelligence on radiation risks after 3.11. *The Asia-Pacific Journal, 12*(7), 5, Japan focus, Feb 2014. Retrieved from http://apjjf.org/2014/12/7/YasuhitoAbe/4077/article.html..

Yamashita, S., & Takamura, N. (2015). Post-crisis efforts towards recovery and resilience after the Fukushima Daiichi Nuclear Power Plant accident. *Japanese Journal of Clinical Oncology, 45* (8), 700–707.

Videos

IRSN. (2012). *Contamination of environment*. Retrieved from http://www.irsn.fr/EN/publications/thematic-safety/fukushima/Pages/2-fukushima-understanding-environment.aspx.

Risk Communication Between Companies and Local Stakeholders for Improving Accident Prevention and Emergency Response

Michael Baram and Preben Hempel Lindøe

Abstract Hazardous industrial areas pose major accident risks. In recent years, two innovative approaches have been used for improving accident prevention and emergency response beyond conventional regulatory requirements: the Seveso and RMP models of local involvement in state regulation. Both promote information sharing and enable direct engagement between companies and local stakeholders, and therefore involve extensive risk-related communications. The authors examine the two approaches in detail by using case studies of their application to hazardous industrial sites in Norway and the US and identify obstacles to their implementation. Nevertheless, they conclude that the approaches advance corporate social responsibility and make risk governance more democratic, respectful, and responsive to the population sectors that are most vulnerable to major industrial accidents.

Keywords Hazardous industry · Risk governance · Risk regulation
Risk communication · Major industrial accidents · Emergency response
Safety regulation · Local stakeholders · Seveso Directive
Risk management plan rule

Introduction

Hazardous industrial activities pose risks of major accidents, as shown by occurrences at AZF-Toulouse (2001), BP-Texas City (2005), and Chevron–Richmond (2012). Those most likely to be injured or killed are workers, emergency responders, and neighboring residents. In addition, there is usually substantial damage to the environment and property.

M. Baram (✉)
Boston University Law School, Boston, USA
e-mail: mbaram@bu.edu

P. H. Lindøe
University of Stavanger, Stavanger, Norway
e-mail: preben.h.lindoe@uis.no

M. Bourrier and C. Bieder (eds.), *Risk Communication for the Future*, SpringerBriefs in Safety Management, https://doi.org/10.1007/978-3-319-74098-0_5

The regulatory toolbox for preventing such accidents includes prescriptive- and performance-based regulations on workplace safety and safety management (Hood et al. 2001; Aven and Renn 2010; Baldwin et al. 2012). It also includes rules that require risk information sharing between a hazardous enterprise and its host community in order to foster their constructive engagement in emergency preparedness, with the EU Seveso Directive (2016) and the US Risk Management Plan Rule (2016) as the leading examples. These approaches stimulate extensive risk communications and, in some cases in the US, have led to the negotiation of a "Good Neighbor Agreement" (Kenney 2004) between local stakeholders and companies that stipulates specific accident risk-reducing initiatives for company implementation.

In a FonCSI research project, the authors examined the Seveso Directive (SD) and the Risk Management Plan and Good Neighbor Agreement (RMP/GNA) approaches and developed several case studies. Our findings indicate that these approaches for informing and engaging communities and local stakeholders are at the forefront of progressive policies that promote corporate social responsibility for public safety. In theory, they promote transparency, information sharing, dialogue, and respect for community concerns and local knowledge. But their implementation encounters several obstacles due to institutional structure and regulatory practices of risk governance, and disputes about risk assessments, differing goals of local participants, and cultural contexts. We also gained insights about risk communication and the trust-building issues that need to be addressed for such communications to lead to acceptable outcomes. These are among the main features of this chapter.

Analytical Framework

Governance of major accident risks involves many types of social controls, including regulation, self-regulation, liability law, values and behavioral norms, and private decision-making by investors, insurers, and consumers (Baram and Lindøe 2014). Each type of social control is a dynamic subsystem that coexists with, but does not necessarily complement the other controls. Some are international in scope, such as the collective wisdom of experts in a particular knowledge domain who contribute to the development of standards and safety management systems.

The SD is a key part of such governance in the EU, as is the RMP in the US. Each requires a hazardous enterprise to disclose and share accident risk information with host communities and local stakeholders, and thereby creates a direct linkage for further communications between the enterprise and the local public. This fosters subsequent risk communications, dialogue, and can lead to voluntary initiatives for improving accident prevention and emergency response. Neither approach prevents regulators from enforcing safety rules and addressing residual risks.

Figure 1 depicts the main actors, their relationships, and pathways of risk communication.

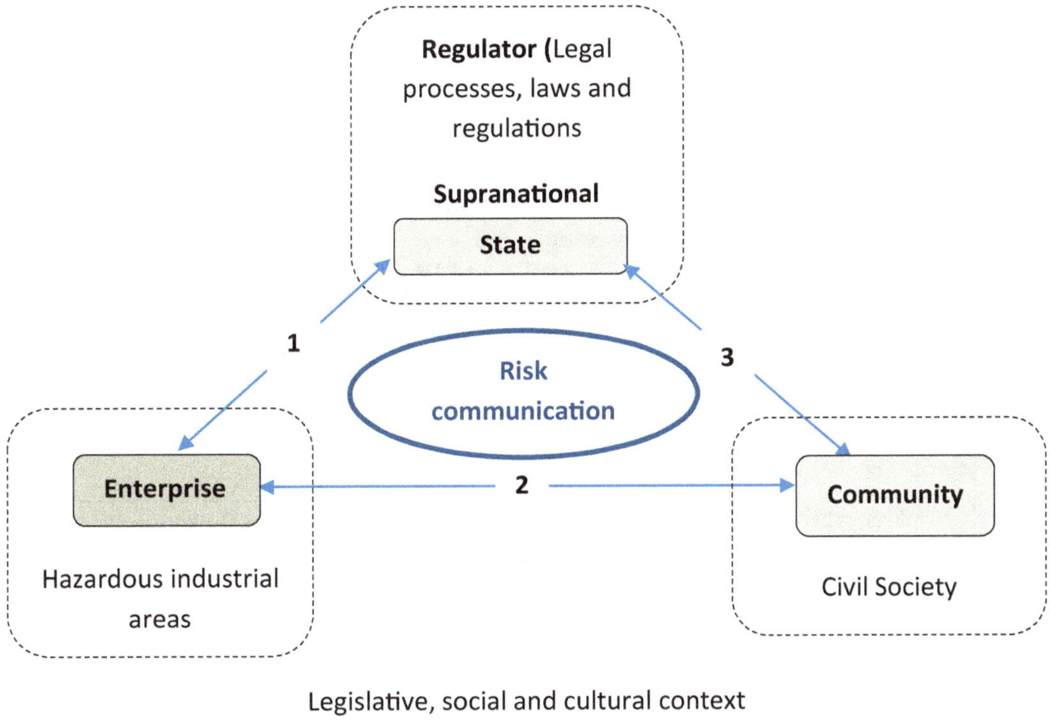

Fig. 1 Analytical framework

The state as regulator oversees and enforces the SD/RMP approach and can intervene with additional information when necessary (1, 3). The hazardous enterprise must share specific types of accident risk information with the state, the community, and local stakeholders (1, 2). The community and stakeholders have the right to provide local knowledge and other risk information to the enterprise and the state, and have dialogue with both (2, 3). What is special about the SD/RMP model is that it clearly establishes the important linkage (2) between enterprise and community or local stakeholders for risk communication, engagement, and dialogue that can lead to voluntary risk-reducing arrangements (OECD 2016). Thus, safety may be improved beyond the requirements of conventional regulations.

Finally, the analytical framework encompasses other social controls. Those that may be particularly influential in shaping the roles and communications of the actors under the SD and RMP regimes are listed in Fig. 2.

Mandates for Information Sharing and Dialogue

The Seveso Directive

Major industrial accidents have occurred worldwide. In Europe, the Seveso accident in 1976 prompted EU adoption of a Directive aimed at the prevention and control of

Characteristics	Examples
Enforceable Laws	Administrative Law Land Use Law & Permit Requirements for Siting and Operating Hazardous Facilities and Activities. Regulation of Workplace Risks & Safety Management Rules on Public and Worker Right to Know
Voluntary Policies	European Eco-Management and Audit Scheme Company Safety Management and Internal Controls ISO 14001 -a generic management system standard Global Reporting Initiative
Generally Accepted Guidances	International Risk Governance Council model ISO 26000 Guidance on Social Responsibility

Fig. 2 Influences on SD and RMP implementation

such accidents. The latest version of the Seveso Directive (SD) now applies to around 10,000 industrial establishments where dangerous substances are used or stored in large quantities, mainly in the chemicals, petrochemicals, storage, and metal refining sectors.

The SD obliges member states and affiliated countries like Norway to ensure that facility operators have a policy in place to prevent major accidents. Operators handling dangerous substances above certain thresholds must regularly inform the public likely to be affected by an accident, provide safety reports, and have a safety management system and an internal emergency plan. EU members and affiliates must ensure that emergency plans are in place for the surrounding areas and that mitigation actions are planned. Account must also be taken of these objectives in land-use planning.

There is a tiered approach to the level of controls: the larger the quantities of dangerous substances present within an establishment, the stricter the rules. Therefore, "upper-tier" establishments with larger quantities than "lower-tier" establishments are subject to tighter control.

The SD has been amended over the years, most recently as Seveso III in July 2012. The Directive has technical updates to take account of changes in EU chemicals classification, affirms that member states and affiliates must ensure that operators have a policy in place to prevent major accidents, and sets stricter standards for inspections of establishments to ensure more effective enforcement of safety rules. The SD also affirms the legitimacy of public stakeholder involvement in its expansive approach to risk governance, and is thereby complementary with laws such as Norway's "working environment" law which establishes roles for the workforce in various aspects of workplace risk governance. Local stakeholders are further empowered by amendments in the SD III that provide (1) better access for citizens to information about risks resulting from nearby companies, (2) requirements about behavior in the event of an accident, (3) more effective rules on participation by the public concerned, in land-use planning projects, and (4) access to justice for citizens who have not been granted appropriate access to information or participation. There will also be legitimate roles for public access to risk governance proceedings. Industrial parks and the risk of domino effects of incidents and accidents have been one of the areas addressed in the enforcement and implementation of Seveso inspection. A number of innovative strategies for proactive risk management have been employed by inspection authorities to encourage cooperation among the actors (Larsen et al. 2012).

The Risk Management Plan Rule and Negotiated Agreements

Several US laws and regulations require industrial disclosure of risk information to persons exposed to hazardous industrial activities (Baram 1990). The Worker Right to Know rule ensures that workers have access to information about the hazardous substances in their work settings. The Community Right to Know law provides that states and communities have access to company reports on the types, volumes, storage, and emissions of the hazardous substances at their facilities. And the Risk Management Plan rule (RMP) was subsequently enacted and requires some 15,000 companies using specified types and quantities of chemicals, and who thereby pose risks of major accidents, to provide the Environmental Protection Agency (EPA), states, and host communities with a report containing an accident history, worst-case and alternative release scenarios and their estimated consequences, a program for preventing accident risks, an emergency response program, and a plan for implementing the programs.

At the time the RMP was enacted, Congress and EPA envisioned that the reported information would enable dialogue between communities and companies that would lead to improved emergency response capabilities and voluntary risk-reducing initiatives by the companies. However, fear of terrorist incidents and their manifestation on September 11, 2001 caused high-level officials and EPA to restrict open public access to some of the RMP information, especially with regard to analyses of the offsite consequences of the accidental release scenarios (Beierle 2003). Nevertheless, RMPs, some with scenario consequence information, are usually provided to a host community's Local Emergency Planning Committee (LEPC) and made available to the public at some 50 federal reading rooms across the country (Risk Management Plan Rule 2016). In addition, the RMP rule has encouraged LEPCs in major industrial area to work closely with companies on improving and coordinating emergency response plans, take an active role in reviewing RMPs and securing further gap-filling information, and help community officials and local stakeholders engage in dialogues with companies about risk-reducing measures (Walter 1998).

These informational developments have also activated groups of local stakeholders and community leaders to press companies to make operational changes that reduce accident risks and improve emergency response capabilities. In a number of communities, dialogues with industry have occurred and led to negotiation of "Good Neighbor Agreements" (GNAs) with companies (Kenney 2004; Baram 2016). The negotiation process typically involves addressing a cluster of concerns over proven and perceived risks and impacts, unlike traditional risk regulation that requires a separate agency-managed proceeding for each risk or impact. It often involves demands for company internal information that exceed what is required in regulatory proceedings, and draws the attention of the media and public support. Agreements with risk-reducing and emergency response commitments have been negotiated with many types of companies, including global majors with US facilities such as Shell, Rhone-Poulenc, and Chevron.

Overall, studies of GNAs show that many company commitments were implemented, especially commitments which focused on preventing the recurrence of a prior injurious event and improving emergency response services. Perhaps, the most notable achievements of many GNAs are informational and involve company commitments to allow and pay for independent health and safety audits of the company's operations, to act upon audit recommendations for improvements, and to accept public involvement in the audit process and public review of relevant documentation.

Case Studies

Three case studies are briefly summarized here by characterizing the industries and local communities (*cf.* Relation 2 in Fig. 1). All the cases involve production, storage and transport of gas, and oil and chemical products where leakage, loss of control, and other foreseeable circumstances could lead to explosion, fire, and harmful discharges resulting in loss of lives, injuries and severe health consequences among workers, emergency responders, and local residents. These hazardous activities are in or close to urban areas with housing, public areas, and vital public infrastructure such as transport. Figure 3 gives some characteristics of the cases.

Risavika, Sola Municipality

The Hazardous Industry

As a regional, national, and international logistics hub Risavika covers 400,000 m^2, with 120 enterprises and about 7000 workplaces (DSB 2015b), the harbor has been developed since the 1950s, and it includes seven quays with three different owners

Case:	Norway: Seveso Directive		US: RMP-rule
	Risavika, Sola municipality	South Port, Oslo	Chevron, Richmond
Activity	LNG-production, storage of goods, harbor and passenger terminal.	Storage and transport of chemicals, gas and oil products	Production and storage of oil products
Industrial structure	One LNG producer and a diversity of 120 companies.	35 major and minor companies	Chevron as the only major actor
Governmental actors	LNG-producer and harbor with public ownership. State level regulators.	Ports and industrial areas with public ownership. State level regulators.	City of Richmond, Contra Costa County, California, & national regulators.

Fig. 3 Characteristics of the cases

operating 25 ships day and night. The production in the area is divided between three main activities: industrial production (30%), storage and transport (25%), and service providers (20%). Some major companies within the petroleum sectors are located in the area: ConocoPhillips, Baker Hughes, Schlumberger, Halliburton, and Norwegian Shell. In 2005, the Lyse Group, owned by 16 municipalities in Rogaland County, planned to establish an LNG plant in Risavika with a production of 300,000 ton of LNG per year. The gas is temporarily stored in a 30,000-m^3 tank before being transported by road or sea. For a more environmentally friendly fuel source, Norway and EU policies require a shift from diesel oil to LNG for maritime transport. In line with the new policy, new passenger ferries powered by LNG have been developed. Due to their travel scheme, they have to be loaded with liquid gas while passengers are embarking.

Surrounding Community and Risk Communication

North of the industrial area, there is a dense housing area, kindergarten, schools, churches, and public playing areas. Further away, a local center with shops and service facilities are located. In 2006, protests and complaints were raised against the plan of locating the LNG plant in the area. In the public consultation, process citizens requested more specific analyses of possible impacts and risks. Formal complaints were addressed to the County Governor and state agencies, notably the Directorate for Civil Protection (DSB 2015b), which is responsible for the fire and explosion legislation and for coordinating the enforcement of the Seveso Directive, as the plant would clearly be subject to these regulations. The public debate in the press between these key actors opened a public space for risk communication and mobilized more stakeholders in the local community (Vinnem 2010). Lyse engaged experts and organized public consultations in which focus group meetings were held, including residents living close to Risavika, enterprises located in the area, emergency services, and other experts on risk appraisal and evaluation (Drottz-Sjöberg 2008). Criticisms spanned the whole spectrum of conditions, decision-making processes, and perceived risks. In particular, the quality of the initial risk assessments was questioned in terms of assumptions and scope, and the availability of information and the involvement of stakeholders in the process were severely criticized. Further, they reviewed the existing risk assessments and how the planned and implemented measures would reduce the risks to a presumably tolerable level (Vatn 2010). Series of meetings, consultations, complaints, and decisions took place involving a number of actors, from local citizen groups to responsible ministries and even the EFTA Surveillance Authority (ESA).

When ferries were planned to be loaded with LNG at the terminal building, a new round of public controversy took place. Regulation for fueling LNG to passenger ferries falls between onshore and maritime rules. LNG is transported by trucks 1600 km through Southern Norway and Sweden to the ferry's destination port in Denmark. A new regulation developed especially for Risavika came into force in December 2013.

The South Port, Oslo

The activities in the South Port, just 3 km from central Oslo, began at the end of the 1930s (DSB 2015a). Since then, the scope of activities has gradually increased. The port is arguably Norway's most important logistics and transport hub, with well-established residential areas to the south, and a large residential area is in progress to the north. In the late 1990s, it was decided to develop the waterfront to increase public access to the harbor areas. The so-called Fjord City Project is the largest urban development project in Oslo and includes residential areas, enterprises and workplaces, hotels, restaurants, cafeterias, parks, and promenades.

The Hazardous Industry

Today, the South Port comprises all or most of the industrial activities in the Oslo harbor area. The port is the largest container port in Norway and the largest terminal for the storage and distribution of petroleum products, including all jet fuel for Oslo Airport. About 40% of the national consumption of road traffic fuel goes through the port. The area comprises some 35 firms with port-related activities. Encompassing a large number of enterprises with varying degrees of interdependence and requirements for coordination, South Port became an area with increased risk. Many risk-prone activities are concentrated in a small area, in particular, the transport and storage of petroleum products. There is a possibility of domino effects. In sum, this can result in lack of oversight and consistent management, and insufficient clarification of interfaces and responsibilities. During the last 15 year, a variety of incidents and accidents have taken place in the area: explosion in the underground storage of oil, collision between train and tank truck, overfilling of diesel oil when unloading from ship, three workers killed, and major damage when a set of railway wagons rolled uncontrolled into the harbor (DSB 2015a, pp. 84–85).

Surrounding Community and Risk Communication

The South Port is located close to districts in Oslo with a population of approximately 100,000.

Due to the development in downtown, the population expects to increase with 4–5000 residential units and approximately 20,000 workplaces. The Port of Oslo administers the harbor area on contract relations based on a "shopping mall model" and their own role as "landlord". In terms of safety, this implies that tenants are kept at arm's length, with each enterprise responsible for its own safety and risk management. As a consequence, a systematic dialogue among stakeholders on risk issues regarding neighboring populations or the development of "Fjord City" and the South Port has taken place before DSB raised the issue in their report. The worst-case scenarios, described in the report, include an ignited leak of gasoline and an oil fire with gas driving toward downtown Oslo. The case was reported in headlines in one Oslo-based newspaper, but no further media coverage or public debate followed. As a follow-up to the report, and as an element in increasing emergency preparedness related to incidents at the South Port, a full-scale exercise among responsible actors and emergency agencies was initiated in 2015 (DSB 2016).

Chevron, Richmond

Richmond, nearby San Francisco, is home to one of the biggest oil refineries in the United States. Now owned by Chevron Corporation, the refinery was built in 1902 in a "tiny railroad settlement". As the refinery and port facilities grew, so did the town, which now has over 100,000 residents. Chevron has long been the largest employer as well as one of the biggest polluters. Its troubled history includes fires, explosions, spills, and other accidental releases of toxic chemicals, significant leaking ("fugitive emissions") of air pollutants, unsightly premises, unwillingness to engage with local stakeholders, and attempts to finance and influence political developments (Chevron Wikipedia 2016; Mattera 2016).

Richmond is a diverse community with different factions competing for political primacy. After the refinery was identified as the San Francisco Bay Area's largest polluter in 1982, Richmond residents began "Environmental Justice" activism. In the mid-1980s, the National Toxics Campaign sent an organizer who helped create a local stakeholder group, the West County Toxics Coalition (WCTC) in North Richmond, a chronically impoverished area. WCTC activities have continued and focus on holding Chevron accountable for its accidents and pollution impacts. Another national organization, Communities for a Better Environment (CBE), also set up a local branch in Richmond and published an influential study of environmental justice issues (Kenney 2004).

In July 1993, a safety valve ruptured on a railroad car located on Chevron property. The valve leaked aerosolized sulfuric acid into nearby communities over a range of fifteen miles, causing 24,000 local residents to seek medical treatment. In the following year, Chevron and the community signed a Memorandum of Understanding (MOU) in which Chevron committed to taking action on several concerns including plant-wide replacement of valves, fenceline monitoring of specified air pollutants for data that would lead to further controls, waste cleanup and aesthetic improvements, areas for recreation, and funding for several community needs (Macey and Susskind 2003).

Nevertheless, accidents and emissions of pollutants that threatened public health and safety continued and actually worsened over the following years. In 2007, the EPA reported that Chevron had produced over 900,000 lb of toxic waste and that the Refinery was in "high priority violation" of EPA standards. Then, in 2012, a major fire took place at the refinery. After a leak was observed in a corroded carbon steel pipe containing hydrocarbon process fluid and several repair attempts failed, the decision was made to shutdown the refinery. But prior to shutdown, "hot work" repairs on the corroded pipe caused an explosive release of a vapor cloud that immediately ignited, causing a fire that sent a large plume of pollutants across the Richmond area. Nearby residents were instructed to take shelter with their windows and doors closed. 15,000 people from the surrounding community subsequently sought medical attention for respiratory complications due to the fire (Chemical Safety Board 2013a).

Residents claiming they are "disproportionately impacted" joined a multi-organizational protest March that gained international publicity. Community groups have brought several lawsuits against Chevron and the City of Richmond also went to court to seek orders that would bring about a new safety culture at the refinery. Several state and federal agencies and the national Chemical Safety Board (CSB) investigated the accident and presented findings at public meetings.

CSB reports identified technical, organizational, emergency response, and safety culture deficiencies at the refinery and inadequacies in the relevant industry codes. They also noted that the failed pipe should have been replaced earlier with an inherently safer corrosion-resistant alloy that the leak should have led to shutdown of operations before repair was attempted, and that reluctance among employees to use their "Stop Work Authority" and substandard equipment maintenance were evidence of a deficient safety culture (Chemical Safety Board 2015). The final report was presented at a public meeting in Richmond on January 15, 2015. Chevron refused to attend but responded in a letter in which they accepted most of the CSB findings and recommendations but disagreed with other findings as an inaccurate depiction of its process safety culture.

Public Engagement and Risk Communication

In this section, we will look at characteristics and findings from, respectively, the Norwegian and US cases with the aim of exploring public engagement in assessing, interpreting, and responding toward hazard accompanying industries within the communities.

Learning from the Norwegian Cases

The two Norwegian cases can be described both with similar and different characteristics. The similarities are *structural* with locations nearby urban areas, public ownership, a major seaport, and a complex diversity of companies with a variety of hazardous activities. The differences are *processual* and *communicative,* showing how state agencies and local actors respond, respectively, reactive and proactive in assessing and communicating risk issues. By using our analytical framework, three factors seem to be of relevance for the outcomes: First, limitations of the regulator in preventing and handling critical incidents and accidents creating domino effects affecting surrounding communities and environment; second, the conflicting roles with public ownership and third, the contextual and cultural basis for engagement within "local risk society" (Lindøe and Kringen 2015).

First, in Norway the state-managed approach to regulatory tasks is distributed horizontally as well as vertically among several ministries and national regulatory agencies. County governors at the regional level and local authorities including municipal planners give permission for locating hazardous industries. Emergency responses including fire services are organized at the municipal level. National port regulations specify the economic independence of the ports, and the ISPS Code imposes port security requirements.[1] The Seveso Directive and other safety regulations are in place for the storage, handling, and transport of dangerous substances. The two cases highlight a major weakness within the regulatory framework, as shown in Fig. 1. Most safety regulations are implemented either by the state directly or delegated to county or municipality (1) are directed toward an individual enterprise. They do not call for an overall or holistic risk governance process when several enterprises or activities are sited in close proximity to each other. As a consequence, no holistic risk assessment regarding vessel traffic activity has been provided either by the Port of Oslo or Risavika, or by national coastal authorities. Although the county governor coordinates governmental regulation of municipalities,

[1]The International Ship and Port Facility Security Code (ISPS Code) is a comprehensive set of measures to enhance the security of ships and port facilities, developed in response to the perceived threats to ships and port facilities in the wake of the 9/11 attacks in the United States. The ISPS Code is implemented through Chap. XI-2 Special measures to enhance maritime security in the International Convention for the Safety of Life at Sea (SOLAS), 1974.

administration of the regulations is fragmented, and the regulations are less suited for addressing the composite risks that are encountered in industrial parks and ports. In Risavika, the locations of the LNG plant and the ferry terminal were largely handled as separate issues and the aggregated accident risks were insufficiently evaluated. However, the SD III has potential value because it addresses the clustering of hazardous enterprises and domino effects by requiring member states to identify groups of enterprises where the danger of a major accident is increased because of their location, activities, and the proximity of dangerous substances. In such cases, the exchange of information and cooperation among the enterprises is required and the coordinating mechanisms are anchored in enforcement of the SD, and to some extent in Norwegian HSE regulations.

Second, the public ownership of the harbor and industrial areas introduces multiple and partly conflicting goals, likely creating role conflicts for key stakeholders, particularly at the local level. Ports are often part of municipal developmental schemes that involve tradeoffs between benefits and risks, and socioeconomic considerations may tend to overshadow risk concerns, as in the South Port case. Public involvement and ownership should normally ensure democratic and trustworthy control mechanisms. The information on which public actors must base their decisions relies largely on risk studies from companies that have been developed by their contracted experts. These raises concern about the objectivity of risk assessments and risk communication. Such processes can lead to public mistrust as seen in Risavika. When the public is unable to deal with theoretical risk estimates related to their “real world”, or with disagreement among risk experts, mistrust may escalate and risk communication became a vicious circle. In Risavika, conflicts afflicted “the social contract” between the owner of the LNG plant and the municipality on one side and stakeholder groups and individuals within the local communities on the other side. The most contentious issues were the quality and relevance of the risk assessments, and the decision process for locating the LNG plant. The case illustrates the ambivalent and contested power of knowledge in proceedings where experts differ over risk assessments and frustrate the public’s quest for certainty.

Questions raised in the community were “Is the location correctly selected, and can we live with this industry close to our door?”. While a risk expert from the local university brought the risk issue onto the public agenda with strong criticism of the enterprise and the municipality, he was opposed by other experts (Vatn 2010). The heated public debate that followed appeared to be a reaction to uncertainties regarding the risk of possible events and to the mixed roles and interests of stakeholders in the project.

Third, different social climates in the two cases may have influenced perceptions of risk among stakeholders and civil society. In this respect, the two regions differ. Risavika is in the county of Rogaland, which also includes Stavanger, an exceptional area because it is the “Oil and Gas Region” of Norway. Industries, professionals, and media have over the years fostered a strong public awareness and attention to risk with extensive media coverage of incidents and accidents. This region also has considerable clusters of experts in safety research, education, and consulting. These factors may have contributed to the public engagement, media debates, and interventions among local citizens. The Oslo region lacks most of these features and is mainly focused on developmental benefits rather than on risks. A worst-case scenario indicates that an accident caused by a major leak of petroleum from a tanker in South Port and ignition and the spread of smoke and gas would endanger the whole area toward downtown Oslo including housing, public areas, and the iconic Opera building. Although a greater worst-case risk is posed in South Port than in Risavika, there has only been one newspaper article and no public engagement or debate followed.

Learning from the Chevron–Richmond Case

Chevron's Richmond refinery is subject to a multitude of safety and environmental regulations that are enforced by federal and state (California) agencies. It must also secure several permits from county, regional, and community (Richmond) units of government that set operational requirements. This regulatory framework includes the RMP rule and is supplemented by other components of risk governance (CCHS 2016).

Nevertheless, refinery operations have caused hundreds of accidents, spills, and other harmful events over several decades, with many attributed to regulatory violations. As a result, Chevron is continuously defending against enforcement actions and lawsuits, and has paid tens of millions of dollars in penalties and damage awards (Mattera 2016). Our research, which included the review of extensive reports (Macey and Susskind, Kenney, etc.) and other documentation and numerous interviews in Richmond, leads to the conclusion that the company, in aggressively implementing its business plans, subordinates regulatory compliance and avoids engaging with the public and taking other voluntary actions except when it needs a permit to continue or expand operations.

In the modern era of industrial safety, the Richmond refinery ranks as a worst case. As such, it provides an opportunity to understand the circumstances that undermine the effectiveness of the RMP rule and enable the continuation of its accident-causing operations. The undermining circumstances arise mainly from (1) the high socioeconomic value of the refinery and the low economic condition of the community, and (2) national security policies and the failure of the oversight agency, EPA, and the company to provide the factual information and analyses needed for effective risk communication and dialogue.

Federal and state regulators, knowing that the refinery's operations are of considerable importance to the national and state economies, dutifully take enforcement actions to punish noncompliance but tailor them to avoid impacting operations to the extent that their societal value would be impaired. Absent the threat of severe sanctions, this highly profitable company absorbs the penalties and other monetary loss consequences of their accidents and violations as costs of doing business, continues to subordinate regulatory compliance, and sees little need to engage in risk communications and dialogue with local stakeholders.

Similarly, local officials with permit granting authority know that refinery operations are essential to the Richmond economy (e.g., jobs, tax revenues, and local suppliers). They also know that despite many factions in the city with different objectives and conflicts between them, there is an underlying position shared by most if not all in Richmond, namely to keep the company in Richmond and not drive it elsewhere. As a result, permit requirements are carefully crafted to address issues by means that are acceptable to Chevron. Company promises to provide jobs and job training, and contribute funds for social services and other community betterments have also influenced community decision-making. The company has also made political contributions to change community leadership.

In addition, the potential value of the RMP rule for promoting meaningful, risk communications, engagement, and dialogue between the company and local stakeholders has not been realized. One reason is that national security policies have constricted information sharing, making it more difficult for local stakeholders to access critical information about a particular facility's accident hazards, safety management program, and offsite consequences, as noted earlier (Beierle 2003).

Another reason is that RMP implementation by the EPA has been weak. As reported by the Chemical Safety Board (CSB), EPA has not required accident risk reduction nor required that the company demonstrate that its safety systems are functioning, and the EPA regional office lacks sufficient resources to fully inspect and audit the numerous high hazard facilities within the area. The CSB concludes that the RMP program as applied by EPA to refinery operations has not resulted in Chevron's development and documentation of sufficient factual information and analyses needed for control of major accident hazards and risks (Chemical Safety Board Regulatory Report 2013b). Thus, EPA, as well as Chevron, has deprived local stakeholders of the factual information and detailed studies needed for effective risk communication and dialogue.

Finally, it is instructive to consider the case in which Chevron secured the permits it needed to change and expand refinery operations in order to meet new federal requirements for an environmentally friendly reformulated gasoline (Kenney 2004; Macey and Susskind 2003). Permit approvals were granted in 1994 by the City Council and a regional regulator despite Chevron's performance record, the occurrence of a spill and a major accident at the refinery during the permit application process, and deep mistrust and hostility among Richmond residents. In addition, a Mitigation Task Force comprised of three environmental organizations and Chevron negotiated a GNA that contained additional company commitments.

Some of the Chevron commitments expressed in the permits and the GNA involved reduction of emissions of toxic chemicals, replacement of leaking valves, and cleanup of contaminated and unsightly premises. But many others involved its funding of community social and health services, recreational facilities, and other community betterments. This patchwork approach, sweetened by company donations, did not provide a foundation for continuing engagement, communications, and dialogue, nor did it contribute to building a safety culture at Chevron. As a result, the company continues to incur accidents, polluting occurrences, and community hostility.

Conclusion

Our point of departure has been conflicts that arise when companies with hazardous activity cause local concerns about risks, impacts, and their consequences for the safety of workers, public health, and the environment. The analysis has identified different approaches and "modeling" of the risk governance process and the company–community relationship. The Norwegian cases with industrial areas and harbors represent a "regulatory model" that is administered by the state, involving many regulatory agencies and addressing the interest and concerns of stakeholders within the national legal framework as well as the European Seveso Directive. The US case with a huge refinery operation similarly involves national regulation, including the RMP rule, and also involves regional and local permit granting authority. It leaves the door open for company and community (or citizen groups) to voluntarily negotiate an agreement on specific steps to be taken to resolve residual risks and community concerns. It also enables negotiation of company donations for improving the community's social programs. Each model has special features, contextual circumstances, and implications which differ from the familiar features of traditional regulatory and permitting procedures.

As presented in the analytical framework (Fig. 1), the SD and RMP components of state regulation should be viewed as complementary policies for information sharing and promoting engagement and dialogue between a company and its community, including the workforce and local stakeholders. They also enhance transparency of proceedings and respect for community concerns and local knowledge (Lindøe 2017).

Our assessment has shown that obstacles to implementation can arise. They include the following:

- Insufficient coordination of the regulatory framework causing a fragmented approach to risk,
- Technical complexity and stakeholder confusion arising from competing experts,
- Competing or conflicting interests of multiple stakeholders,
- Concerns about security that restrict the flow of risk information and communications,
- Prioritization of economic and developmental interests that subordinates local concerns about health and safety,
- Lack of factual detail in the company information provided.

Nevertheless, the societal benefits being gained, despite these troubles, justify robust implementation of the SD and RMP approaches. They move corporate social responsibility from theory to practice and establish a pathway for discourse between company and community. They confirm the legitimacy of local stakeholders for participation in risk decision-making on hazardous industrial operations and thereby enable a more sensitive and holistic approach to risk issues by regulators and companies. Overall, they contribute to making risk governance more democratic, respectful, and responsive to the population sectors that are most vulnerable to major industrial accidents.

References

Aven, T., & Renn, O. (2010). *Risk management and governance*. Berlin: Springer.

Baldwin, R., Cave, M., & Lodge, M. (2012). *Understanding regulation*. Oxford: Oxford University Press.

Baram, M. (1990). *Risk communication as a regulatory alternative for protecting health, safety and environment, administrative conference of the United States*.

Baram, M. (2016). A new social contract for governing industrial risk in the community. *Jurimetrics Journal, 56,* 223.

Baram, M., & Lindøe, P. (2014). Modes of risk regulation for prevention of major industrial accidents. In M. Baram, P. Lindøe & O. Renn (Eds.), *Risk governance of offshore oil and gas operations* (pp. 34–55). New York: Cambridge University Press.

Beierle, T. (2003). *Environmental information disclosure: Three cases of policies and politics, resources for the future*.

CCHS. (2016). RMP-Chevron Richmond Refinery, Contra Costa Health Services.

Chemical Safety Board. (2013a). *Interim investigation report: Chevron Richmond refinery fire* (April 2013).

Chemical Safety Board. (2013b). *Regulatory report: Chevron Richmond refinery pipe rupture and fire* (December 2013).

Chemical Safety Board. (2015). *Final investigation report: Chevron Richmond refinery pipe rupture and fire* (January 2015).

Chevron Corporation, Wikipedia. (2016).

Directorate for Civil Protection. (2015a). *Sydhavna (Sjursøya)—an area with increased risk*. Tønsberg.

Directorate for Civil Protection. (2015b). *Risavika - helhetlig risikostyring i områder med forhøyet risiko* (*Risavika - holistic risk management in areas with increased risk*). Tønsberg.

Directorate for Civil Protection. (2016). *Evaluation report HarbourEx15*. Tønsberg.

Drottz-Sjöberg, B. M. (2008). *LNG-anlegget i Risavika. Kommentarer og synspunkter fra risikoanalytikere, bedriftsnaboer, brannvesen og beboere i Tananger* (LNG-plant in Risavika. Comments and viewpoints from risk experts, neighbors, fire brigade and residents in Tananger). Trondheim: NTNU.

Hood, C., Rothstein, H., & Baldwin, R. (2001). *The government of risk*. Oxford: Oxford University Press.

Kenney, D. S., Stohs, M., Chavez, J., Fitzgerald, A., & Erickson, T. (2004). *Evaluating the use of good neighbor agreements for environmental and community protection*. Final report. University Colorado Law School Scholarly Commons.

Larsen, R. G., Olsen, A. L., Wood, M., & Gyenes, Z. (2012). *Chemical hazards risk management in industrial parks and domino effect establishment*. Luxemburg: Publication Office of the European Union.

Lindøe, P. H. (2017). Risk regulation and resilience in offshore oil and gas operation. In A. Herwig & M. Simoncini (Eds.), *Law and the management of disaster. The challenge of resilience* (pp. 105–123). Routledge.

Lindøe, P. H., & Kringen, J. (2015). Risk governance of hazardous industrial ports and areas: A case study of industrial areas and harbors in Norway. *Journal of Risk Research, 18*(7), 931–946.

Macey, G., & Susskind, L. (2003). *Using dispute resolution techniques to address environmental justice concerns*. Consensus Building Institute.

Mattera, P. (2016). *Chevron: Corporate rap sheet*. Corporate Research Project.

OECD. (2016). *Trends in risk communication policies and practices*. Organization for Economic Cooperation and Development.

Risk Management Plan Rule. (2016). US EPA. https://www.epa.gov/rmp.

Seveso Directive. (2016). http://ec.europa.eu/environment/seveso/.

Vatn, J. (Ed.). (2010). *Issues related to localization of an LNG facility risk and safety: Theory and applications*. Leiden: Taylor & Francis.

Vinnem, J. E. (2010). Risk indicators for major hazards on offshore installations. *Safety Science, 48,* 770–787.

Walter, R. (1998), *Local emergency planning guidebook: Understanding the EPA risk management program rule*.

Part II
When Reality Strikes Back: Tough Lessons to Be Learned from Crises

How Risk Communication Can Contribute to Sharing Accurate Health Information for Individual Decision-Making

An Empirical Study from Fukushima During a Post-emergency Period

Mariko Nishizawa

Abstract Risk communication is an established concept within the risk analysis framework. It is a tool for conveying the results of the scientific assessment and management of risk, for sharing safety-related information, and exchanging views and values amongst varying stakeholder groups. Its ultimate aim is to build trust through social interaction. However, the nature of effective risk communication is yet to be fully understood and, consequently, gaps in perception about risks between experts and nonexpert remain significant. In order to address this issue and suggest how risk communication can contribute to the creation of shared awareness of the risks and benefits of nuclear energy in Japan, this chapter will show an empirical study conducted in Japan between 2011 and 2012 in the post-Fukushima accident period. In the study, scientists explained nuclear safety and health effect of radiation to local residents evaluated from radiation-affected areas in Fukushima. It concludes that a carefully designed risk communication programme can serve as an effective tool to narrow gaps in perception between experts and nonexperts about risks, and as a useful and trustworthy source of safety information for individual decision-making.

Keywords Nuclear disaster · Fukushima · Public communication
Participation

M. Nishizawa (✉)
Litera Japan Corporation, Tokyo, Japan
e-mail: nishizawa@literajapan.com

M. Bourrier and C. Bieder (eds.), *Risk Communication for the Future*, SpringerBriefs in Safety Management, https://doi.org/10.1007/978-3-319-74098-0_6

Introduction

It is widely agreed that the accident at the Fukushima Daiichi nuclear power plant was triggered by natural events combined with technical failures and was a human-induced disaster as well (National Diet of Japan 2012; Investigation Committee 2012). From this unfortunate accident, we have learned that human and organisational factors associated with emergency planning, response and decision-making for nuclear safety need to be more carefully reviewed and enhanced. Contributions from the social sciences, especially from risk management and risk communication, play key roles.

Risk communication is an established concept within the risk analysis framework. It is a vital tool for conveying the meaning of scientific assessments and risk management, for sharing safety-related information and exchanging views and values amongst various stakeholder groups, or for triggering behavioural change and resolving conflicts. Its ultimate aim is to build trust through dialogue and social interaction (Rosa et al. 2014).

However, it would not be an overstatement that the nature of effective risk communication is yet to be fully understood. As a result, risk communication is sometimes only partially integrated into risk management practice or is not considered at all. This marginalisation of risk communication is observed in a variety of risk communication practices, or more evidently, in the perception gaps that exist between the lay public and experts about risks.

This chapter will address this pressing issue and suggest how risk communication can contribute to create shared awareness about the risks and benefits of nuclear energy by illustrating an empirical study in Japan conducted between 2011 and 2012 in the post-Fukushima accident period. In the study, scientists explained nuclear safety and health effect by radiation to local residents during a series of risk communication practices planned for the evacuees from a disaster-affected region, Iitate Village of Fukushima Prefecture. The author was directly involved as the planner and as the facilitator as well. This exploratory study investigated why communication between professionals and laypersons often fails and, ironically, how it can sometimes lead to a mistrust of science.

Before presenting the empirical study, the next section reviews literature on risk communication and public participation in general and about Japan in particular.

Risk Controversy and Dialogues: Literature Review

Science and technology are inevitably associated with uncertainty. Neither 100% safety nor zero-risk exists. In other words, risk can be reduced but it can never be zero. What we need to achieve is not a situation of 'zero risk' but to a degree that society deems acceptable. In addition, society demands that risk managers are in control of the risk and not subject to reoccurring surprises, i.e., such as financial meltdowns and system failures.

Studies of risk communication in the past have shown that risk-related controversies depending on their characteristic (Rosa et al. 2014). And it is known that those in which even experts are divided on safety issues, or those that are closely bound with values, ethics, religious beliefs, or world views, tend to be intense. This makes forming a consensus more difficult. Worldwide disputes over genetically modified crops are a symbolic example (Krebs 2013; Nishizawa and Renn 2006). The debate over low-dose radiation exposure from the reactors at Fukushima is another example—risk perception remains high in contrast to expert's scientific risk assessment.

Social theorists have long recognised the existence of a new constellation of attitudes and concerns about risks derived from complex and uncertain aspects of science and technology such as the long-term and irreversible effects of global warming or economic impacts on agriculture by the application of genetic engineering; and they have pointed to the need for new ways of handling risk-related issues in the face of changing social circumstances (Beck 1992; Giddens 1991).

In this context, dialogue-based risk communication and citizen participation in risk controversies has increasingly come to be seen as a useful response. Scholars such as Forester (1999), Renn et al. (1995) and Schön (1983) suggest that it leads to critical self-reflection on the part of key actors and a greater mutual understanding between them, and that this in turn creates a more favourable environment both for problem-solving and for democratic governance. It is suggested that dialogue-based risk communication and participatory methods likely to be effective in risk debates that are complicated and for which scientific conclusions about the risks are ambiguous (Renn 2008).

In recent years, there has been more attention to dialogue-based communication in Japan. An example is a health communication practice for the residents during the volcanic eruption in the mountains on Miyake Island in 2000. A communication programme about health effects of volcanic gas was carried out by a team of university researchers (Kikuchi et al. 2006). There are also reports on community-based participatory disaster planning, as in the case of a village in Tottori (Okada et al. 2013; Okada 2015).

Notwithstanding of these, typical communication practices in Japan are still designed to be top-down. Hence, truly participatory and dialogue-based risk and crisis communication is limited (Nishizawa 2005; Nishizawa and Renn 2006).

It was therefore not surprising that the initial emergency communications on the events at Fukushima Daiichi nuclear plant by the central government were largely one-way. It was symbolised in a frequently quoted phase, 'no immediate impact (tadachini eikyoha nai)'. This was criticised by the public as well as the media who both felt that the central government and scientists were trying to make the effects of the radiation look less severe (Nakanishi 2014; Nishizawa 2013). Subsequently, local residents in Fukushima demanded their local governments provided them with more reliable safety information.

It was in this context that, 6 months after the accident, the author was appointed to be a risk communication advisor by Iitate Village Municipality of Fukushima from September 2011 to March 2012 and involved in implementing a public communication programme for its concerned residents.

Risk Communication for the Residents of Iitate Village, Fukushima 2011–2012

Initial Group Interview in September 2011

Iitate is a small village in northern part of Fukushima that used to be known for its organic farming and for raising cattle. However, after the accident, it became to be known domestically and internationally as a village badly affected by the nuclear fallouts. The village is located 25–45 km from the Fukushima Daiichi Nuclear Power Plant. Initially, it was outside the mandatory evacuation zone that was set right after the explosions. Nevertheless, it was discovered a few months later that the radiation level was higher than initially estimated due to nuclear fallouts blown by the wind. Of the approximately 6500 people who lived in the area before the accident, virtually all left the village as a precautionary measure when the evacuation zone was widened 2 months after the disaster. As of April 2013, the level varied from 4.5 μ (micro) Sv/h in a heavily contaminated area to 1.4 μSv/h in a less contaminated area.[1]

Consequently, many village residents had become sceptical of both scientists and officials both from the central and the local governments—they had been initially told to remain in the village but later the entire village was advised to evacuate the area. They felt betrayed by the authority, left behind, frustrated and scared, without being given any substantial safety information to protect their families for half a year. The municipality was at a loss about how to convey accurate safety information onto the village residents, because it was unfamiliar with techniques for communicating with the public about radiation. It was in this context that they invited a group of experts who had expertise on radiation science and public health.

The Iitate Village municipality asked the Risk Communication Advisory Group, which consisted of four experts including scientists and a medical doctor, to plan and implement an emergency communication programme. The author was its primary architect as its only expert on risk communication. Its role was to help scientific experts explain the science of radiation and the health effects from exposure to radioactive materials to local residents who had been evacuated from areas contaminated by nuclear fallout from the Fukushima Daiichi nuclear plant. The Municipality agreed not to intervene in the programme and its structural and content-wise design was left fully to the hands of the Advisory Group.

---

[1]By January 2016, the value had decreased even more, to less than 1 μSv/h, at the majority of measured areas; according to the official data from Fukushima Prefecture (Fukushima Prefecture 2016).

Risk communication needs to be well-designed and the cost of poorly design communication is high (Baruch and Kadvany 2011). As noted in a preceding section, risk communication aims to create mutual trust through its process, yet, if such a programme was run primary one-way, it would raise scepticism that its hidden aims are to persuade participants towards certain directions and could result in creating distrust instead.

In order to conduct a pilot study, the author selected one particular residential complex (Y) in Fukushima City where approximately 250 had taken refuge. Nearly 40% of the refugees were children under the age of twelve. Parents and grandparents were particularly concerned about the health effects of radiation on their children. In order to design such a programme, the author visited the sheltering site with a graduate student for initial group interviews in September 2011. Twenty residents, ranging in age from 25 to 80, voluntarily participated in and were interviewed to assess their level of knowledge of radiation and to determine their needs. The interviews lasted for a day.

The interviews revealed that interviewees had received little information about radiation from the local government or from schools during the six months after the accident. When asked about their sources of information, they said it was primarily television or the Internet. They expressed anger, disappointment and fear and said that they needed safety information that was trustworthy. The information they had received from the media was contradictory or largely frightening and, consequently, they could not fully trust it. Many felt abandoned, frustrated and scared without any substantial safety information to protect their families.

Communication Programme with a Radiation Expert in October 2011

Together with another communication advisor who was an expert in radiation science, the author attempted to implement a communication roundtable at the sheltering living complex, inviting about 20 local residents to participate, ranging in ages from 25 to 80 years.

The communication session lasted one and half hours, with a 60-min lecture about radiation and its health effects, followed by a Q&A session. The attendees, the lecturer and the author (facilitator) sat together on tatami mattresses. This created a friendly atmosphere in which participants could readily ask any questions or express their concerns.

Initially, the session looked to be successful. Feedback by questionnaire demonstrated that the participants had improved their understanding of radiation, and their fears about health effects were lessened. Yet, when the author conducted follow-up telephone interviews with several participants after the initiative, it was revealed that the programme had had little real influence on their thinking. They remembered very little from the lecture with a few exceptions. For example, in the lecture, it was mentioned that bananas naturally contain a radioactive material, potassium 40. However, rather than calm her one woman's fears about radiation, she said that she would not give her daughter bananas anymore. Hot springs that naturally contain radon were also mentioned in the talk and people remembered this. Fukushima has several radon hot springs. In other words, people remembered some things from the programme, but these were not the things that would help them make better personal decisions about living in Fukushima. Accordingly, the communication programme needed to be changed so it better suited the needs of the attendees.

Follow-up Interviews: More Active Listening Necessary

In order to implement a more adequate and effective programme, the author conducted another group interview in January 2012 with 11 volunteers. Interviewees were separated into two groups; a group of the elderly (average over 60 years old, $N = 7$) and a group of mothers (average 30–39 years old, $N = 4$).

The results of the interviews with the former group, the elderly, showed that this generation was more interested in prospects for rebuilding lives than radiation-related information. They saw the decision to return to the village as in the hands of the younger generation. They showed little interest in knowledge about radiation. A frequently referred sentence was: 'We want to know when we can return (home)'. Their primary concerns were not about radiation.

On the other hand, the results of interviews with the mothers illuminated two issues. The first was that they are seriously concerned about the health effects of radiation on their children and based on this, they had taken actions to protect them by changing the food that the children ate. The second was that a divergence occurred between what they actually wanted to know and what they actually heard from experts. What mothers wanted was hands-on information that they could use to help them protect their children and not the more detailed and scientific information provided by the experts.

The failure of the initial communication programme deployed in October 2011 made us realise that an effective communication programme can be planned only after active and careful listening to the target audience. The interviews with the group of mothers highlighted that they had a high interest in practical radiation-related information, but not in the *science* of radiation. They found it difficult to understand the science of radiation and its relevance to their situation. They wanted crucial information on how to protect their families, and not an academic classroom lecture. In particular, they wanted reliable information on the risks of consumption of radiation-contaminated food and the measures that they could take to limit their radiation exposure. In risk decisions, people feel safer when they have personal control over a risk (Slovic 2000). The group of mothers expressed its disappointment because they were yet to be given such hands-on information by the scientists.

Attentive listening is also important in risk communication for trust building. Earle et al. (2007) demonstrate that shared values are immensely important to public trust. Active listening conveys an unspoken message: 'We care, and therefore we listen to you'. Charles (Chuck) Casto, former United States Nuclear Regulatory Commission (NRC) executive who provided support to the Japanese government and U.S. Ambassador after the Fukushima accident, suggests that explaining science to local residents can be only possible after carefully listening (Casto 2016). His observation corresponds to the experience that the author had in Fukushima.

In summary, the attendees of communication exercises in Fukushima felt frustrated because the information provided by the scientists was not what they expected and wanted. It was either too scientific, and thus difficult to grasp, or not relevant to what they needed for their everyday life.

Furthermore, the author realised that the two groups involved, the elderly and mothers, needed to be approached separately. Among other things, the younger generation expressed a reluctance to talk frankly and give honest views in front of the older generation. It is understandable, since Iitate is a small village and its social structure is strong and conservative unlike cities like Tokyo. In particular, the behavioural expectation for females to be silent and obedient prevails in Iitate. Without active listening, such important elements could have been easily overlooked.

Revised Communication Programme in February 2012

Based on the results of the group interviews, the author formed a small study and designed and piloted a communication initiative that involved a study hour on 'foods and radiation'. The programme took place in February 2012. Four mothers volunteered to take part. Three had participated in the earlier group interviews and the author was acquainted with them.

The author prepared information material on 'How to deal with radioactive material in foods'. This explained that eating locally grown vegetables and drinking tap water was safe and why. In addition, the author asked a mother who acted as a quasi-leader of the group to bring in foods like milk and banana, to make it more participative, hands-on and more visibly clear. The discussion of how to deal with foods was deliberately slow paced and took almost 2 h. The author provided them with her email address and promised to answer any questions that they had later.

Before starting the discussion, the author asked participants what they wanted to know regarding the food they eat. Their interests varied; some wanted to know about the safety of eating local fish and others about drinking tap water. The author did not begin with a description of the risk of radiation, but instead, explained that there is no such thing as zero risk in foods. Some natural toxins are found in many vegetables, and non-pasteurised milk and raw eggs have certain risks that can be fatal. Conventional foods contain carcinogenic and neurotoxicants, such as acrylamide in potato fries, coffee and burnt bread. Hijiki (a sort of seaweed seen as a healthy food in Japan) contains inorganic arsenic and is banned from being sold in the UK.

The level of risks can be more readily grasped by being compared to accepted risks. The primary chemical of concern from Fukushima was caesium. However, potassium 40 has similar pharmacokinetics (ICRP 1990) and is a naturally occurring radioactive isotope in many foods. So, the author discussed that many foods, such as potato chips, milk and banana, contain 'natural' radioactive potassium 40 and that we consume as much as 100 Bq per a day of such radioactive material. That is, 20 Bq of potassium 40 is consumed from one bag potato chips, 20 Bq by eating a large-sized banana, 50 Bq by drinking 1 L milk, and 5 Bq by drinking a large can of beer; according to the Japanese Ministry of Education, Science and Technology (MEXT) (2011). In order to make this seem more real to participants, food was placed on the table in front of everyone.

This was followed by showing the results of sampling of vegetables that had been conducted by the Ministry of Health, Labour and Welfare of Japan. The current and future regulatory values of radioactive caesium in Japan were then explained. Finally, the author showed the results of monitoring tests conducted by Coop Fukushima that measured the actual amount of radioactivity found in cooked meals at home. The measurement conducted at 51 households in Fukushima prefecture demonstrated that the detected radioactivity came predominantly from potassium 40 and only a limited amount of caesium was detected (Fig. 1). Those households where caesium was found were reported to have used vegetables not on the market, but rather from edible mushrooms and plants taken from wild sources by the households themselves.

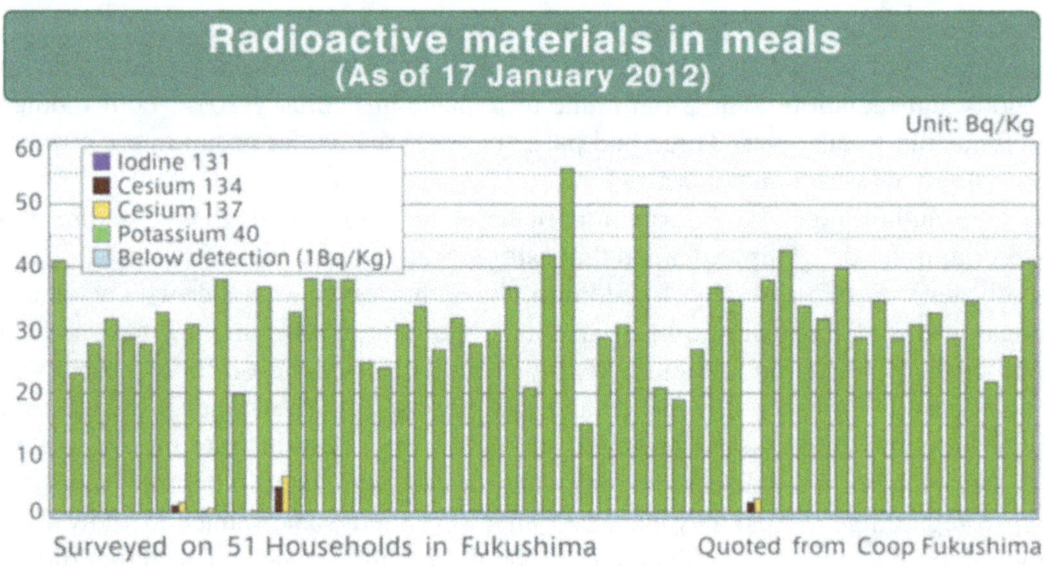

Fig. 1 Radioactive ceasium in meals in January 2012 (Study on 51 households in Fukushima Coop.) *Source* Fukushima Coop (2012) www.fukushima.coop/kagezen/2011.html

The participants said that the dialogue was more helpful and practical than the conventional explanations they had heard from the scientists visiting Fukushima. They said that they had overestimated the risks from radiation and said they would change the way they choose foods and water. An example was the way they chose drinking water. Originally, they were afraid of giving tap water to their children and usually bought more expensive bottled water. However, after the dialogue they said they would stop purchasing bottled water. The dialogue appeared to deliver credible safety information and help households decide what to consume.

Discussion

Effective risk communication delivers to its audience a clear and convincing view of risks by appealing to it emotions and needs; people interpret information largely using intuitive (emotion-based) heuristics. Scientists tend to explain facts using numbers and logic but this approach is not consistent with intuitive heuristics. In other words, risk communication needs to be designed so that it speaks to System 1 (intuition (emotion)), rather than to System 2 (logic); as psychologists or behavioural economists like Kahneman (2012) discuss.

Another key element in risk communication is risk comparison as noted in a preceding section (Nakanishi 2014). There is a tendency that when focused on one risk, people tend to perceive that the level of the risk is higher than it actually is (Nakada et al. 2012). Therefore, the author tried to explain the strength of the risk from radiation in comparison to other socially accepted risks; particularly radioactive potassium 40 in foods.

There is a persistent misunderstanding that the primary goal of risk communication is to 'persuade' the public, so that they will accept the risk in question, or to accurately convey scientific facts (Nishizawa 2015). In fact, the goal should be to give the information that people need to make appropriate decisions about their lives and community. As was argued in a preceding section, one needs to listen to those involved, so that risk communication can be tailored to their concerns, needs and interests. This is to say that risk communication starts by listening.

Creating an atmosphere where one can ask 'dumb' questions is also an important factor, and one which is often neglected in practice. It was the reason that we all sat on the tatami floor together, drinking tea. This allowed the conversation to be sometimes derailed by talk about the weather, families and even fashion. However, it allowed it to flow and provided a platform for questions that were about risk and of importance to the participants. The session was set in the early afternoon before their children came home; this helped mothers attend the session.

In paying attention to the 'risk-information route', it is also essential to make risk communication programme more effective. It is known that risk-related information is conveyed mainly through two communication channels: the mass media and by word of mouth (Renn et al. 1995). In fact, the mothers in the study said they felt that the most reliable source of information was their mothers' friends. Hence, it was hoped that accurate and useful information about radiation would pass on amongst the mothers' circle; ripple effects in the horizontal connection. They did say that they would pass the information further onto their friends who were not able to come to the session. This experience illustrates the importance of peers for adding credibility to messages and demonstrates that people are more likely to believe important safety information from familiar and/or trusted sources/persons. Trust is of utmost importance.

From the series of largely exploratory studies in Fukushima, we may argue that common failures in providing safety information were identified not in scientific information itself, but in the ways such information was conveyed to lay people. As discussed in the preceding sections, scientists primarily try to explain the science of radiation by the use of numbers and logic. However, lay people understand health-related safety information by images and emotions in the context of their needs. Experts want to be scientifically correct whereas the public need hands-on, clear and concise explanation of practical use. Scientists' adherence to scientific accuracy is understandable but communicating scientific information requires a different skill set and objective. This lay–expert gap is an element of mistrust of science and needs to be more readily acknowledged. In order to narrow the gaps, experts need to deliver the safety-related information that is asked for, tailoring their language to be more readily understood by their lay audience.

Our experience in Fukushima made us realise that more frequent science-lay encounters will help scientists become more aware of the needs of the lay people and of how they understand information. We also learned that it is best that the first encounter occurs during a noncrisis situation and not during a crisis itself. Furthermore, we learned that, before talking science, experts need to express empathy and concerns in front of the affected audience. This will lead to a more honest and trustworthy dialogue between them.

Conclusion

The present chapter discussed how to provide information that is both accurate and of practical use for local residents in relation to nuclear risk. The present case was complicated as the local residents felt abandoned and had persistent mistrust towards scientists and authority. As a result, one-way communication failed. Hence, interactive and a dialogue-based communication was used not only to deliver accurate information but also to create mutual understanding and build trust. In the event of an emergency, it is essential to deliver information concisely and within a short period of time. However, when a certain amount of time has elapsed, it becomes more important to consider delivering information tailored to the characteristics, emotions and needs of each population group. As reported in this chapter, demands for information about radiation information were notably different between the child-rearing generation and the older generation. It was the former group that needed hands-on and practical advice about radiation, not the latter. The programme used must to be tailored to the needs of its target audience. Therefore, it is necessary to actively listen to audience in the design of the programme in order to make it more useful and credible. It is good to remember that good communication starts from good listening.

With the increasing deployment of nuclear technology in developing countries in Asia and elsewhere, as well as the persistent negative perceptions within and outside Japan about agricultural products grown or caught in Fukushima and neighbouring regions, the bitter lessons from Fukushima need to be shared on an international basis. This will hopefully contribute to the creation of emergency communication programmes that are more robust, resilient and trustworthy. We learned from Fukushima that we can communicate more effectively regarding risks during noncrisis situations in a way that cannot be achieved during a crisis. Accurate safety information therefore needs to be shared during noncrisis situations and, in order to pursue this, the creation of truly participatory and dialogue-based public 'spheres (platforms)' for science-lay encounters need to be rigorously developed during noncrisis situations. Such platforms are also paramount for creating an atmosphere of trust and confidence that provide the basis for joint decision-making during crises. More fundamentally, risk communication needs to be paid more attention from the spheres of science and technology.

Acknowledgements The author is especially grateful to the local residents of Iitate Village who cooperated with the interviews and participated in the 'food and safety' study session. I also thank the Editors of this book and David Cragin and Ortwin Renn for their useful suggestions about this chapter.

References

Baruch, F., & Kadvany, J. (2011). *Risk: A short introduction*. Oxford: Oxford University Press.

Beck, U. (1992). *Risk society: Towards a new modernity*. London: Sage.

Casto, C. (2016, March 14). Presentation given at a Litera Japan discussion session "Banogiron". Tokyo: Litera Japan.

Earle, T., Siegrist, M., & Gutscher, H. (2007). Trust, risk perception and the TCC model of cooperation. In Siegrist et al. (Eds.), *Trust in cooperative risk management*. London: Earthscan.

Forester, J. (1999). *The deliberative practitioner: Encouraging participatory planning processes*. Cambridge, Mass: The MIT Press.

Fukushima Coop. (2012). Measurement of radioactive material by conducting Kagezen testing for the years 2011–2012. Retrieved from http://www.fukushima.coop/kagezen/2011.html.

Fukushima Prefecture. (2016, January). *Radioactivity in Fukushima*. Retrieved from http://fukushima-radioactivity.jp/.

Giddens, A. (1991). *Modernity and self-identity: Self and society in the late modern age*. Standford: Stanford University Press.

ICRP. (1990). Age-dependent doses to members of the public from intake of radionuclides—Part 1. ICRP Publication 56. Annals of the ICRP 20(2).

Kahneman, D. (2012). *Thinking, fast and slow*. London: Penguin Books.

Kikuchi, Y., Takebayashi, T., & Omae, K. (2006). Miyakejima kizonnimuketeno kenko risk communication. *Nihon Kyobu Rinsho, 65,* 252–260.

Krebs, J. (2013). *Food: A short introduction*. Oxford: Oxford University Press.

MEXT. (2011). *Hoshasen niyoru eikyo*. Retriebed from http://www.mext.go.jp/component/b_menu/other/__icsFiles/afieldfile/2011/11/04/1313005_10_1.pdf.

Nakada, H., Shinya, H., Yeung, L., & Kakeya, H. (2012). *Fukushima daiichi genpatujikoyuraino hoshasennikansuru risk communication no kenkyu*. Retrieved from the 8th Seminar on the Society for the Analysis of Media Information (CD-ROM).

Nakanishi, J. (2014). *Genpatsujikoto hoshasen no risk gaku*. Tokyo: Nihon hyoron sha.

Nishizawa, M. (2005). Citizen deliberation on science and technology and their social environments: Case study on the Japanese consensus conference on GM crops. *Science and Public Policy., 32*(6), 479–489.

Nishizawa, M. (2013). *Risk communication*. Tokyo: Energy Forum. (Japanese).

Nishizawa, M. (2015). Why scientists should get involved. *Journal of the Atomic Energy Society of Japan, 57*(9), 21–25.

Nishizawa, M., & Renn, O. (2006). Responding public demand for assurance of genetically modified crops: Case from Japan. *Journal of Risk Research, 9*(1), 41–56.

Okada, N. (2015). *Hitorikarahajimeru koto okoshino susume*. Hyogo: Kanseigakuin Shuppankai.

Okada, N., Fang, L., & Kilgour, M. (2013). Community-based decision making in Japan. *Group Decision Negotiation, 22,* 45–52.

Renn, O. (2008). *Risk governance: Coping with uncertainty in a complex world*. London: Earthscan.

Renn, O., Webler, T., & Wiedemann, P. (Eds.). (1995). *Fairness and competence in citizen participation: Evaluating models for environmental discourse*. Dordrecht, The Netherlands: Kluwer Academic Publishers.

Rosa, E., Renn, O., & McCright, A. (2014). *The risk society revisited: Social theory and governance*. Philadelphia, Pennsylvania: Temple University Press.

Schön, D. (1983). *Reflective practitioner: How professionals think in action*. New York: Basic Books.

Slovic, P. (2000). *The perception of risk*. London: Earthscan.

The Investigation Committee on the Accident at the Fukushima Nuclear Power Stations of Tokyo Electric Power Company (Government-led Investigation Report), (2012). Final Report. Available on: http://www.cas.go.jp/jp/seisaku/icanps/eng/final-report.html

The National Diet of Japan. (2012). National Diet of Japan Fukushima Nuclear Accident Independent Investigation Commission (NAIIC). The official report of The Fukushima Nuclear Accident Independent Investigation Commission. Tokyo: NAIIC.

Crisis Communication During the Ebola Outbreak in West Africa: The Paradoxes of Decontextualized Contextualization

Loïs Bastide

Abstract As organizations involved in the 2014–2016 Ebola virus disease (EVD) outbreak response in West Africa are now drawing lessons from the crisis, the "manufacture of consent" (Burawoy 1979) emerges as an important issue. Recommendations and public health interventions developed during the response were met with suspicion and often resistances by affected populations, pushing involved organizations and actors to reflect about the validity of their risk communication tools and concepts. These difficulties stressed the numerous shortcomings of risk communication practices, which proved inefficient in an unfamiliar social and cultural context. Many reasons can be pointed-out to explain this failure to communicate risks and public health measures effectively under these circumstances. They include: unrealistic goals for communication; lack of integration of social science skills and knowledge in communication guidelines and human resources; underestimation of the breadth of communication-related tasks; over-segmentation and lack of clarity of communication concepts and expertise (risk communication, crisis communication, social mobilization, and health promotion are all but a few of these categories). Among all these possible lines of inquiry, I want to address what can arguably be considered the most fundamental flaw of crisis communication during the West African EVD episode: its inability to take into account and analyze efficiently the *context* of the intervention.

Keywords Ebola · Public health interventions · Risk communication
Social mobilization

L. Bastide (✉)
Institute of Sociological Research, University of Geneva, Geneva, Switzerland
e-mail: lois.bastide@unige.ch

M. Bourrier and C. Bieder (eds.), *Risk Communication for the Future*, SpringerBriefs in Safety Management, https://doi.org/10.1007/978-3-319-74098-0_7

Introduction

As organizations involved in the 2014–2016 Ebola virus disease (EVD) outbreak response in West Africa are now drawing lessons from the crisis, the "manufacture of consent" (Burawoy 1979) emerges as an important issue. Recommendations and public health interventions developed during the response were met with suspicion and often resistances by affected populations (Fribault 2015), pushing involved organizations and actors to reflect about the validity of their risk communication tools and concepts. These difficulties stressed the numerous shortcomings of risk communication practices, which proved inefficient in an unfamiliar social and cultural context.

Many reasons can be pointed-out to explain this failure to communicate risks and public health measures effectively under these circumstances. They include: unrealistic goals for communication; lack of integration of social science skills and knowledge in communication guidelines and human resources; underestimation of the breadth of communication-related tasks; over-segmentation and lack of clarity of communication concepts and expertise (risk communication, crisis communication, social mobilization, and health promotion are all but a few of these categories). Among all these possible lines of inquiry, I want to address what can arguably be considered the most fundamental flaw of crisis communication during the West African EVD episode: its inability to take into account and analyze efficiently the *context* of the intervention.

To discuss this point, I will start by proposing an informed definition—to the extent that social sciences are concerned—of what a "context" might be. Drawing on this definition, I will then extract a few significant characteristics of the response context, by applying proper analytical tools assembled from the disciplinary archives of social sciences (thus, showing that the issue is more about *heuristics* than knowledge of local circumstances per se). In the last section, I will contrast this analytical framework with the techniques of inquiry available to health emergency communication experts. These tools and related practices were identified and investigated during different fieldworks involving interviews with risk communication experts at the World Health Organization (WHO) and at the US Centers for Disease Control and Prevention (CDCs), as well as observations at WHO's Department of Communications (DCO).[1] This will allow to show that these

[1]Part of these fieldworks took place in the context of the *Organizing, communicating and costing in risk governance: learning lessons beyond the H1N1 pandemic* research project (2013–2017), funded by the Swiss National Science Foundation, with a core research team composed of scholars from the Department of Sociology, University of Geneva, and the Haute Ecole de Gestion, Geneva. Other observations and interviews were conducted in the context of a joint research project between the Department of Sociology, University of Geneva, and WHO's DCO, titled "Generating evidences by capturing field experience from WHO-led deployment of risk communication experts do West Africa" (2015).

techniques tend to erase contexts by taking an individual, psychological and behavioral perspective on affected populations, in the spirit of Evidence-Based Medicine (Brives et al. 2016).

Understanding "Context"

Looking back as far as at Jakobson's famous scheme of the functions of language (1960), which identified the context as a pivotal determinant of human communication, it is striking to see how communication, as a professional domain and practice, has paid little attention to this very dimension. In this respect, the Ebola outbreak in West Africa certainly acted as a powerful reminder: Most of international responders did not understand where they stood during the first months of the response, thus falling in all sorts of traps and pitfalls, causing much delays in necessary interventions: Ebola patients escaped; families and communities hid their ills; dead bodies were silently buried (Faye 2015; Moulin 2015); international funds vanished in the maze of national and regional bureaucracies. Puzzled by these facts, a common reaction among responders was to attribute these failures to backward beliefs, in affected countries, and to a lack of rationality (personal interviews, WHO; for a media account see *Malagardis* 2014). This kind of stereotypes outlines the lack of understanding of local circumstances in West Africa. Dangerously, these assumptions often served as a base for the development of public health interventions.

As Simmel (2007) has shown, stereotyping is a basic social process: it is a cognitive strategy aiming at offsetting a lack of knowledge about unfamiliar interactional partners, at the beginning of a relationship. When encountering new "others", stereotypes facilitate interactions as they serve as a baseline to draw expectations and possible lines of conduct, thus structuring an incipient relationship. As the relationship unfolds, *actual* knowledge about interactional partners is gathered through recurring encounters. It then progressively substitutes the necessary but highly biased information encoded in the stereotype. This process of learning through interaction is obvious in the response to the Ebola crisis in West Africa. A good example is the idea of African people living in traditional *communities* rather than being constituted of highly mobile *individuals*. This pervasive social representation, permeated with primordialist assumptions, prevented understanding early enough that affected areas were crisscrossed by intense human circulations—rather than being composed of still, enclosed tribal entities—spreading the virus along roads, routes, and paths. This view also caused an underestimation of current political and economic dynamics across national borders. Realization that the concept of community was misplaced and might have had a problematic effect on the response slowly emerged as a result of actual experiences on the field, which proved the concept to be misleading. However, this understanding came late and it was just starting to develop as an emerging topic among the leading actors of the response when WHO started to engage in a process of after-action analysis in order to draw lessons from the crisis, in November 2015.[2]

Rather than developing systematic analytical tools to investigate actual social and societal patterns in affected and "at risk" areas, responding institutions thus relied on such basic, lay social representations (stereotypes) to develop their actions, as no system was in place to gather and process the necessary information, not only in "real-time" but by tapping into existing knowledge on best-practices to deal with an Ebola outbreak (Bourrier forthcoming). This failure to analyze the social determinants of the crisis points toward a lack of understanding of contextualization, as a basic and pivotal building block of human communication (Winkin 2001). To analyze these difficulties, let me first outline a rudimentary conceptualization of what a "context" might be, as far as social sciences are concerned. By identifying relevant analytical tools, I will then be able to contrast a scientifically informed definition of contextualization process with the actual cognitive and communicative processes developed by responding institutions to characterize their field of operations.

Speaking of contextualization is recognizing that actions—communication being considered a specific type of action, and actions always having a communicative component (Winkin 2001)—are *embedded* in specific situations, which contribute to configure their semantic contents. Actions are always sited, and they aim at specific outcomes, *in a given situation*. Conversely, actions also contribute to *shape* situations, as they carry on their own effects. Situations are thus a condition, a dimension, and a product of actions.

Understanding action thus involves delineating how local situations are *socially* and *cognitively* constructed. Similar in this to what Dodier (1993, 66) calls a "sociological pragmatics", I propose that this effort involves understanding how social dynamics, in a broad sense (as encompassing cultural, political, and economic phenomena) aggregate and interact locally to frame expectations about/according to specific circumstances, by conveying meaning from past events and framing anticipations, *considering the structuring necessities of unfolding events* (Abbott 2016; Bastide 2015a; Tsing 2005).[3] Contextualizing is thus a matter of relocating the present (unfolding events) in this *tensed*, multilayered temporality. In this analytical framework, the present thus has a logical precedence over the other time-spaces (past and future) since it is the only possible locus of action and cognitive operations, where past and future are linked according to the requirements of the here and now of social life (Abbott 2016).

Understanding local situations thus involves looking at (1) Current circumstances—how a specific event operates and reconfigures existing institutions and social arrangements, by introducing new stakes; (2) History, as a collection of past, individual and collective experiences, which can be used to attribute meaning to

[2]Personal observation, workshop on post-Ebola reorganization, WHO headquarters, Geneva.

[3]Understanding these meanings, expectations and anticipations is critical since they form the base for action.

current circumstances (Abbott 2001, 2016; Schutz 2011); and (3) Anticipations—based on "social imaginaries" framing the perception of possibilities and probabilities contained in the present (Appadurai 1996, 2013). Thus, for instance, one cannot understand the EVD outbreak in West Africa without clarifying its relation to colonial and postcolonial medical practices across the region; in the same spirit, it is difficult to understand the crisis without looking at prevailing social imaginaries to understand vernacular rationalizations of the event, involving culturally and socially formed expectations; and it is difficult as well to make sense of the situation without looking at how the event reshuffles social arrangements and draws a line between a before and an after (Bensa and Fassin 2002)—as when Ebola intersected with political elections, or with social relations by restricting body contacts or disturbing funeral rituals.

Therefore, I want to use this basic conceptual toolbox to look at each of these different time frames (present/past/anticipations) in order to analyze the logic of action deployed by affected populations. This, in turn, will allow shedding light on the "motives" (Mills 1940) underpinning action courses, thus pointing toward specific forms of rationality. However, I need to stress that my expertise concerns outbreak response rather than local societies and histories; thus, I want to show that, by applying a relevant set of analytical tools, one is able to map out and look for relevant information in any given situation, in a sensitive, meaningful and efficient way, *in spite of* knowledge gaps regarding local circumstances—social, cultural, political, and economic patterns.

Current Circumstances, Past, Anticipations

Current Circumstances: Mapping the Stakes

The EVD outbreak opened a period of high uncertainty. As with every crisis of such scope, deep uncertainties created all kinds of new political, economic or social stakes, and opportunities (Klein 2007). Within affected localities, power relations were reconfigured by the epidemic: for example, some fractions of the people were able to seize working opportunities and contributed to staff the response; local political or moral figures, who were hired in the response to create trust between responders and communities, saw their social prestige increase or erode due to this position (Faye 2015); Ebola became a political stake during parliamentary elections in Liberia (*NYT*, December 4th, 2014), Guinea (*Al Jazeera*, October 10th, 2015),[4] as in the US during 2014 mid-term elections (*Politico*, October 10 2014; personal interviews at the US CDCs in Atlanta) due to an imported case and the development of a local transmission chain in Dallas. Communicators lamented about what they

[4]http://www.aljazeera.com/indepth/features/2015/10/deadly-clashes-flare-guinea-election-151010132336700.html.

understood as political interferences; they also complained about media coverage, thus effectively ignoring that both politicians and the media conform to logic of actions articulated around different stakes and interests that those regulating public health experts' practices.

Stakes were also high within and among institutions and organizations involved in the response. Indeed, the organization of an emergency response structure had deep effects on organizations' processes, as specific organograms were drafted, put in place and populated to structure the response. Negotiation about appropriate functions and expertise to be involved fostered competition between different departments, and available positions sustained competition between different individuals, within individual organizations. The fact that Bruce Aylward was officially appointed as the head of Ebola response at WHO as late as January 26, 2015, six months after WHO's declaration of Ebola as a Public Health Emergency of International Concern (PHEIC), is a testimony of the intensity of underlying negotiations. In one of our interviews, an informant framed this issue in telling terms: "Ebola makes careers" (personal interview, MSF Swiss member, December 17, 2014).

As in any "humanitarian space" (Hilhorst and Jansen 2010), Ebola also shaped an "arena" (Céfaï 1996) where different stakeholders—national institutions, international organizations, local, and transnational NGOs—competed for different types of resources—to enhance their profile as emergency experts; for funding; in order to increase their authority; to capture existing or emerging fields of action; and so on. For instance, a competition developed around the issue of communication, as prevailing "social mobilization" and "health promotion" techniques failed to convince people to comply with the prescriptions of involved institutions. Social mobilization thus shifted toward "community engagement", that is a more interactional way of negotiating interventions. The opening of this new domain of action drove struggles around the definition of this new, still blurry, field of expertise, both within organizations, as it foreshadowed the reorganization of communication capacities, and at an inter-organization level as it opened a new cluster in emergency response systems, in need of staff and leadership.

Responders usually failed to consider these overlapping dynamics, integral to affected populations and to responding organizations. And, as a consequence, they also failed to recognize that the response itself, as a set of specific practices and interactions, created new social networks and collectives involving *both* responders *and* local societies.[5] Such social interactions and dynamics framed the *situations* in which individuals and collectives dug into the past to make sense of current circumstances.

[5]Considering this, analyzing the response itself as a specific social formation involving and cutting across responders and local populations, with its own social dynamics, would be interesting. Clues to this approach can be found in Ong and Collier (2005).

History, Expectations, Anticipations: Mapping Conflicts

Among the numerous historical "lineages" (Abbott 2016) which combined to frame Ebola as a public issue in the different countries, let me mention just a few.

First, the legacy of colonial medicine (Anderson 2014; Marks 1997) and the logic of postcolonial global health (King 2002) probably played a significant role in raising people's mistrust while confronting the massive public health enterprise swooping down on them. Historical work has shown, for instance, that colonial public health was not predicated upon the will to better colonized populations' welfare, or only in minor ways. It rather aimed at ensuring the biological well-being of European settlers (Lachenal 2014), at safeguarding the productivity of the local workforce, or at experimenting with hygienist utopias involving, for instance, segregated urban planning, or epidemiological or medical techniques such as mass vaccination against trypanosomiases (Lachenal 2010). In Liberia and Sierra Leone, British colonial medicine did little to better local population's circumstances (Cole 2015). In this context, it is easy to understand that the massive influx of organizations and individuals from advanced industrial countries was met with caution, to say the least.

This kind of reactivation of old, asymmetrical relations of exploitation could only be reinforced by the militarization of the response, with the deployment of the US, British, and French troops and/or logistical capacities in Sierra Leone, Liberia, and Guinea, which gave an obvious neocolonial twist to the intervention, while old colonial powers reinvested past dominions.

It would be useful also to investigate the effects of pharmaceutical companies' dubious practices in the region (Chippaux 2005), which might have further contributed to frame social imaginaries regarding Western medicine and to raise suspicion.

Last, internal tensions within countries also played a major role in complicating the response. Thus, entrenched conflicts between the central government and affected communities, in Guinea, fueled suspicion toward the response as a whole, be it domestic or international, since outsiders were being seen as working with the State, and since the State was often seen as a Trojan horse for foreign interests (Faye 2015).

Anticipations and expectations were thus framed against this backdrop, making people's individual and collective behavior toward the response all the more *rational*.

Re-assembling Rationality

Thus, if conflicts and violence arose between affected populations and actors of the response, one of the most striking features of the crisis was the conflict of *rationalities* at play between responders and affected populations. More challenging, misunderstanding arose from the entrenched idea, across response apparatuses that local citizens were acting erratically, irrationally, or at best according to obsolete traditional beliefs. Thus, many professionals deployed in the field more or less explicitly relied on sets of binary representations to characterize the relationship between response apparatuses and local populations: Us and Them, cutting-edge science versus traditional healing practices, rationality versus beliefs, expertise versus primitive knowledge, and so on. To explain sometimes violent encounters between intervention teams and affected populations, one of our respondent at WHO thus put forward the cultural violence entrenched in local cultural practices, mentioning cases of cannibalism—a claim which proved untrue. Her own fear was thus predicated upon misleading expectations, themselves related to phantasmagorical lineages and stereotypes. Thus, misaligned expectations due to stereotyping and superficial knowledge prevailed on *both sides* of the response. Developing a "symmetrical anthropology" (Faye 2015; Latour 1997) of the response would thus have helped debunking mutual stereotypes and relativizing West African people's putative lack of rationality.

Indeed, as some anthropologists have shown, popular resistance to public health interventions surely retained their own rationality (Faye 2015)—a given for any social scientist. In relation to the proposed conceptualization of "context", rationality can be understood as a cognitive path developed by social actors to *process* the relation between current events, history, and anticipations in order to make sense of the situation and to act consistently. Thus, as it has been clarified in social sciences at least since Weber's seminal delineation between different types of rationality—i.e., value-oriented or means-ends oriented (Weber 2003)—the problem is not to draw a line between rationality and irrationality, but to recover and outline the internal logic of specific forms of social action (Bastide 2015b).

This conceptualization helps understanding why the biomedical logic of the early response in West Africa was met with resistance. If it surely needs to be empirically documented, it is clear that affected populations could only relate to this deployment by referring to the past—hence, the importance of considering the legacy of colonial medicine, the intricacies of postcolonial global health, to reflect on the postcolonial aspect of the response and to consider local political dynamics —to ascribe specific motivations and intentions to the actors of the response, and by drawing anticipations according to this understanding. In this respect, the fear of entrusting one's relatives to medical staff dressed in awe-inspiring Personal Protective Equipment (PPE), knowing that, at the beginning of the crisis, most of these patients would be buried without ever returning to their families, are easily understood. As one of our respondents at the Geneva University Hospital phrased it, this reluctance is very easy to grasp with a simple thought experiment, by transposing the situation in our own countries and families (personal interview, December 19, 2014). However, this individual understanding did not diffuse within collective practices developed across response structures. Furthermore, it is important to stress again that, on the side of responders, social imaginaries about Africa played a symmetrical role to this of local populations' own expectations and anticipations, further blurring the response, as a *social relation*.

Framing popular behaviors as irrational bore important consequences. Referring to the issue of traditional funerals, a high-risk practice considering that rituals involve close contact with highly infectious bodies, M. Osterholm, a prominent US expert on emerging infectious diseases wrote:

> Public health workers haven't been able to curtail this traditional practice; it's a challenge that puts religious and cultural beliefs in direct conflict with infection control. (*The Washington Post*, August 1st, 2014)

Trying to *redress* what medical practitioners widely perceived as obsolete, dangerous, and backward beliefs, by means of social mobilization and public marketing, rather than *leveraging* on this rationality to renegotiate biologically safer funeral practices in ways respectful of and meaningful to affected populations, caused much delays in the response. Indeed, communicators were very slow to understand that, for many, the very real risk associated to the transgression of funeral practices could well exceed the perceived risk of dying from Ebola (Brives et al. 2016). Conflicting definitions of risks were thus at play, between a biomedical risk and a moral risk associated with breaching rituals.

Conceptualizing Populations, Analyzing the Crisis

The purpose and methods of crisis communication developed at the onset of the outbreak failed to consider these different dimensions. At the same time, however, the fact that emergency response faced different forms of resistance among affected population also stressed the importance of putting professional communication specialists at the forefront of the response. This move was unprecedented in public health. It was the first crisis of this magnitude that saw communicators being embedded in the US CDCs health "swat teams" (Anderson 1994) deployed in the field, at the request of technical teams who had long looked down upon them (personal interview, CDC Headquarter, August 18th, 2015, Atlanta). At WHO as well, communicators quickly gained momentum within the response structure, for the very same reason, since biomedical interventions were often rejected by affected population, a refusal sometimes escalating into violent attacks (see for instance: Afrik.com, February 13th, 2015). Communication was expected to bridge the all too apparent divide between the logic of action enacted by responders, and their perception by affected populations. As a matter of fact, it only brought mixed results. Let me focus on this semi-failure. I will proceed by contrasting the proposed conceptualization of "context" with the tools available to communicators, across organizations, during the EVD outbreak in West Africa. These tools are indeed remarkably standardized and consistent.

When the international response deployed in West Africa, organizations behaved as if they had reached a *terra incognita*. Ebola was not an expected pathology in this region, and it displayed unusual features such as multiple epidemic locations and its spread to capital cities. In an emergency setting, organizations were usually unable to identify, consider or to tap into available knowledge, including local knowledge and previous scientific surveys, to develop an accurate understanding of the situation.[6] What they usually did, in order to quickly assemble information on the *local context*, was to run Knowledge, Attitudes, and Practices (KAP) surveys to design "evidence-based" communication strategies. This type of survey, originally developed in the 1950s to measure attitudes and practices with regards to family planning, has gradually become a ubiquitous technique to plan and to measure the outcomes of a broad range of public health interventions in countries in the South. They aim at measuring a population's knowledge, attitudes, and practices around a specific issue, through the use of questionnaires, and to assess the impact of implemented interventions, by being ran at regular intervals. This excerpt from an end of mission report (organization cannot be named for confidentiality reasons) illustrates these following points:

> – Analysed an existing KAP survey in [Location name] and integrated findings into communications and social mobilization strategy; and supported and reviewed proposals for two new KAP studies:
> a. one in [Location name] to set a baseline for communications and social mobilization work there,
> b. and the second a repeat of the one done previously in [Location name] to measure against the existing baseline survey to evaluate the outcomes of communications and social mobilization work there.

KAP surveys thus framed public health interventions throughout the crisis: they acted as a context-making practice, allowing organizations to stabilize an understanding of their field of action; they also played the role of an evaluation device, providing a feedback on the efficacy of implemented interventions. KAP surveys thus made action possible, by generating information, allowing to identify needs and gaps, and to design appropriate strategies. Critically, it allowed gathering data *in a speedy way*. As such, they proved well fitted to the time-frame of an emergency. And indeed, speed, cost-effectiveness, and the production of seemingly hard data, under the form of statistics, is what makes them popular among health-oriented organizations.

However, this technique suffers from numerous flaws. Let me mention a few, extracted from a paper by Launiala (2009): first, KAP surveys only measure people's *biomedical* knowledge; as such, they neglect vernacular practices and knowledge about health, diseases, and cure. Moreover, the information they produce is over-reliant on language and formal knowledge, thus neglecting more practical, less formalized types of knowledge. Being framed as standardized questionnaires, they also raise issues in terms of translation and the use of an appropriate language with local populations. Eventually, they rely on personal knowledge, thus individualizing knowledge and practices by abstracting them from their embeddedness in social networks and dynamics.

[6]This stresses the issue of *knowledge management* rather than knowledge production per se. Knowledge was available, but institutions were not able to retrieve it in a timely manner. More than a scientific issue, we are thus faced with an *organizational* problem.

This conceptual privilege of the individual over collectives is reflected also in available crisis communication guidelines. A look at the latest CDC's Crisis and Emergency Risk Communication guide (CDC 2014), the most comprehensive institutional resource for risk communication in the field of public health emergencies, helps grasp this issue: in the document, public behaviors in health crises are depicted in purely psychological terms, in a chapter entitled: "Psychology of a crisis". The context is reduced to a series of *stimuli* inducing a narrow variety of psychological states, aroused by specific events, namely: uncertainty; fear, anxiety, and dread; hopelessness and helplessness; denial; panic. These states then translate into a limited a number of behaviors. This model empties social and cultural patterns of all substance, as it draws on very basic versions of behaviorist psychology, typical of the professional literature on risk communication: the link between message production and emission and behavior change is understood in terms of simplistic causal relations. Just as KAP surveys, this model is well fitted to the specific temporality of a crisis as it provides a base for a speedy reaction by allowing to design simple algorithms of the type, in *this case,* implement *that intervention* in order to produce *the following outcome.* In terms of communication, KAP surveys provide the baseline to define the case, under the form of a situational assessment. Once the situation is characterized, it becomes possible to design a specific *stimulus*, aimed at producing a *behavioral twist*—the outcome. Another KAP survey then reassesses the situation, by including previous outcomes. Like KAP surveys, these plans are action (rather than knowledge)-oriented; like KAP surveys, they leave "responders" with the feeling of developing evidence-based actions and strategies.

However, as an interviewee at the CDCs rightly underscored, conflicting needs emerge in such a crisis between speed and accuracy of information, and between rendering complexity and the need for operational decision instruments. It is easy to see that, during most crises, the urge for quickly actionable information prevails over the need for depth and precision. KAP surveys can thus be seen as a middle-road in the highly constrained environment of an emergency: it provides speed, actionability, entitlement (they produce the *evidences* needed for *evidence-based* interventions). However, they also produce low-quality data. While my conceptualization of the context stresses the need to look at current individual and collective dynamics, in relation to past events and to culturally framed expectations and anticipations, this type of tools shapes the context as a collection of timeless and socially disembedded individual opinions and knowledge. Therefore, the need for speed somehow results in the production of what can be termed, quite paradoxically, a *decontextualized contextualization*, where individuals are abstracted from their social embeddedness in social networks, in lineages of past events, and in a specific cultural horizon and are reinscribed as simple parameters in the realm of *evidence-based* interventions.

As a matter of fact, the dramatic emergence of the context as a prominent agent in the crisis underlines the weakness of these models. And institutions and individuals enrolled in the response were ill-equipped to face this challenge, as they lacked appropriate analytical tools to deal with this dimension. Hence, the belated and somehow improvised resort to anthropologists when affected populations' resistance derailed the deployment of response systems (see for instance: NPR, September 28, 2014). The current reflection, at WHO, to integrate social scientists within emergency response human resources is a clear recognition of this fact (SciDevNet, April 29, 2015): failing to consider and analyze sociocultural patterns plagued the response and pointed toward the need to shift from quantitative data collection, informed by a reductionist, solipsist behaviorist bias, toward more qualitative, inclusive ethnographic research practices. Of course, behaviors evolved during the crisis, making infection control easier as it unfolded. However, in the absence of reliable data, it is impossible to attribute these changes to implemented communication interventions. Most likely, they are in good part the result of populations' own agency and capacity to draw lessons from their experience in dealing individually and collectively with the crisis.

Conclusion

In a context of high uncertainty, information is gold; as mentioned in most public health emergency communication plans and guidelines, the first step to be taken during a crisis is to make sense of the situation, in order to establish evidence-based response strategies. Hence, the critical role attributed to *situational assessments*, and the need for ready-made tools and algorithm-like plans of action: they allow speeding-up the process of data collection, to trigger action, and to orientate the response. However, the EVD episode in West Africa showed that these techniques produce low-quality data, with few remaining relations to the complexity of actual social dynamics. It is partly when anthropologists were brought into the response structure that relevant issues could be mapped and addressed. Yet, many responders expressed frustration with the lengthy temporality required by the logic of ethnographic inquiry. Thus, we witness a two-fold movement taking place as after-action evaluations are being developed: first, anthropological consultant firms and anthropological staff in organizations advocate the development of a new field of "emergency anthropology"; their first requirement is to develop methodologies consistent with the high pace of a crisis, combining the production of accurate *and* actionable knowledge, in a speedy way. However, this tendency is not without raising concerns among more critical, academic anthropologists.[7] Second, organizations such as WHO are thinking about shifting their recruitment policy in the area of communication staff, by hiring less public communication specialists in favor of a more social science-oriented workforce. It remains to be seen, however, whether sound survey methodologies are compatible or not with the time compression that characterizes emergency situations. What can be said, at least, is that, after all, much

[7]This is somehow a classical dynamic of professionalization, well documented in the sociological archive.

time was lost, in this episode, by *not resorting* to these qualitative survey techniques: speeding-up action based on too fragile knowledge is a risky business.

References

Abbott, A. D. (2001). *Time matters: On theory and method*. Chicago, Ill.: University of Chicago Press.

Abbott, A. D. (2016). *Processual sociology*. Chicago, Ill.: University of Chicago Press.

Anderson, C. (1994). Sentinel health unit surveillance system. *The Canadian Journal of Infectious Diseases, 5*(5), 207–209.

Anderson, W. (2014). Making Global Health History: The Postcolonial Worldliness of Biomedicine. *Social History of Medicine*, hkt126. https://doi.org/10.1093/shm/hkt126.

Appadurai, A. (1996). *Modernity at large: Cultural dimensions of globalization*. Minneapolis, MN: University of Minnesota Press.

Appadurai, A. (2013). *The future as cultural fact: Essays on the global condition* (Vol. 1-1). London, New York: Verso.

Bastide, L. (2015a). *Habiter le transnational: Espace, travail et migration entre Java*. Lyon, ENS éditions: Kuala Lumpur and Singapore.

Bastide, L. (2015b). Faith and uncertainty: Migrants' journeys between Indonesia, Malaysia and Singapore. *Health, Risk & Society, 17*(3–4), 226–245. https://doi.org/10.1080/13698575.2015.1071786.

Bensa, A., & Fassin, E. (2002). Les sciences sociales face à l'événement. *Terrain. Revue d'ethnologie de l'Europe, 38,* 5–20. https://doi.org/10.4000/terrain.1888.

Brives, C., Marcis, F. L., & Sanabria, E. (2016). What's in a context? tenses and tensions in evidence-based medicine. *Medical Anthropology, 35*(5), 369–376. https://doi.org/10.1080/01459740.2016.1160089.

Burawoy, M. (1979). *Manufacturing consent: Changes in the labor process under monopoly capitalism*. Chicago, Ill.: University of Chicago Press.

CDC (2014) Crisis Emergency Risk Communication, US Centers for Disease Control and Prevention, Atlanta, 2014

Céfaï, D. (1996). La construction des problèmes publics. Définitions de situations dans des arènes publiques. *Réseaux, 14*(75), 43–66. https://doi.org/10.3406/reso.1996.3684.

Chippaux, J. P. (2005). L'Afrique, cobaye de Big Pharma. (2005, juin 1). *Le Monde diplomatique*. https://www.monde-diplomatique.fr/2005/06/CHIPPAUX/12513. Accessed on March 17, 2016.

Cole, F. (2015). Sanitation, disease and public health in Sierra Leone, West Africa, 1895–1922: Case failure of British colonial health policy. *The Journal of Imperial and Commonwealth History, 43*(2), 238–266. https://doi.org/10.1080/03086534.2014.974901.

Dodier, N. (1993). Les appuis conventionnels de l'action. *Eléments de pragmatique sociologique. Réseaux, 11*(62), 63–85.

Faye, S. L. (2015). L' « exceptionnalité » d'Ebola et les « réticences » populaires en Guinée-Conakry. Réflexions à partir d'une approche d'anthropologie symétrique. *Anthropologie & Santé. Revue internationale francophone d'anthropologie de la santé*, (11). https://doi.org/10.4000/anthropologiesante.1796.

Fribault, M. (2015). Ebola en Guinée: Violences historiques et régimes de doute. *Anthropologie & Santé. Revue internationale francophone d'anthropologie de la santé*, (11). https://doi.org/10.4000/anthropologiesante.1761.

Hilhorst, D., & Jansen, B. J. (2010). Humanitarian space as arena: A perspective on the everyday politics of aid. *Development and Change, 41*(6), 1117–1139. https://doi.org/10.1111/j.1467-7660.2010.01673.x.

Jakobson, R. (1960). Closing statement: Linguistics and poetics. In T. A. Sebeok (Ed.), *Style in language* (pp. 350–377). Cambridge, Mass: MIT Press.
King, N. B. (2002). Security, disease, commerce ideologies of postcolonial global health. *Social Studies of Science, 32*(5–6), 763–789. https://doi.org/10.1177/030631270203200507.
Klein, N. (2007). *The shock doctrine: The rise of disaster capitalism*. London: Penguin.
Lachenal, G. (2010). Le médecin qui voulut être roi. *Annales. Histoire, Sciences Sociales, 65e année*(1), 121–156.
Lachenal, G. (2014). *Le médicament qui devait sauver l'Afrique: un scandale pharmaceutique aux colonies*. Paris: la Découverte.
Latour, B. (1997). *Nous n'avons jamais été modernes: essai d'anthropologie symétrique*. Paris: La Découverte.
Launiala, A. (2009). How much can a KAP survey tell us about people's knowledge, attitudes and practices? Some observations from medical anthropology research on malaria in pregnancy in Malawi. *Anthropology Matters, 11*(1). http://anthropologymatters.com/index.php/anth_matters/article/view/31. Accessed on March 25, 2016.
Malagardis, M. (2014, Septembre 20). Entre fantasmes et sorcellerie, Ebola tue aussi par l'ignorance; En Guinée, une délégation de prévention a été assassinée à la machette. *Le Temps*. https://www.lexisnexis.com/uk/nexis/docview/getDocForCuiReq?lni=5D5T-0151-JBSTY1NV&csi=257973&oc=00240&perma=true. Accessed on September 22, 2014.
Marks, S. (1997). What is colonial about colonial medicine? And what has happened to imperialism and health? *Social History of Medicine, 2,* 205–219.
Mills, C. W. (1940). Situated actions and vocabularies of motive. *American Sociological Review, 5* (6), 904–913. https://doi.org/10.2307/2084524.
Moulin, A. M. (2015). L'anthropologie au défi de l'Ebola. *Anthropologie & Santé. Revue internationale francophone d'anthropologie de la santé*, (11). https://doi.org/10.4000/anthropologiesante.1954.
Ong, A., & Collier, S. J. (2005). *Global assemblages: Technology, politics, and ethics as anthropological problems*. Malden: Blackwell.
Schutz, A. (2011). Phenomenology and the social sciences. In L. Embree (Ed.), *Collected papers V*. Berlin: Springer.
Simmel, G. (2007). The stranger. In C. Calhoun, J. Gerteis, J. Gerteis, J. Moody, S. Pfaff, & V. Indermohan (Eds.), *Classical sociological theory* (pp. 295–299). Wiley-Blackwell.
Tsing, A. L. (2005). *Friction: An ethnography of global connection*. Princeton, NJ: Princeton University Press.
Weber, M. (2003). *Economie et société, tome 1 : Les Catégories de la sociologie*. Pocket.
Winkin, Y. (2001). *Anthropologie de la communication: de la théorie au terrain*. Seuil: De Boeck & Larcier/Paris.

Part III
The Collapse of Absolute Trust in Absolute Truth

Transparency in Health Care: Disclosing Adverse Events to the Public

Siri Wiig, Karina Aase, Mathilde Bourrier and Olav Røise

Abstract The topic of transparency has received increasing academic interest in recent years. Transparency can be interpreted as conducting affairs in the open, being subject to public scrutiny, or admitting to problems when they arise. This chapter analyses transparency in disclosing adverse events to the public in Norway. We use the widely publicized Daniel case to show the communication between the regulator and the public, discussing key elements of transparency in the healthcare setting, including the role of media. The Daniel case describes an accidental tonsillectomy characterized by cover-up, failure of the initial regulatory and hospital follow-up, coming to a head when media shone a spotlight on the case. The media coverage caused social amplification of the risk communication resulting in regulatory follow-up having to apply new forms of transparency strategies to rebuild trust in the public. By using the Daniel case as emblematic of Norwegian risk communication strategies in health care, improvements should be made along the lines of direct and adequate information exchange according to patient rights, and efforts to foster open and transparent regulatory and organizational cultures to ensure public trust.

Keywords Transparency · Adverse events · Risk amplification
Health care

S. Wiig (✉) · K. Aase · O. Røise
SHARE—Center for Resilience in Healthcare, Faculty of Health Sciences, University of Stavanger, Stavanger, Norway
e-mail: siri.wiig@uis.no

M. Bourrier
Department of Sociology and Institute of Sociological Research, University of Geneva, Geneva, Switzerland

O. Røise
Division of Orthopaedic Surgery, Oslo University Hospital, Oslo, Norway

O. Røise
Institute of Clinical Medicine, University of Oslo, Oslo, Norway

M. Bourrier and C. Bieder (eds.), *Risk Communication for the Future*, SpringerBriefs in Safety Management, https://doi.org/10.1007/978-3-319-74098-0_8

Introduction

Background

It is commonly claimed that we live in an age of transparency (Hood and Dixon 2015) or in a 'transparency society' (Han 2015). The topic of transparency has therefore received increasing academic interest, resulting in theoretical and empirical propositions. Transparency can be interpreted as conducting affairs in the open, being subject to public scrutiny, or admitting to problems when they arise. Transparency may improve the communication of benefits and risks, and support the spread and sharing of knowledge. There is little doubt that transparency is fundamentally important from democratic and efficiency perspectives, although it may also have negative implications. More information and more communication do not necessarily lead to better decisions about risk, and the call for increased transparency may also increase costs and complicate decision-making processes (Han 2015; Hood and Dixon 2015). Some transparency strategies may involve dedicated web portals, publication of recommendations, introduction of public hearings, establishment of safety and quality committees and disclosure of the minutes of meetings and meeting agendas (Bouder et al. 2015).

In Norway's healthcare context, transparency trends are developing in line with greater international emphasis on holding healthcare providers accountable and relying more on performance indicators (e.g. Kurtzman and Jennings 2008; Tavare 2012). More specifically, more hospitals are making their adverse event rates public and posting hospital infection rates on their websites. Hospitals also disclose the number of patient complaints, their performance on national quality indicators, and waiting times (e.g. AHUS 2015; OUS 2015).

Promoting patient safety using a system perspective has shown promising results in improving health care and reducing adverse events. However, the use of error disclosure and the creation of transparent safety cultures have not been rigorously assessed or implemented (Francis 2015; Liang and Lovett 2013; Waring 2015). Healthcare scandals in several countries have shown that uncaring and ineffective practices can flourish if the organizational context goes wrong (Braithwaite et al. 2015; Francis 2013; Mannion and Davies 2015). There are still intimations of a culture of individual blame within health care, supported by professional cover-ups of adverse events (Johnstone and Kanitsaki 2006; Wiig and Lindøe 2009; Woodier 2015), and a fear of whistleblowing (Mannion and Davies 2015; Waring 2015). Healthcare professionals, managers and regulators alike have been accused, especially by the media, of avoiding transparent and open communication with patients and next of kin after adverse events (e.g. Aase and Rosness 2015; Francis 2013; Hannawa et al. 2016; Helsetilsynet 2015a, b; NOU 2015:11; Woodier 2015).

The nature of communication and regulation of risk has changed in Europe (Lofstedt et al. 2011; O'Connor 2016). Regulatory scandals have resulted in greater public distrust of regulators and policymakers and new models of regulation emerged with focus on public participation, transparency and increasingly powerful non-governmental organizations. The call for greater transparency developed to ensure more open decision-making processes, as regulators and policymakers were no longer trusted. The role of media as an independent 'watch dog' is crucial and implies that journalists may become advocates and take strong stances, and in many cases amplifying the risks associated with the topic that they are covering (Kasperson et al. 1988; Lofstedt et al. 2011).

The Norwegian Board of Health Supervision (NBHS) is the national regulatory body for health and care services. It is a public institution organized under the Ministry of Health and Care Services. At the regional level, 18 county governors oversee services within primary and specialized health care. In 2010, a new investigative group was established as part of the NBHS to improve regulatory follow-up after serious adverse events in Norwegian specialized healthcare services. To ensure transparency, the NBHS publishes anonymized versions of investigative reports, summary reports, and has recently increased its transparency approach by publishing a draft report. The 2015 draft report was based on an in-depth regulatory follow-up investigation of the death of a 3-year-old child after a routine tonsillectomy (the Daniel case) in 2009 (Helsetilsynet 2015a, b). The regulatory follow-up and the police investigation in the Daniel case were initially closed in 2010, but new information from the news media caused the regulatory case to be reopened in 2014 (*Aftenposten*, June, 20, 2014). At that time, the new investigation unit within the NBHS was operative and took on the task.

Aim

This chapter analyses transparency in disclosing adverse events to the public in Norway. We use the widely publicized Daniel case to show the communication between the regulator and the public, discussing key elements of transparency in the healthcare setting, including the role of media.

Theoretical Approach

This paper applies the Social Amplification of Risk Framework (SARF) (e.g. Kasperson et al. 1988; Pidgeon et al. 2003), as the theoretical foundation to understand the role of media in a high-profile case. It identifies how a new regulatory transparency approach has implications for the portrayal of events, interpretation of the event from different societal actors' perspectives and has unforeseen implications. In brief, the SARF is an integrative framework that depicts the dynamic social processes underlying risk perception and response. It is founded on the belief that hazards interact with psychological, social, institutional and cultural processes in ways that may increase or decrease the perception of risk and shape risk behaviour. The experience of risk is not just an experience of physical harm; it is also the result of a process by which individuals or groups learn to acquire or interpret hazards (Kasperson et al. 1988; Pidgeon et al. 2003).

Hazardous events hold a signal value, which individuals and social groups may perceive differently. These signals are subject to transformations as they are filtered through individual and social amplification stations (e.g. mass media, groups of scientists, governmental agencies, and politicians). Social amplification may have repercussions far beyond the initial impact of the event, bringing effects such as demands for regulatory constraints, litigation or loss of credibility and trust. These processes imply that diverse hazards are given more or less attention due to the diverse understanding of signals among individuals and groups, causing an amplification or attenuation of risks (Pidgeon et al. 2003).

Methods

We apply a retrospective case study strategy in the ‘Daniel case’ to understand the trajectory of the event and its implications for different stakeholders between 2009 and 2015 (Stake 1994). In this study, we conceive the case as the adverse event and the following activity among the stakeholders in the aftermath of Daniel’s death. This paper is based on a qualitative content analysis (Pope et al. 2006) of publicly available data material on the Daniel case. The data material includes newspaper articles, news briefs from national media, and the preliminary draft version and the final investigation report published by the Norwegian Board of Health Supervision (NBHS). The main data sources are the draft version and the final version of the investigation report from the NBHS. The newspaper articles and news briefs have been used as a supplement to the investigative reports, adding narratives and voices related to the event, and also to provide insight into details, not covered by the mandate of the NBHS’s investigative reports. All of the data material was downloaded from the Internet, and the study did not require ethical approval for collecting and analysing the data. The institution names, occupational positions, roles and responsibility were all present in the data material as it appeared in the published public documents. We have not disclosed any new information in this case. We analysed the material using a thematic approach where we read all of the material and then categorized the data according to the themes emerging from the data (Pope et al. 2006). We analysed the data to gain insight into (a) the chronological process between the regulator and the public, (b) the implications of a new transparency approach and (c) the influence of the media on the development and escalation of the case from the beginning of 2009 when Daniel died, to the end of 2015, after the NBHS published the results of the final investigation.

Findings

In this section, we present the findings chronologically. We begin with a description of the adverse event, the internal follow-up, and the regulatory and police investigations in 2009. Then, we describe how media dug up new information in 2014, the reopening of the case, and the implications of the new transparency policy in 2015. Figure 1 gives the timeline of the Daniel case.

The Daniel Case: What Happened?

Daniel, aged 2 years and 11 months, was referred for chronic tonsillitis to the otorhinolaryngeal unit of Molde Hospital in north-western Norway. He had been having monthly throat infections, snoring, difficulties with speech and food intake and was accepted for surgery by the chief consultant. At admission for surgery January, 16, 2009, the patient was re-examined by a resident who classified the large tonsils as grade 3–4 according to Friedman's four-grade scale and confirmed the indication for surgery. No documented information was given to the parents on the particular risks associated with this surgery on such a young child. The patient underwent an uncomplicated adenotonsillectomy and was discharged from the hospital the next morning.

On day three after surgery, the patient was readmitted for bleeding. At admission, the bleed had stopped and the patient was prophylactically treated with antibleeding medication and surveyed fasting at the recovery unit. The patient was treated with penicillin due to elevated CRP. Neither blood screening nor reservation

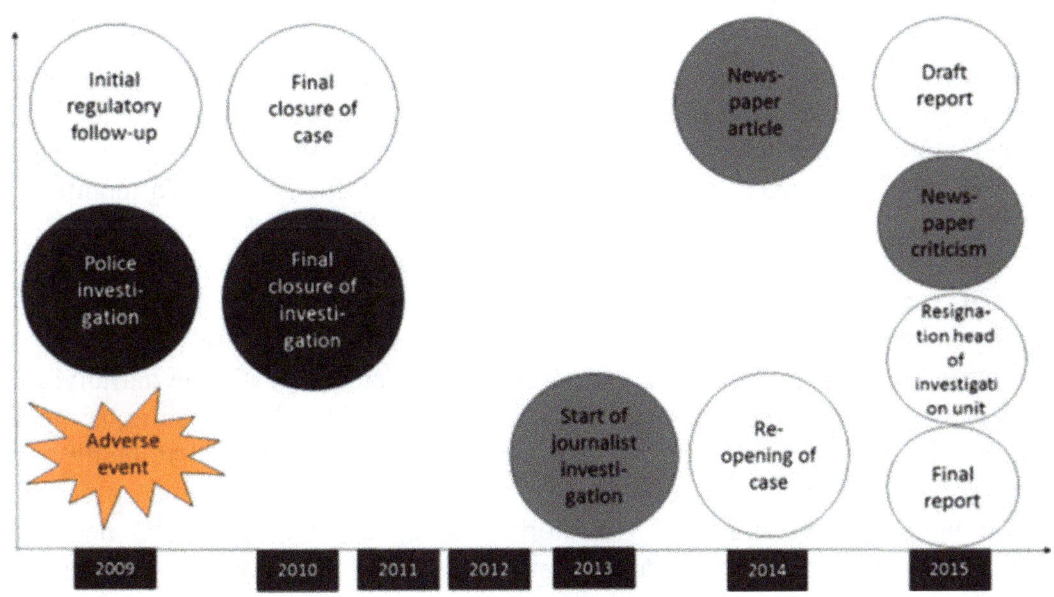

Fig. 1 Timeline of the Daniel case

of blood for potential transfusion was ordered. After 3 hours, the patient was transferred to the general ward and observed in a four-bed room close to the nurses' guardroom. The patient's mother was concerned and uncomfortable with the nurses' lack of observational behaviour. At approximately 3:30 a.m., the patient's father became alarmed when the patient vomited blood. The nurse called the operating theatre team. According to the patient's father, they entered the operating room 20 min after he alarmed the nurses at 3:50 a.m. According to the nurse anaesthetist, the patient was in shock, but according to the surgeon the patient was still awake. The patient was unsuccessfully intubated with a tube without cuff guided by laryngoscope in general anaesthesia as blood hindered visualization of the deep part of the throat. The second intubation attempt was successful in terms of correct tube placement. A few seconds later the patient had cardiorespiratory collapse and cardiorespiratory resuscitation was started. During ongoing resuscitation, a bleeding spot was secured with compression and diathermia. The senior consultant surgeon, who arrived at the operating theatre at 4:12 a.m., heard a strange sound and suspected a tube dislocation that was corrected. Several attempts of venous access restoration were unsuccessful so fluid transfusion was not possible. The ATLS-trained (Advanced Trauma Life Support) resident surgeon was then called to assist the resuscitation. He established intraosseous access in the left tibia and transfusion of fluid, medication and blood was immediately started. Two hours later the patient was transferred to the Regional University Hospital, St Olav Hospital in Trondheim, where he died 4 days later. Autopsy showed massive brain oedema. Death was caused by severe hypoxemia due to bleeding shock with cardiac arrest (Helsetilsynet 2015a, b).

Internal Follow-up Immediately After the Adverse Event

Several critical issues for the case development were raised shortly after the adverse event. The hospital management did not carry out any formal debriefing. After Daniel's transfer, the involved healthcare professionals at Molde Hospital gathered, and the otorhinolaryngeal surgeon requested data from the anaesthesia monitoring equipment. However, this was impossible, as the data had already been deleted. The reason for this is not clear, but the nurse anaesthetist could not rule out that she had pressed 'the finish patient button', deleting all patient data. On February 2, the deputy managing director of the hospital called a joint meeting for all anaesthesia and otorhinolaryngeal doctors. There were major discrepancies in the narratives of the adverse event between the two professional groups. The chief otorhinolaryngeal doctor, who had not been present during the adverse event, argued that the meeting should not be held, partly due to old professional conflicts, and partly because of the upcoming police investigation. The otorhinolaryngeal perspective was negative, and they did not have an open and constructive discussion about the treatment of the patient. The meeting became a discussion of the reason for the patient's cardiorespiratory collapse. The anaesthetists suggested a loss of blood. The resident otorhinolaryngeal surgeon and the chief otorhinolaryngeal doctor were not given the opportunity to counter this suggestion. In addition, memories from a similar meeting in 2006 involving personal attacks on the otorhinolaryngeal staff revived old conflicts and the atmosphere was experienced as tense. According to the investigative report (Helsetilsynet 2015b), the anaesthetists claimed that the meeting as being normal. No minutes were written.

A few days later, the anaesthesia consultant visited the resident otorhinolaryngeal surgeon and asked him to reconsider the information he had included in the medical record. In addition, the resident explained that the anaesthesia consultant, who chaired the library meeting, had said, 'Remember that everybody did a good job', just before the resident went into the police interrogation. The resident felt threatened and pressured to revise information (*Aftenposten*, June, 5, 2015; Helsetilsynet 2015b). Shortly after this episode, the chief otorhinolaryngist explained that the chief anaesthesia doctor had come to his office. They had a rough discussion on causality, the rumours spreading through the hospital and challenges of developing common procedures between the otorhinolaryngeal and anaesthesia units. The discussion degenerated into a scolding, according to the chief otorhinolaryngist (Helsetilsynet 2015b). The investigative report does not present data on the chief anaesthetist's perception of this situation.

Process of Police Investigation and Regulatory Follow-up in 2009

In 2009, a regulatory follow-up and a police investigation were initiated. Both closed the case and concluded that there was no reason for regulatory sanctions or prosecution. The Regional Board of Health Supervision in the county and the police received reports from the hospital on an unnatural death, as required by law. Almost 6 months later, the Regional Board of Health Supervision requested the National Board of Health Supervision (NBHS) to assess prosecution. The NBHS did not find sufficient grounds for prosecution under the Health Professional Act, and the decision was upheld after a review of the documents from the police investigation (Helsetilsynet 2015b). The police had interrogated the healthcare professionals involved and consulted an expert in children's diseases. Based on the expert's opinion, and because the NBHS did not find sufficient evidence to prosecute, the police dismissed the case, concluding that there was no evidence of a crime. The expert on children's diseases concluded that even though mistakes had been made, no individuals were to blame. The hospital did not follow up the expert report with a learning perspective strategy and plan (*Aftenposten*, June, 22, 2014).

Media Push Causing a Reopening of the Regulatory Case in 2014

The Daniel case was subject to regular media coverage in local and national news press and TV. A turning point came in June 2014 when media released new and highly relevant information:

> In the documents that Aftenposten [*newspaper*] has access to, severe allegations are put forward indicating that hospital employees coordinated their depositions to the police. There moreover appear allegations on pressure and intimidation of healthcare professionals who refused to conform. Several at the hospital feared the results of the police investigation. (*Aftenposten*, June, 20, 2014)

Moreover, the parents expressed a need to clarify several unanswered questions, and the media information described a culture of fear, cover-ups, and claimed that healthcare professionals involved in Daniel's surgery had given incorrect information about his care. Based on the new media information in June 2014, the NBHS investigation group reopened the case and conducted an in-depth regulatory investigation to assess if the healthcare services provided in January 2009 had been done according to legal requirement of sound professional practice (a legal standard involving both institutions and individual healthcare professionals) (Helsetilsynet 2015b). The targets of the investigation included duties of documentation, internal follow-up of the event and whether the information and follow-up with the next of kin complied with the law.

A New Transparency Strategy—Publishing a Preliminary Regulatory Investigation Report in 2015

In June 2015, the NBHS chose a new transparency strategy, by publishing the draft version of the investigation report. The published draft concluded that the health care had been provided according to sound professional practice, but the internal follow-up and the hospital's error management and learning system had not met regulatory standards. The draft report, however, did not go into detail about the culture of fear, and the negative psychosocial work environment. The Daniel case was a high-profile case, and the conclusion created extensive media interest. The analysis, methods and perspectives applied by the regulator were heavily criticized by the public for leaving out the key subject of a negative psychosocial work environment (*Aftenposten*, July, 6, 2015; June, 19, 2015). The NBHS countered by saying that the work environment was outside of its mandate (*Aftenposten,* June, 19, 2015).

Taking Public Input into Account—Major Revision of the 2015 Final Report

In November 2015, the NBHS published its final report. The NBHS explicitly stated that by publishing the draft report, it wanted to promote openness and obtain input on the draft report to shed new light on the case. As was customary in similar investigations, the health trust (providing specialist healthcare services, teaching and research), involved health professionals, and the next of kin can give feedback on the draft report. In this case, the media and several actors were able to provide new input on the draft. The NBHS also invited different stakeholders (Daniel's parents and grandparents, experts on clinical leadership, anaesthesia and law, patient ombudsman, patient association) to meetings to elaborate or clarify their input:

> We have invited several of those who provided input [*to the draft report*] to meet us and elaborate their points of view, to ensure we have a correct understanding of their view. (Helsetilsynet 2015b: 14)

The NBHS changed its conclusion about the effects of the negative psychosocial work environment on patient safety. In the final report, several amendments appear. One key amendment is how the NBHS elaborates on the management's responsibility for ensuring a sound psychosocial working environment, as a prerequisite for patient safety. The establishment of this link between managerial responsibility, working environment and patient safety appears to be required if working environment issues are to be incorporated under the NBHS jurisdiction. The report, moreover, states that the supervisory follow-up of issues in the working environment falls under the jurisdiction of the Labour Inspection Authority, but when the working environment affects patient safety and the public trust in healthcare services, it will require an interface with the NBHS's supervision (Helsetilsynet 2015b). In the conclusion of the final report, the conclusion regarding sound professional practice, documentation requirements and follow-up with the next of kin remained the same, but the NBHS added a new paragraph on the psychosocial working environment:

> After publishing the draft report, we have received new information indicating that there are still challenges related to working environment, which is of relevance for patient safety. We will therefore ask the County Governor [*regional regulatory body*] to follow up this issue as a specific case [*new*]…. The further supervisory activity on how the health trust ensures the psychosocial working environment will be in collaboration with the Labour Inspection Authority. (Helsetilsynet 2015b: 79)

An additional amendment addresses the suggestions for future safety recommendation for learning purposes. Most of the recommendations pertain to the revision or establishment of procedures related to tonsillectomy on children; storage of data in anaesthesia monitoring equipment and surveillance units; information to and taking care of next of kin after severe adverse events; and handling of professional conflicts and personal clash of interest to prevent them from developing into conflicts that may threaten patient safety. The NBHS, moreover, suggests considering the establishment of new national guidelines for tonsillectomy, including an assessment of which hospitals should offer this surgery, their competence needs and guidelines for observation of post-operative haemorrhage. At last, the future recommendations state that NBHS will initiate dialogue with the Labour Inspection Authority regarding the overlapping jurisdiction concerning the psychosocial working environment in relation to sound patient treatment.

Details on the Role of Media and Public Critique

The final report provided amendments related to the media coverage of the Daniel case. In the draft report (Helsetilsynet 2015a), the role of media is described in one short paragraph. The comparison between the draft (Helsetilsynet 2015a) and final report (Helsetilsynet 2015b) illustrates much greater attention to the details of the media's role. In particular, we find more information on how the *Aftenposten* journalist worked on the case. The journalist claimed that in 2013, an employee who was not involved in the case tipped him off about 'war-conditions' between doctors at Molde Hospital, after a child's death following a routine operation in 2009. The journalist met with the child's parents and relatives, who described a situation of total repudiation of liability. He also obtained a disc containing all files in the case. The investigative report does not say anything about how the journalist got access to the disc, but he presented it to a lawyer and two doctors. Based on their feedback on the content, the journalist focused his attention on accusations of collusion and pressures and on why the regulatory authorities had closed the case in 2009 (Helsetilsynet 2015b).

After publication of the draft report, one of the experts that *Aftenposten* asked to comment on the case (co-author Olav Røise) argued that NBHS did not go into details on several issues in the report, including the accusations of pressure to adapt their version of the story to the police. Possible reasons for this could be a lack of competence or clinical experience among the investigatory team members, as he explained in the newspaper interview (*Aftenposten,* July, 6, 2015). Shortly after this critique, the head of the investigatory unit in NBHS called the expert. In a letter to the director of NBHS, the expert explained how the head of the investigative unit had approached him (*Aftenposten*, Sept. 3, 2015):

> In the letter [*Expert*] writes that [*head of investigation unit*] told him that it could "harm him" if he presented the critique in public. She pointed out that this would harm doctors at Molde Hospital as well. According to the letter, [*Head of investigative unit*] also said, that [*expert*] had made "horrific accusations" about her unit, not holding the correct competence to assess if Daniel had received sound professional treatment at Molde Hospital.

Shortly thereafter, the head of investigatory unit resigned (*Aftenposten*, Sept. 3, 2015). The media's role in the Daniel case has been acknowledged both by Daniel's parents and the NBHS. Both the parents and the NBHS argue that the case would not have been reopened, and the conclusions would not have been revised, without newspaper attention (*Aftenposten,* Nov. 19, 2015).

Discussion

Tonsil Surgery—What Do We Know About the Risk from a Medical Perspective?

Tonsil surgery, with or without adenoidectomy, is technically a simple procedure learned at the early stages of surgical training. It is among the most common surgical procedures in the world. However, the procedure is associated with potential severe and lethal complications that are very rare and therefore not considered an important risk factor when operation is offered to the patient or to a child's parents. In a Swedish study based on data from the National Patient Register (NPR) matched with the National Cause of Death Register over an 8-year period (2004–2011), the incidence for lethal outcome after benign tonsil surgery was 1 out of 41,263 operations (Ostvoll et al. 2015). This means that an operation with lethal outcome, based on the Swedish data, will be seen about once every 8 years in Norway, providing that the indications for surgery are the same.

In Austria in 2006 and 2007, five children under the age of six died after tonsillectomy (Sarny et al. 2013). This led to a public and emotional discussion on risk after tonsil surgery resulting in a consensus paper with the goal of making the procedure safer. The indication for doing tonsillectomy was restricted and tonsillotomy—a less invasive procedure—was advocated for children younger than 6 years of age. This consensus strategy was followed up with—to our knowledge—the only large-scale register study including all tonsil surgeries in Austria for 9 months in 2009—2010 disclosing safety data (Sarny et al. 2013). In their series, a haemorrhage rate of 12.3% for tonsillectomy and 2.3% for tonsillotomy was reported. Four percent of the patients with haemorrhage after tonsillectomies needed secondary surgery. Almost none in the tonsillotomy group needed secondary operation. The study also showed that repeated episodes of minor post-operative bleeding were a warning sign for further bleeding. According to the authors, the Austrian experience brought changes in education prior to surgery. Patients were given detailed information about what to watch for after a child's operation and what to do in case of haemorrhage.

Media as Whistleblower in Risk Communication

By exploring the Daniel case, we have seen how a tonsillectomy case characterized by cover-up, failure of the initial regulatory and hospital follow-up, came to a head when media shone a spotlight on the case (Hinchcliff et al. 2012; Mannion and Davies 2015; Millenson 2002; Waring 2015). By bringing new information to the table including critique of regulatory follow-up, the regulatory body appeared left with no other option than to re-open the case. They then continued with a strategy of transparency (Bouder et al. 2015), uncommon in a Norwegian setting, releasing draft report to the public, inviting experts to provide input, reflecting upon the media role and by making new safety recommendations to a wide range of actors.

The role of journalism in patient safety is interesting (Hinschcliff et al. 2012; Millenson 2002), and our study is reminiscent of findings from the early days of the patient safety movement. Millenson (2002) argued that until journalists took an interest in patient safety, it had not received much attention. As our study showed, this has similarities with the Daniel case where the regulator and the police closed the case, despite having collected information on possible cover-ups and professional battles after the event. News media gave the Daniel case renewed urgency. Moreover, the 'people-like-you' perspective in Millenson's (2002) study, is part of the Daniel case, where people like the readers or their children could die from a routine tonsil surgery. This framing places a human face on the formal parties involved (hospital, healthcare professionals and regulators).

Amplification of Events and Transparency

The regulator applied a new strategy of transparency in the Daniel case. The Social Amplification of Risk Framework (Pidgeon et al. 2003) claims that the social and economic impacts of an adverse event like Daniel's death are determined not only by the direct physical consequences of the event but also by the interaction of psychological, cultural, social and institutional processes amplifying or attenuating public experience of the event, resulting in secondary impacts (Pidgeon et al. 2003; Renn et al. 1992). By publishing new information and consulting powerful experts, we contend that the news media started an amplification process with consequences of loss of credibility in the initial regulatory follow-up, causing the case to be reopened and the findings in the final report substantially changed. This new transparency can be interpreted as a way of reconstructing the credibility of the regulatory investigation (Lofsted 2010) by making the process as open and transparent as possible in terms of information sources, regulatory assessments and rationality, use of input from journalists, experts, healthcare professionals and next of kin. In the transparency literature (Bouder, et al. 2015; Coglianese 2009), this approach is termed a *reasoned form of transparency*.

This is different from *fish-bowl transparency*: full disclosure without explanatory information or contextualization. Reasoned transparency accepts that transparency, as information disclosure alone, is not a solution. Reasoned transparency policies demand that regulators or government officials 'offer explicit explanations for their actions', the facts and evidence they base decisions on (Bouder et al. 2015; Coglianese 2009). In our case, we revealed several links to the reasoning approach, for example when and why the NBHS initially excluded psychosocial working environment from the draft report, and then argued why it had been added to the conclusion of the final report. The media coverage and reasoned transparency approach had societal impacts (Pidgeon et al. 2003). The safety recommendations manifest some of the societal impacts by suggesting new procedures, guidelines and clearer interface between regulatory authorities (Board of Health and Labor Inspectorate) and the coordination of inspection activities.

Transparency related to the adverse event is high on the agenda in Norwegian health care and elsewhere (Blomgren 2007; Kurtzman and Jennings 2008; Tavare 2012). The development can be interpreted as part of a risk communication strategy focusing on openness to patients and the public (Bouder et al. 2015; Kasperson et al. 1988; Lofstedt et al. 2011). Under the Social Amplification of Risk Framework (Pidgeon et al. 2003), the increased demand for transparency is not necessarily welcomed by healthcare professionals or regulators. These actors may fear the role of media and wish to go under the radar to avoid negative publicity and reputation risk, following media's role in risk communication and amplification processes. We saw this in the Daniel case when healthcare professionals were pressured to align their explanations, and when the director of the investigation unit at NBHS called one of the experts, and warned him that public criticism in the media would damage him and other doctors at the hospital. We can interpret these reactions, as an attempt to reduce the expected amplifications and ripple effects (Pidgeon et al. 2003) caused by fleshing out the event and critics in the media.

Conclusion

Transparency is not a panacea and involves trade-offs. More democracy, more freedom of information and more efficiency are expected from transparency, but may cause a society of control, with few confidential spaces (Han 2015), and escalating costs to meet performance demands (Hood and Dixon 2015). Healthcare innovations, regulation and safety improvement processes involve conflicts, professional discussions, mistakes and new ideas. Healthcare professionals and regulators need confidential space for debate and disagreement (Becker 1999). This is not the same as a cover-up or collusion to conceal an adverse event from the public. By using the Daniel case as emblematic of Norwegian risk communication strategies in health care, improvements should be made along the lines of direct and adequate information exchange according to patient rights, and efforts to foster open and transparent regulatory and organizational cultures to ensure public trust.

Declaration of interest Co-author, Olav Røise, was involved in the media coverage of the Daniel case as a clinical expert who was asked to give an assessment of the draft report described in the results section: *Details on the role of media and public critique*.

References

Aase, K., & Rosness, R. (2015). Organisatoriske ulykker og resiliente organisasjoner i helsetjenesten – ulike perspektiver. In: Aase, K. (Ed.), *Pasientsikkerhet - teori og praksis*, (pp. 25–47). Oslo: Universitetsforlaget. (Title: Patient Safety—Theory and Practice).

AHUS. (2015). AHUS web page on patient safety including 3-3 reports and quality indicators. http://www.ahus.no/fagfolk_/temasider_/Sider/pasientsikkerhet.aspx.

Becker, G. (1999). From theory to practice—On the difficulties of improving human-factors learning from adverse events in an inhospitable environment. In Misumi, J., Wilpert, B., Miller, R. (eds) (1999). *Nuclear Safety—A human factors perspective*. London: Taylor & Francis.

Blomgren, M. (2007). The drive for transparency: Organizational field transformation in Swedish healthcare. *Public Administration, 85*(1), 67–82.

Bouder, F., Way, D., Löfstedt, R., & Evensen, D. (2015). Transparency in Europe: A quantitative study. *Risk Analysis, 35*(7), 1210–1229.

Braithwaite, J, Wears, R. L., & Hollnagel, E. (2015). Resilient health care: Turning patient safety on its head. *International Journal for Quality in Health Care*, 1–3. https://doi.org/10.1093/intqhc/mzv063.

Coglianese, C. (2009). The transparency president? The Obama administration and open government. *Governance, 22*(4), 529–544.

Francis, R. (2013). *Report of the mid staffordshire NHS foundation trust public inquiry executive summary*. London: The Stationery Office.

Francis, R. (2015). *Freedom to speak up*. London: TSO. http://webarchive.nationalarchives.gov.uk/20150218150343/, https://freedomtospeakup.org.uk/wp-content/uploads/2014/07/F2SU_Executive-summary.pdf.

Han, B.-C. (2015). *The transparency society*. Stanford: Stanford University Press.

Hannawa, A. F., Shigemoto, Y., & Little, T. D. (2016). Medical errors: Disclosure styles, interpersonal forgiveness, and outcomes. *Social Science and Medicine, 156,* 29–38. https://doi.org/10.1016/j.socscimed.2016.03.026.

Helsetilsynet. (2015a). *Utkast til rapport i tilsynssak—dødsfall etter postoperative komplikasjoner etter tonsillektomi*. (Draft investigation report).

Helsetilsynet. (2015b). *Tilsynsrapport etter alvorlig hendelse (Danielsaken)*. (Final investigation report).

Hinchcliff, R., Westbrook, J., Greenfield, D., Baysari, M., Moldovan, M., & Braithwaite, J. (2012). Analysis of Australian newspaper coverage of medication errors. *International Journal for Quality in Health Care, 24*(1), 1–8.

Hood, C., & Dixon, R. (2015). *A government that worked better and cost less? Evaluating three decades of reform and change in the UK central government*. Oxford: Oxford University Press.

Johnstone, J., & Kanitsaki, O. (2006). The ethics and practical importance of defining, distinguishing and disclosing nursing errors: A discussion paper. *International Journal of Nursing Studies, 43*(3), 367–376.

Kasperson, R. E., Renn, O., Slovic, P., Brown, H. S., EMel, R., Goble, J.X. et al. (1988). The social amplification of risk: A conceptual framework. *Risk Analysis, 8*, 177–187.

Kurtzman, E. T., & Jennings, B. M. (2008). Trends in transparency. *The Journal of Nursing Administration, 38*(7/8), 349–354.

Liang B. A., & Lovett K. M. (2013). Error disclosure. In Agrawal, A. (Ed.), *Patient safety—A case-based comprehensive guide* (pp. 329–340). New York: Springer Science and Business Media New York.

Lofsted, R. (2010). Risk communication guidelines for Europe: A modest proposition. *Journal of Risk Research, 13*(1), 87–109.

Lofstedt, R., Bouder, F., Wardman, J., & Chakraborty, S. (2011). The changing nature of communication and regulation of risk in Europe. *Journal of Risk Research, 14*(4), 409–429.

Mannion, R., & Davies, H. T. O. (2015). Cultures of silence and cultures of voice: The role of whistleblowing in healthcare organizations. *International Journal of Health Policy Management, 4*(8), 503–505.

Millenson, M. L. (2002). Pushing the profession: how the news media turned patient safety into a priority. *Quality and Safety in Health Care, 11,* 57–63.

NOU. (2015:11). *"Med åpne kort – forebygging og oppfølgning av alvorlige hendelser i helse – og omsorgstjenesten"*. Departementenes sikkerhets- og serviceorganisasjon Informasjonsforvaltning.

O'Connor, R. E. (2016). Transparency and the regulatory process in Europe and the United States: Two research priorities. *Journal of Risk Research, 19*(9), 1129–1140. https://doi.org/10.1080/13669877.2015.1071866.

Ostvoll, E., Sunnergren, O., Ericsson, E., Hemlin, C., Hultcrantz, E., Odhagen, E., et al. (2015). Mortality after tonsil surgery, a population study, covering eight years and 82,527 operations in Sweden. *European Archives of OTO-Rhino-Laryngology: Official Journal of the European Federation of OTO-Rhino-Laryngological Societies, 272*(3), 737–743.

OUS. (2015). Oslo University Hospital's web page on patient safety. http://www.oslouniversitetssykehus.no/fagfolk_/kvalitet_/pasientsikkerhet_/Sider/side.aspx.

Pidgeon, N., Kasperson, R. E., & Slovic, P. (Eds.). (2003). *The social amplification of risk*. Cambridge, Mass: Cambridge University Press.

Pope, C., Ziebland, S., & Mays, N. (2006). Analysing qualitative data. In C. Pope & N. Mays (Eds.), *Qualitative research in health care* (pp. 63–82). Oxford: BMJ Books.

Renn, O., Burns, W. J., Kasperson, J. X., Kasperson, R. E., & Slovic, P. (1992). The social amplification of risk: Theoretical foundations and empirical applications. *Journal of Social Issues, 48*(4), 137–160.

Sarny, S., Habermann, W., Ossimitz, G., & Stammberger, H. (2013). What lessons can be learned from the Austrian events? *ORL; Journal for OTO-Rhino-Laryngology and Its Related Specialties, 75*(3), 175–181. PubMed PMID: 23978805.

Stake, R. E. (1994). Case studies. In N. K. Denzin & Y. S. Lincoln (Eds.), *Handbook of qualitative research* (pp. 236–247). Thousand Oaks: Sage Publications.

Tavare, A. (2012). Where are we with transparency over performance of doctors and institutions? *BMJ, 345,* e4464.

Waring, J. (2015). When whistle-blowers become the story: The problem of the third victim. *International Journal of Health Policy and Management, 5*(2), 133–135.

Wiig, S., & Lindøe, P. H. (2009). Patient safety in the interface between hospital and risk regulator. *Journal of Risk Research, 12*(3–4), 411–427.

Woodier, N. (2015). Moving from Safety I to Safety II, but what about the media? *BMJ Quality & Safety, 24,* 178. https://doi.org/10.1136/bmjqs-2014-003827.

How Safety Communication Can Support Safety Management: The Case of Commercial Aviation

Michel Guérard

Abstract Commercial aviation traffic has increased so dramatically over the past decades that virtually everyone can identify him/herself to a passenger or a passenger's relative. With the evolution of communication means and pace, every accident or incident induces an unprecedented amount of reactions and communication from many actors outside the aviation community. These newcomers on the safety communication scene challenge the historical safety management world and actors, traditionally limited to aviation professionals.

Keywords Safety management · Aviation · Safety communication

Introduction

Air travel has grown steadily since the end of the Second World War, doubling every 15 years. This industry is still expanding at roughly the same rate thanks to the emergence of new markets as well as to the development of new business models such as low-cost carriers.

Had the accident rates of the 60s and the 70s been kept at the same levels, the air transport safety situation would have become unacceptable to the travelling public and the development of the air travel industry would have unavoidably been severely impacted. The average fatal accident rate during the 60s was 4.4 per million flights, compared with 0.15 per million flights in 2016. An American researcher named Curt Graeber published in 1995 a study in which he applied the then prevailing accident rates to traffic projections and concluded that unless something was done in terms of safety, the industry would have to cope with one serious accident every week by 2010 (Graeber 1995). This conclusion did not go unnoticed and strongly contributed to the promotion of safety enhancement initiatives within the air travel industry.

M. Guérard (✉)
Toulouse, France
e-mail: michel.guerard@airbus.com

M. Bourrier and C. Bieder (eds.), *Risk Communication for the Future*, SpringerBriefs in Safety Management, https://doi.org/10.1007/978-3-319-74098-0_9

This reasoning was perfectly sound but this terrible prophecy never materialized, because in the meantime safety drastically improved. However, this frightening warning had been heard worldwide and positively contributed to the increased mobilization of the entire industry towards a safer air transport system. Graeber's study was not only about safety projections; it was also about communicating them to all stakeholders in a powerful and effective way.

With the spectacular development of commercial air transport around the world in the past decades, a growing number of people feel concerned by aircraft accidents. Air transport is an international activity by nature, and from an outsider's vantage point, nothing looks more like an airline, an airport or an aircraft than another airline, airport or aircraft. Almost everyone can identify him/herself to a passenger or a passenger's relative.

In addition, the accelerated development of information and communication means and channels makes each and every event, especially significant incidents or accidents known to almost everyone on the planet, and its interpretation by whoever communicates on it as well.

Over the years, safety-related topics have progressively been dealt with by new audiences, such as Internet sites, independent experts, lawyers, victims' associations, social media groups, pilot unions. The objectives were not the same and comments could sometimes be critical towards the air transport industry. This has opened new issues for air travel industry safety communications specialists, who found themselves facing higher levels of criticism than ever before.

In parallel, the overall image of the aviation industry has changed. Air transport began as a dream, even though only a few people were initially directly concerned. The early years of aviation triggered considerable enthusiasm among vast portions of the population. As it became a more banal way of moving around, the acceptability of accidents decreased and the identification of the public at large to air travellers increased, since more and more people could afford travelling by air.

The enthusiasm that initially surrounded air travel progressively faded and new environmental preoccupations arose. Aviation has been progressively associated with noise, pollution and global warming. Building a new airport or simply adding a runway to an existing one can be a major challenge in many countries. The difficulties encountered in Japan in the 70s concerning Narita airport and those concerning Heathrow's fifth terminal in the 80s or recently in France for the projected new Nantes airport illustrate this situation.

This changing environment is a challenge for the air travel industry in terms of communication. In other words, the perception framework of commercial air transport safety has evolved significantly.

If safety communication has always existed, its scope, actors and pace have changed, thus modifying its impact on safety management. It is therefore in the interest of this industry to better understand the ongoing changes in order to address them in the best possible way.

Safety Communication Among Industry Actors: A Historical Driver for Safety Enhancement

Organizing activity in commercial air transport dates back to its earliest years, after World War II. Indeed, ICAO was created in 1944 and IATA followed in 1945. As for Authorities, they were already in place in the countries where air transport had begun. Most legacy carriers were created around that time and the then big manufacturers (Lockheed, Douglas, Boeing, De Havilland, etc.) were already producing airliners.

One can say that a solid frame was in place and ready to be used for safety matters as well. In fact, aviation actors realized fairly early that safety was not a matter of competition but rather a condition for the survival and the development of the industry as a whole. Indeed, whatever the area of the world, the aircraft operated and regulations are similar, as are air traffic control mechanisms. In other words, sharing information about safety has been identified as a crucial need for a long time.

The US National Transportation Safety Board, for example, has been keeping records of civil aircraft accidents since 1967. The National Aeronautics and Space administration administers a confidential and voluntary Aviation Safety reporting System since 1976.

However, with the evolution of technology and culture, the types of information gathered and shared as well as sharing practices evolved over time. It started with the lessons learned from accidents identified as an obvious source of information to contribute to improve safety. This sharing between operators did indeed help to identify major hazards, such as the metal fatigue phenomenon that was only understood after the De Havilland Comet fatal crashes in the 50s, and 'deep stalls' that were not known until the 1963 BAC 1-11 accident.

Experience feedback has always been and still is a vital flow, especially in aviation, because airliners are complex machines which are flying in increasingly large numbers. In addition, every new aircraft experiences its lot of early problems, but it will stay in service for 20 to 30 years; ageing problems will in turn feed this experience feedback. In other words, disseminating across the entire industry the lessons learned from adverse safety events has always been and will remain of prime importance to enhance safety.

As a matter of fact, in order to further improve safety, authorities have made it mandatory to report significant events, regulating in a sense one of the aspects of safety communication. In Europe, for example, occurrence reporting is defined in a document called AMC 20-8. However, the resourcing of aviation authorities is variable and this basic two-way flow of information is not always in place. It nonetheless forms the basis of a learning process that constitutes the foundation of industry-driven safety communication. If accident and serious incident investigations enable us to learn from what happened, they fortunately remain very rare events. All potential safety events do not end up in incidents or accidents.

The main stake for an industry growing at such a pace became to learn from other sources of information in order to try to further enhance safety. Therefore, voluntary reports from crews were encouraged by Authorities and within airlines in order to gather additional information on actual practices possibly inducing safety issues. This new form of safety communication involved setting up a specific framework. Indeed, voluntary reports were much more numerous in environments where they were not systematically punished when reporting mistakes, i.e. where 'just culture' principles (Havinga and Dekker 2014) translated into practice. A blame culture does still exist in certain parts of the world and deprives organizations and the industry as a whole of an opportunity to learn from experience. Safety communication is a powerful tool in terms of safety enhancement, but it must be fed.

With technological progress in terms of data recording and processing, another source of information was made available to further enhance safety: flight data analysis. A number of parameters are systematically recorded all along a flight and deviations from a safe envelope defined a priori are pointed out. Therefore, even in the absence of any incident or accident, safety-related information can be retrieved, processed and the outcome of the safety analysis disseminated. In a more recent approach, an auditor may also fly with a crew in order to attend the flight and evaluate the general performance of the pilots.[1]

This shows how far the air transport industry is ready to go in order to learn from day-to-day operations and to collect safety-related information. These various sources of information are potentially a very effective way of enhancing safety, but require a good safety communication system both within the operator and outside. In fact, practices in terms of communication to feed the analysis and disseminate the safety lessons learned may vary significantly around the world.

It is worth noting that most of these safety enhancement practices were put in place by numerous operators even before they became mandatory. In other words, safety communication is regulated between individual aviation actors and the Authorities. However, as mentioned earlier, the industry has soon realized that safety is a matter of survival of the activity as well. Therefore, additional safety communication practices developed with time on a voluntary basis.

In the US, a system was launched in October 2007, and an associated forum as well, for all aviation actors to share their safety information and perform joint analysis: Aviation Safety Information Analysis and Sharing (ASIAS). Volunteer airlines, airports and air traffic control centres get together on a regular basis, share their flight data analysis, incident reports and other sources of information to collectively learn lessons from operations. A similar approach is currently under study at European level.

Aircraft manufacturers also communicate about safety on a regular basis with airlines. It is done through technical bulletins, safety conferences and magazines. Similarly, airlines report operational occurrences to manufacturers on a voluntary basis. The number of events reported increases regularly, because airlines increasingly understand the benefits of reporting and communicating about their events. More generally, the awareness of all aviation actors of the benefits to learn from as much experience as possible is increasing. Indeed, even though each airline

[1]A mechanism known as Line Operations Safety Assessment, or LOSA.

operates a limited number of aircraft, in a limited number of operational conditions, the overall experience accumulated by the industry is huge, since there is more than one aircraft taking off every second around the globe. However, as mentioned earlier, even if the safety communication system collects more and more data, with again some variations among actors, making sure that the appropriate safety information reaches the relevant targets is a different story.

Indeed, experience has shown that sometimes safety lessons were shared among safety managers but stayed with them, without reaching the operational people concerned.

This internal aspect of safety communication is now addressed by a recent regulatory requirement. Indeed, safety promotion within an organization is one of the four pillars of the Safety Management System (SMS) regulation. SMS is basically a new approach to safety which asks aviation actors to identify and evaluate their risks in order to mitigate them and therefore enhance safety. It is detailed in the International Civil Aviation Organization Annex 19 (ICAO 2013).

It includes the dissemination of lessons learned as well as the enhancement of safety culture. In this area as well, practices may vary significantly from one actor to another.

In order to dispatch safety-related information, the air travel industry has progressively launched a number of initiatives. An overall frame has been provided by the ICAO and enforced by local Aviation Authorities but numerous steps in safety communication have been taken by other organizations, resulting in a number of conferences, exchange forums, safety programs and training initiatives.[2]

For a rather long period of time, the major part of safety-related communication took place within the air travel industry itself, including official organizations. It was consistent and to a large extent consensual. The state of air travel safety was clear, as well as the priorities. No external party was interfering and safety was indeed progressing on a continuous basis as proven by statistics. More recently, aviation safety has come increasingly under scrutiny, especially from new stakeholders, not belonging to the traditional circles within this industry.

New Actors, New Safety Communication, New Influences on Safety Management

Today, other stakeholders, such as victims' associations, law firms, pilot unions, social media, have entered this arena and have earned their share of voice. Through safety-related communication, they claim a right to access all the information and sometimes to perform their own analysis of an event. It is the advent of a system of checks and balances on the historical select club of professionals. Two worlds, two types of practices, one strictly regulated based on a technical approach to safety, the

[2]https://flightsafety.org/category/safety-calendar/.

other one 'self-regulated', often driven by reactions to an accident (general public, associations of victims' families such as FENVAC in France, politics, etc.) with different timelines (delayed response due to ongoing investigations vs. immediate response under public pressure).

Aviation accidents have always generated strong media coverage. There are many reasons for this, but we first of all have to recognize that aviation accidents generally result in a significant number of victims. In this respect, they can be considered as big industrial accidents. The overall perception that air travel is an extremely safe means of conveyance also contributes to making each accident a kind of exceptional event. Everybody expects no accident and the safety rate is indeed very high, with one fatal accident every ten million flights for the latest generation of airliners.

When an accident occurs, it contradicts this expectation to a certain extent and the general public, not only aviation professionals and the travelling public, are eager to know what might have happened. This interest in air crashes and subsequent investigations is a well-known fact which materialized in an impressive number of TV reports, films, books and event theatre events.

Back in 1999, a play named Charlie Victor Romeo (CVR also stands for Cockpit Voice Recorder) was created on the basis of audio recordings from several fatal accidents. Actors installed in a cockpit mock-up on a stage would replay the last moments of these crew members. It was a very successful enterprise and *Time* magazine included Charlie Victor Romeo in their 2004 Best Plays of the Year list. A number of TV series such as 'Air Crash Investigation' produced by Cineflix since 2003 and many others also account for this wide interest in air accidents and the associated investigations. Back in 2012, the famous American actor Denzel Washington played a captain in 'Flight', a successful drama based on a jetliner accident. In 2016, Tom Hanks appeared in the film 'Sully' which related the successful landing of a jetliner in the Hudson River after having hit a number of geese.

Travelling by air is no longer reserved to the wealthy, and millions of people can therefore identify themselves to the unfortunate victims of an airplane accident. There are many reasons for the public at large to be interested in air accidents, but it is a fact and every new unfortunate event confirms this situation. As mentioned previously, accidents are statistically extremely rare but air traffic volume is large and continuously growing. More than 100,000 commercial flights are performed every day, this means more than one aircraft taking off every second.

However, what the public remembers are absolute numbers, not relative ones. And accidents are absolute numbers. It means that safety must progress in proportion as traffic grows if we do not want the general public to develop the feeling that the air transport industry is no longer delivering its promises in terms of safety. Obviously, air accidents coverage always highlights a failure of the safety system at some point. It is clearly negative publicity for the air transport community.

Beyond the general public and its overall interest in these catastrophic events, a number of persons took a far more active share of voice in recent years. It is the case first of all of victims and relatives. The way these communities were treated in the past has not always been to the credit of the air travel industry. Authorities have been made aware of the need to clarify everyone's duties and a number of rules have been specified in order to ensure that care, respect and dignity prevail following an accident. The US Federal Family Assistance Plan for Aviation disasters illustrates this approach (NTSB 2008).

Following the accident of the Asiana aircraft in the US, in July 2013, the airline was fined by the Federal Aviation Administration for not providing the expected assistance to families in due time. Victims of an air accident and their families have rights. This is also made more concrete by the level of financial compensation following an aircraft accident, especially in the USA.

Such accidents often generate legal proceedings and some law firms such as Kreindler and Kreindler have specialized in aviation disasters. Because civil damages are substantially higher in the USA, lawyers will often try to sue in this country. The recent accident of Germanwings (March 2015) illustrates this. Some families tried to sue Lufthansa, the parent company of Germanwings, on the basis that the suicidal First Officer was initially trained in the USA. Obviously, law firms will have their own strategies and therefore their own communication objectives following an accident.

Another recent evolution has also seen the growing implication of political staff. On the occasion of the Germanwings accident, three heads of state (President François Hollande from France, Chancellor Angela Merkel from Germany and Prime Minister Mariano Rajoy from Spain) gathered on the crash site for the memorial service. Such a strong presence creates a precedent and is likely to be expected again in comparable cases. This trend can be seen as the reflexion of sociological trends in modern democratic societies. It is nonetheless a confirmation that victims now have a specific and recognized status. This status gives them more influence and their opinions are better heard than before.

Politicians make laws and can change the framework in which safety investigations or justice, for example, are pursued. These are medium to long-term evolutions but they are real possibilities. The family assistance act in the USA is a relevant example of such regulations being introduced. Victims' associations will form quicker than before thanks to the Internet and social media and also because they receive official support from governments. In France, bodies such as INAVEM and FENVAC are officially backed by the authorities in their support to victims and their associations.

Other groups, such as pilot unions, may also get involved in order to protect the reputation and the interests of their members. As a matter of fact, the vast majority of accidents are due to operational factors in which crews often play a part. It is quite common to read articles putting the blame on either the aircraft or the crew. Accident investigations most of the time demonstrate that truth is more complex. Beyond the main cause of an accident, a number of contributing factors may place the event in a different perspective. Understandably, pilots' unions will focus on issues such as Human–Machine Interface in order to explain and defend crew behaviour.

Traditional media will logically follow the move and reflect these numerous activities surrounding an accident whereas social media will generate additional communication involving more actors. The multiplication of 24 h news channels has also increased the coverage of events such as aircraft accidents. The media investigation into the potential causes of the accident will start almost immediately with the support of numerous private experts who quickly elaborate possible scenarios even in the absence of consolidated facts.

It has now become current to see dedicated sites launching their own investigations with limited information from various origins such as flightradar24, weather reports, pictures and videos. One of these groups is Aviation Herald, a site based in Austria and run by Simon Hradecky. It is extremely reactive and has become a kind of reference for several media. Other communities share extensive information quite quickly following an accident or a serious event.[3]

While communication from the aviation community during an accident investigation is highly regulated by the ICAO Annex 13 (ICAO, 2016) which specifies the conditions of an investigation following an accident or a serious incident, the emerging 'new' communication is not subject to such constraints. However, a kind of self-regulation can be observed, especially on social media with common intense exchanges and challenges of untrue statements. This phenomenon by the way leads to the emergence of some influencers recognized by a large community for their expertise.[4] They enjoy a real status and are taken very seriously by airlines as well as other aviation stakeholders such as Original Equipment Manufacturers.

Eventually, safety communication has progressively increased leading to more information exchange with more actors among aviation professionals, taking place in a continuous manner, silent and invisible to the public. What changed dramatically over the past decade is the safety communication landscape following an accident.

To What Extent Does the Evolution of Safety Communication Impact Safety Management?

The emergence of new safety communication actors such as victims' associations, justice, political staff, social media has led to an evolution of pressures, stakes and power that eventually influence the way safety is managed. It is worth noting that these new actors' primary motivation is not necessarily to contribute to safety enhancement. Motivations include the right to know, the request to perform an independent analysis, but also an opportunity to promote convictions about technology, training or any other aspect of the aviation industry.

With the strict rules imposed by ICAO Annex 13 on communication about accident investigations (ICAO 2001), requiring an exclusively consolidated factual

[3]See for example: http://www.airliners.net/forum/; http://www.pprune.org/.

[4]See for example the following significant influencers on twitter:
Jason Rabinowitz https://twitter.com/AirlineFlyer
Alex Macheras https://twitter.com/AlexInAir
Mary Kirby « Runway Girl » https://twitter.com/RunwayGirl.

basis, the pace of official communication induces a timing that leaves an empty space for too long a time with respect to the current communication and societal landscape. The delay of official communication often creates frustration from media and families and feeds impressions that there is a lack of transparency and that pressure might be applied on authorities in order to protect industrial interests. Such a situation is often observed and may undermine the credibility of investigating authorities.

This lack of trust in investigation bodies also involves an almost systematic challenge of their accident reports. This pressure on investigation authorities may delay the publication of accident reports and sometimes influence the content. Eventually, whatever the motivation of the emerging safety communication actors, their share of voice is consequential on safety management.

First of all, the growing appetite for real-time information encourages speculation to compensate for the lack of facts available immediately after the event. In this respect, it is adding pressure on investigation authorities who generally take more time to communicate their first findings, for they need to rely on validated information.

Every accident leads to the expression of a variety of logics with respect to safety. A rational one turned towards safety enhancement that of the industry and more specifically of the investigation body; an emotional one, that of the victims and families of victims; a rational but more individual one, that of individual experts or critics whose visibility will obviously increase on these occasions.

As previously mentioned, all these logics do not share the exclusive objective to enhance safety. It is therefore almost inevitable to see controversies, polemics, delayed decisions, misperceptions. Moreover, the two latter logics sometimes lead to decisions which do not obviously and directly contribute to safety. For example, following the Sharm El Sheikh accident in which 134 French passengers were killed in January 2004, a parliamentary commission was created in France as a response to public emotion. Forty proposals were made the same year.[5]

Among these 40 proposals, some were by nature doomed to failure whereas others were heavily challenged. Indeed, because air travel safety depends on an international system, it is quite challenging for any country to act independently and efficiently. Therefore, the proposals challenging ICAO recommendations for example about pilots licensing were not realistic. Another proposal was made in order to enforce the exclusive use of English in exchanges between crews and air traffic control in France. It was in fact never enforced because of opposition from some pilots' associations in France. Eventually, despite the publicity made around these 40 proposals, it does not seem that this work had an obvious influence on air travel safety.

Later on, following the crash of the Rio-Paris flight in 2009, a law was proposed in order to create an Aviation Safety Authority ('Haute autorité de la sécurité aérienne'). The objective was to control investigation authorities through a board of nine members. The law was not passed but it illustrates how public emotion and political reaction could impact safety management.

[5] http://www.assemblee-nationale.fr/12/rap-info/i1717-t1-05.asp#P6209_573114.

On the other hand, one can argue that the existence of a counter-power, through emerging safety communication actors, can support safety enhancement by putting the aviation industry under scrutiny and forcing it to do even more. Up to now though, it has not led to the identification of new safety issues.

It seems that the contribution is rather in terms of pressure applied to the overall safety system. One can see this as a recurrent move that will prevent the air travel industry from becoming complacent. Given the extremely low rates of accidents achieved by the industry, the public could fear that air transport actors see themselves as having reached a 'good enough' level in terms of safety. From this point of view, new safety communication actors could be seen as a useful power, a kind of watchdog. However, to keep this role that could contribute to safety enhancement, this counter-power needs to keep an appropriate balance. Indeed, going too much in the direction of negative communication impacts the industry, the authorities and their credibility. It may even give credit to alternative and private accident investigations carried out with less expertise and objectivity. This may result in blurred pictures concerning what needs to be done in order to enhance safety.

Within the framework defined by the ICAO Annex 13, investigations are international task forces involving a number of stakeholders with their own objectives and constraints. Any mishandling would be immediately known.

Conclusion

Safety communication has been for a very long time a continuous activity, undertaken by professionals within the aviation community. It is still the case to a very large extent when it comes to learning from operations and sharing safety-related information in the absence of accidents. However, the communication landscape changes dramatically in case of an accident. If communication used to translate into aviation professionals providing validated information to journalists who in turn informed the public, the sources of information have become diversified, the nature of information as well, not to mention the motivation of those entering the communication scene. In brief, there is on one hand a permanent exercise carried out by professionals, and on the other hand, ad hoc communication triggered by unfortunate events and led by specific and temporary stakeholders.

The safety strategy, and therefore the associated communication delivered by the air travel industry, is a long-term one, somewhat self-centred and raising potential safety issues in a consensual fashion. It is mostly done by aviation experts representing various domains. The other approach is by nature more critical and often challenges the ability of the air travel community to do an effective job in terms of safety. It is done by very diverse actors and increasingly relayed by social media. The industry has no choice but to face this changing and challenging context.

Ignoring it would just make things worse. Some key actors have already started to change their communication practices after an accident, especially investigation authorities. They have realized that a lack of communication could impact their credibility; two important investigation bodies, the NTSB in the USA and the BEA in France, have done a lot over the past years. They now give public information much more quickly than before and they do take care of victims' associations in a dedicated way.

For example, depending on the magnitude of the event, US investigation authorities may decide to organize daily press conferences and sometimes to use Twitter in order to inform the general public in an efficient and fast way. It must be noted, however, that such initiatives are not always welcomed by some stakeholders who believe that more time must be taken in order to prevent hasty conclusions. The French Transportation Investigation Board (BEA), for example, ensures that at all times families learn first about their official communications. They also publish a list of ongoing serious incident and accident investigations in an effort to enhance transparency.

Nonetheless, communication practices around safety vary significantly among aviation actors. It is also fair to say that talking about air travel safety between accidents is not easy for two main reasons: first of all, media are more interested in news than in general speeches. Second, talking about safety indirectly means talking about accidents and companies are not always comfortable with this.

The industry nonetheless needs to find a way to be more present in this new world of safety-related communication. Failing to do so would leave an empty seat and limit its role to firefighting. Every safety communication specialist knows that it is difficult to react when you are in a defensive mode, which is almost unavoidable following an accident. A way forward for the industry seems to be to explain its efforts to a wider public with an appropriate approach, not waiting for accidents to occur to communicate on the public scene. Improving its image in terms of transparency can only help.

References

Graeber, C. (1995). *Accident prevention strategy.*

Havinga, J., & Dekker, S. (2014). Just culture: Reporting, the line and accountability. *Journal of Aviation Management*, 49–57. Published by Singapore Aviation Academy, http://uat-web.saa.com.sg/documents/65465/149063/SAA_Journal_2014.pdf/d06550de-9a92-4632-9746-c2f2e874c556.

ICAO. (2001). Aircraft accident and incident investigation (9th ed.). ICAO.

ICAO. (2013). Safety management. ICAO.

NTSB. (2008). Federal family assistance plan for aviation disasters. NTSB.

Risk Communication from an Audit Team to Its Client

Petra Haferkorn

Abstract The article discusses the paradoxical foundation of a risk decision and the challenges the paradox puts on the management of risk communication. The exploration is done from a social systems theory perspective; a theory that provides a comprehensive theoretical framework for social systems and their communication processes and addresses the complexity, risk and conflicts of interests (Section 'Systemic Audit: Widening the Perspective of Traditional Audit Approaches'). From this theoretical setting, the conclusion is derived that a statement about an organization's risk cannot be proven as a 'true' statement and that a receiver of an audit report (the client) will always have good reasons to question an audit team's risk communication (Section 'The Paradoxical Foundation of a Risk Decision and Associated Challenges for Risk Communication Illustrated by the Example of an Audit Finding'). The article gives some hints on how an audit team can deal with clients' needs by incorporating their requirements in its audit process, using concepts and tools from family therapy, brief therapy and systemic counselling (Section 'Unpicking the Paradox of Risk Communication').

Keywords Risk communication · Risk management · Social systems theory
Notion of risk · Risk perception · Paradox of risk · Meaning dimensions of risk
Connectivity of communication · Audit process design

Systemic Audit: Widening the Perspective of Traditional Audit Approaches

Traditional standards for internal (Standard 2012) and external auditors (ISAs 2012) assign a wide range of responsibilities to a team that audits an organization (cf. Fig. 1, left column), e.g. while being independent and objective (e.g. Code of Ethics 1100 Independence and Objectivity, Standard 2012), auditors are to trustfully interact with clients and auditees (e.g. core Principles for the Professional Practice

P. Haferkorn (✉)
German Federal Financial Supervisory Authority, Bonn, Germany
e-mail: petra@sebastian-haferkorn.de

M. Bourrier and C. Bieder (eds.), *Risk Communication for the Future*, SpringerBriefs in Safety Management, https://doi.org/10.1007/978-3-319-74098-0_10

Traditional approaches	Systemic approaches
Objectivity of an auditor (masking blind spots and contradictions)	Reality is the **construction of an observer** and **based on contradictions**
Successful **risk communication depends on audit team**	Success of risk communication depends on its participants and its current context; **connectivity** might be increased by the audit team
Audits are **steered** by the audit team	Audits are operatively closed, therefore the audit team can only **influence the audit to a limited extend**
Static and cause oriented explanations aiming for **final solutions**	**Dynamic** communication-based, multicausal and recursive explanation models
Risk can be managed and **safety** can be attained	**Risk is a social construct** (which cannot be proven as a "true" statement)

Fig. 1 Traditional audit approaches compared to systemic approaches

of Internal Auditing, Standard 2012). Though the audit is initiated by a client and, in the beginning, the audit team is not in a position to know all the details of its engagement (e.g. 1000 Purpose Authority and Responsibility, Standard 2012), it is nevertheless held responsible for planning and performing the audit (2000 Managing the Internal Audit Activity et seqq., Standard 2012). At the end of the audit, auditors are supposed to negotiate management actions that remedy the organization's deficiencies and make organization safe again (2400 Communicating Results et seqq., Standard 2012).

To handle these challenges, a social systems theory perspective (Luhmann 1984) and related tools and methods of different systemic approaches proved highly efficient (e.g. for family therapy, see Selvini Palazzoli et al. 1977, for brief therapy, see de Shazer 1989; Weakland et al. 1974, for systemic counselling, see Königswieser and Exner 1998). They resulted in the development of systemic audit theory and a systemic audit approach (Haferkorn 2010; cf. Fig. 1, right column).

Social systems theory does not operate with concepts such as 'objectivity' and 'truth', but postulates that every truth depends on an observer and therefore must remain hypothetical (von Foerster and Pörksen 2013; von Glaserfeld 1995, 1996). In this theoretical setting, reality is a cognitive construction derived from an organism's experience (Glaserfeld 1995) and therefore limited to the abilities and experiences of the organism (Maturana and Varela 1987; Luhmann 1990).[1] Every

[1]The doubts and concerns regarding a "total objectivity" or a "complete capture of risk", expressed by social systems theory, are in no way intended to ignore the justified expectations of society on the communication of risk. Quite the contrary, we need a theory which allows for ambiguity and blind spots to develop appropriate tools and measures for risk experts to discover the limits and options of their risk communication and to deal with the expectations of society

observation of the organism draws a distinction, which specifies a unity distinct from a background (Spencer-Brown 1969; Maturana and Varela 1987). Taking a concept from biology, systems theory calls the unseen background 'blind spot' (Maturana and Varela 1987; Luhmann 1990). Every observation has therefore a limited focus and cannot claim to be all-embracing (cf. Fig. 1, second row).

As participants of a social system thus have different perceptions, they cannot take for granted that each party understands the other's viewpoint—misunderstandings between involved parties are therefore likely (Luhmann 1986). For this reason, a systemic audit approach explores the context and conditions of risk communication to the stakeholders of an audit (Haferkorn 2010) and strives for connectivity (cf. Fig. 1, third row).

In this framework, an audit is operatively closed (Haferkorn 2010; Luhmann 1990), i.e. for example audit team depends on the auditees. Consequently, an audit team is not able to steer the audit towards a given objective, but rather focuses on what is possible and feasible in the existing audit context (e.g. available resources in experts, equipment and time) (Haferkorn 2010; Fig. 1, fourth row).

In this theoretical setting, it proved helpful to observe communication processes which can explain the functioning of social systems (Luhmann 2000 in relation to organizations, Haferkorn 2010 in relation to audits). Moreover, organizations are only able to survive when their communication continues to involve and balance the conflicting interests of important demands on the organization (Simon 2007, cf. Fig. 1, first and fifth row). Based on these assumptions, the following section discusses the interpretation of Luhmann's notion of 'risk decision' (cf. last row of Fig. 1) and explores its practical application in audits.

The Paradoxical Foundation of a Risk Decision and Associated Challenges for Risk Communication Illustrated by the Example of an Audit Finding

Power's (2007) research on risk management draws on Luhmann's notion of risk (Luhmann 1991), which implies that future damage is not caused by natural disaster or other external, unswayable events but by a decision.[2] '*Uncertainty is therefore transformed into risk when it becomes an object of management*' (Power 2007, 6).[3] By incorporating more of Luhmann's theoretical program, we can gain an improved

[2]Luhmann presumes the concept of a 'second-order observer'; the decision-maker bases his decision on his observations and is the 'first-order observer' (Luhmann 1991, 235–247).

[3]The following considerations are based on the notion of risk, since an organization that realizes to be threatened by danger (or in Power's word 'uncertainty') should think about the possibilities of protection and thus about a risk decision (Luhmann 1991, 32–40; Haferkorn 2010, 175).

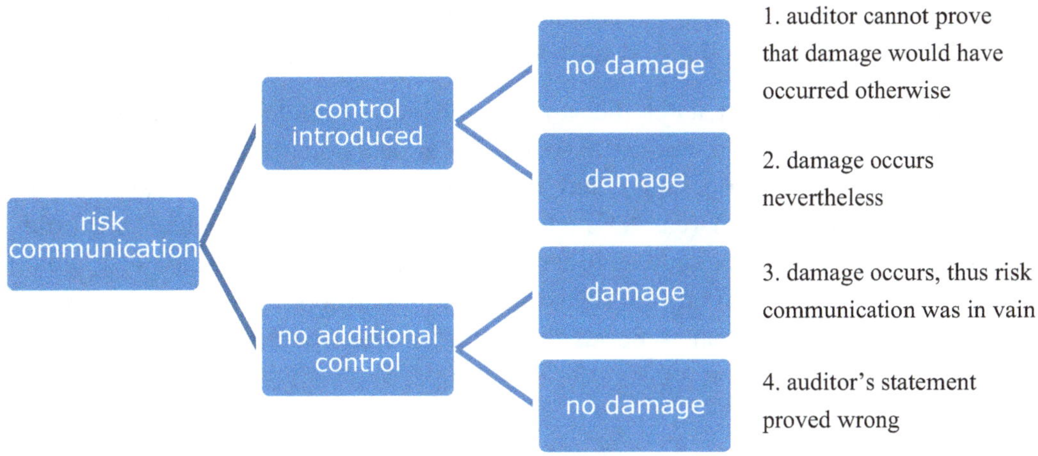

Fig. 2 A statement in risk communication cannot be proven as a 'true' statement (example of an audit finding)

understanding of the paradoxical foundation of a risk decision and the associated challenges of risk communication.

According to Luhmann, a risk decision, i.e. a decision that assumes a relationship between a decision and a probable future[4] damage, has a paradoxical foundation (cf. Luhmann 1991, 9–40 and 1995). This is demonstrated using the following example of an audit team that informs its client about a risk to the organization, which in turn leads to discussions about the audit finding. The audit team informs the client that if a certain decision is taken, e.g. a certain control is not introduced in a workflow of the company, damage will occur within the next 5 months. Figure 2 exposes the four possibilities for future developments:

1. The organization introduces the control mechanism but the damage occurs nevertheless. The forecast—or in Luhmann's words 'the assumption of a relationship between risk decision and future damage'—was wrong.
2. The organization introduces the control mechanism and the damage does not occur. Consequently, the audit team cannot prove that the assumption of a relationship between the lack of a certain control and future damage was correct, as the forecasted damage did not occur.
3. The organization does not establish the control mechanism and the damage occurs. The risk communication was not successful: if the decision-makers had trusted in the audit team's expertise, they would have followed its suggestion.

[4]Remark: The notion postulates a forecast horizon. Some risk communication ignores such a forecast horizon (e.g. some audit findings) and just states that certain damage might occur. I think that the inclusion of a time horizon is essential for the notion of risk (and the core of its difficulties), since otherwise a risk statement will always be true and therefore redundant. This is the parallel case of Keynes' statement: '*The long run is a misleading guide to current affairs. In the long run we are all dead. Economists set themselves too easy, too useless a task if in tempestuous seasons they can only tell us that when the storm is long past the ocean is flat again.*' (Keynes 1923, 80).

4. The organization does not introduce the control mechanism and the damage does not occur. As in the first and second case, the assumption proved wrong.

In summary, Luhmann states that a risk decision is founded on a basic paradox. Either the assumption (relationship between a decision and a future damage) underlying a risk decision holds and the damage occurs—in this case, the risk decision has been in vain (case 3 in Fig. 2), or the assumption does not hold—which means that the decision was based on a wrong assumption (case 1, 2 and 4 in Fig. 2). Since either the final risk decision or the assumption of the relationship is wrong, risk communication is based on a fundamental paradox (Luhmann 1991, 2002, 189, last row in Fig. 1).[5]

Unpicking the Paradox of Risk Communication

For a comprehensible communication of risk, experts often focus on a professional explanation of underlying facts and on the interpretation of corresponding research results for laypersons (e.g. Gigerenzer et al. 2010; Hollands and Lipkus 1999). Though facts play an important role, we have to bear in mind that communication is more than transmitting facts (Luhmann 1986; Roussy 2012 in relation to internal audits, Simon and Weber 2004, 91–97 in relation to systemic therapy).

Moreover, unlike damage, which can be experienced, Luhmann's notion of risk is not a hard and fast fact, since risk is not an observable or demonstrable phenomenon. Risk is rather a social construct and must therefore be dealt with in communication processes. The remaining question of section two is therefore how an audit team can increase the connectivity of its audit findings.

Luhmann's Dimensions of Meaning

Social systems theory assumes that the negotiations taking place in communication can be examined by distinguishing three meaning dimensions: the 'fact dimension of meaning' (**Sachdimension**) refers to the facts and the knowledge exchanged, the 'social dimension of meaning' (**Sozialdimension**) considers the social relationship

[5]In his argumentation, Luhmann adds that the transformation of the logical statement into a probability statement by using the notion 'probable' damage does not unpick the paradox. Both concepts, logic as well as probability theory base their assumptions on a foreseeable and calculable future. Instead of one scenario probability theory uses several (in relation to continuous distributions even infinite) scenarios, but nevertheless the statement is still based on an observer (e.g. a person or a model) to predict future damage. In either case, whether a logical or a probability statement is given, the observer cannot foresee the future and has a blind spot (Luhmann 2002, 189). Thus a statement in risk communication (made by an audit team to its client) cannot be proven as a 'true' statement and its recipient will always have good reasons to question it.

between communication partners and the 'temporal dimension of meaning' (**Zeitdimension**) deals with the timeline of communication processes (Luhmann 1984, 112 et seqq.; Simon 2014, 7 seqq. and 78–84 in relation to counselling).

With this differentiation in mind, I now can establish methods for dealing with challenges that arise within the complex risk communication from auditors to clients, notably the paradox described in the previous section. It should be noted that these dimensions of meaning overlap, for instance when the client does not acknowledge the facts underlying an audit finding (fact dimension of meaning), the audit team can try to gain a better understanding of the client's context and concerns (social dimension of meaning, cf. Collins 2010 in relation to communication between experts and laypersons) and invest time to gather further relevant information (temporal dimension of meaning) and adapt the presentation of audit results to the client's needs. Moreover, as the example indicates and as will be shown later, if connectivity poses problems, it can be helpful to change perspective.

Risk Communication Embedded in an Ongoing Process of Expectation Management

Against this background, it seems necessary to manage the expectations of involved parties (cf. Simon 2014; Königswieser and Hillebrand 2004 in relation to counselling). It is important for the audit department (or audit firm) to build a trustful relationship with the client from the beginning and to establish a generally accepted standing in (and outside) the audited organization (including, e.g. the supervisory body, cf. Roussy 2012). This foundation allows auditors and client (using the temporal dimension of meaning) to develop a common understanding and agreement on their mutual roles during the audit (i.e. a consensus on roles according to the social dimension of meaning, cf. Haferkorn 2013, 35–49).

Given this starting point, the audit team should balance interaction with auditees and other stakeholders in the course of the audit process (Haferkorn 2010, 71–89 regarding auditors' independence; regarding counselling cf. Königswieser and Hillebrand 2004, 94; Pfeffer 2001, 130–132). The team can manage the stakeholders' expectation by respecting their opinion when it seems appropriate (e.g. when asking for the self-image of the organization) and if they comply with the Code of Ethics, but it should also be prepared to politely reject their standpoint later in the process, e.g. when judging the facts underlying an audit finding (cf. Section 'Independence and Need for Social Interaction' in relation to independence of the audit team).

Furthermore, audit actions and observations can change a stakeholder's opinions and attitudes (i.e. the fact dimension of meaning affects the social dimension of meaning). For example, decision-making about the next steps in the audit process would be different if an internal auditor detected fraud. In such a case, he or she would have to be extremely careful in checking all the details of the finding, or would probably think about transferring the issue to an external auditor, who was less dependent on the organization.

Thus, connectivity of the audit finding is not a one-off event occurring at the moment when the finding is disclosed. On the contrary, connectivity is only possible when taking the time for an ongoing gain in knowledge about the needs of the parties involved and about the functioning of the organization audited. (Thus auditors consider the time dimension of meaning.) It is on this gain in knowledge that auditors base their decisions for the next audit step. To increase the audit team's flexibility in aiming for consensus on how to proceed and balancing client's and audit's requirements, the audit is thus not completely planned from the beginning to end, but leaves possibilities to react on unforeseeable information. However, ongoing expectation management and a reasonable involvement of the client in the steering of the audit process are keys to obtain client's confidence and trust in the audit team's risk communication (Haferkorn 2013, 5, 11, 12, 25, 210–212; cf. Bauer 2015, 59–64 in relation to controlling).

The Importance of Audit Preparation

Increasing the flexibility of an audit process by avoiding over-strict planning should not be confounded with lack of preparation. It is a common mistake in practice to think that audit preparation only costs time and is negligible. The earlier an audit team talks to the client, the earlier it can start to manage the expectations of client and auditees, the earlier it is able to evaluate the possibilities and limits of its audit process, and the earlier it can consider diverse scenarios on how to proceed when planning. By gaining a good understanding of its position vis-à-vis the client and the auditees already at the beginning of the audit process, the audit team saves time because it can focus on what is possible and feasible early on (cf. Simon and Weber 2004, 11 in relation to counselling). The audit team therefore uses the temporal dimension of meaning even before starting the on-site audit process and so externalizes part of its expectation management of stakeholders before delving deep into the actual audit work and its fact-finding.

If auditors want to explore which role clients wish to assume for themselves and in which role they see the auditors, they first have to investigate the power structure of the audit including the clients' context (e.g. the organization they work for, their relationship to the audited organization, their participation in relevant subsystems and coalitions and further social relationships observed through the social dimension of meaning). In order to avoid misunderstandings and disagreements during and at the end of an audit, a kick-off meeting proves very helpful, where all parties involved should have the possibility to introduce themselves and present their understanding of mutual roles and of what the audit's aim should be.

Conflicting Demands and How to Deal with Them

Meeting conflicting requirements (Section 'Systemic Audit: Widening the Perspective of Traditional Audit Approaches') on an audit often confronts the audit team with further conflicts of interest. Unpicking the paradox of risk communication thus usually leads to more conflicting demands in practice.[6] The following list includes the most common ones for audits and gives some hints on how they can be negotiated by the audit team (Haferkorn 2010, 35–50; Selvini Palazzoli et al. 1977 in relation to family therapy).

Risk Awareness Versus Illusions of Safety

On the one hand, the reason clients hire an auditor is to get an assurance. On the other hand, the audit team might communicate a dysfunction of the organization. In the latter case, clients might have neglected their oversight responsibility (in case they are part of any controlling or supervisory body) or they could lose money (in case they invested resources). The audit team therefore conveys bad news and clients will have to decide on how to handle the information provided by the auditor. That is why even though the clients order an audit, they often may not be willing to hear the audit result. Auditors thus should be aware of client's paradoxical attitude between hiring an auditor to learn about the organization's risks and not being ready to hear about the actual risk involved (cf. Haferkorn 2010, 43, 44; Weakland et al. 1974 in relation to brief therapy).

In the course of the audit process, the audit team should consequently not expect its findings to be met with an open ear (Beattie et al. 2000) and should prepare the client for a potential risk statement and the uncertainty going along with it (cf. Power 2004, 16; Grote 2011 in relation to the hope that the public will accept the uncertainty going along with a risk statement). Auditors use several approaches to balance this conflict between risk awareness and illusions of safety:

If, in the preparation of the audit, the audit department or firm realizes that the client does not wish to hear about any deficits of the organization audited, it should refuse to contract or outsource the audit respectively (cf. ISAs 2012; Standard 2012). However, if an audit department or firm agrees to conduct the audit after all, it should think about measures to protect the client's and its own reputation. In a social dimension of meaning, it could, in such a case, employ an audit team of inexperienced staff, which does not have the knowledge necessary for relevant audit findings (cf. Ito et al. 2015, 73 the example Toshiba, where inexperienced auditors did not detect overstated profits of 1.2 billion US Dollar). Apart from the auditor

[6]This goes in accordance with the observation that unpicking a paradox by simultaneously keeping the complexity of the topic generally leads to new paradoxes (cf. Luhmann 1993, 203). This is one reason, why social systems theory prefers circular, multicausal and recursive explanation models (Hänsel 2013, 29).

providing limited resources, the client could also play on the temporal dimension of meaning and insist on a short audit. In the case of the Barings Bank failure in 1995, supervisors only spent 2 days at the bank's Singapore branch and had no realistic chance to detect that trader Nick Leeson had been hiding losses of 827 million British pound or 1.78 billion US Dollar (oral statement by a participating auditor made to the author).

Another way to create illusions of safety is to convince the audit team to only produce audit findings which are not important and at best can be resolved quickly during the audit. In the fact dimension of meaning, e.g. the audit department or firm can set up formal and empty requirements, which are prepared in a 'style over substance' manner intended to impress the reader. If, for example auditors are to stick to a checklist (cf. Haferkorn 2010, 222, 223 for a comparison on systemic and rule-based audit approaches), and if the checklist avoids questions that require substantive answers (cf. Power 2011 in relation to 'dumb' questions on risk management), there is a good chance that auditors will create no more than illusions of safety.

Moreover, the audit team has the possibility to communicate the audit finding merely orally and only to certain persons. The decision to take action or to leave things unchanged is then left up to that person. (Here again, conflicting demands are dealt with in the social dimension of meaning.) It is, however, important to point out that to cover up or conceal audit findings is not in accordance with the auditors' code of ethics (ISAs 2012; Standard 2012) and bears a substantial reputational risk for the auditor if a damage occurs and is eventually disclosed. Consequently, audit teams tend to at least allude to the issue in the audit report.

Another way to protect clients would be to merely communicate any deficits of the operational system without linking their potential damage to a strategic decision and thus the clients themselves. (The conflicting demands are then dealt with in the fact dimension of meaning by changing explanations for the predicted damage.) Even though this approach allows auditors to avoid discussions with their clients, there are unwanted side effects, too. First, the employees in charge will be frustrated about a finding, because their handling of the operations in question merely met the given strategic targets. This frustration may lead to conflicts with the auditors and tarnish their reputation or it can result in an undesirable personnel turnover, i.e. the employees concerned leaving the organization. Second, if auditors do not name the (overall) root of the potential damage, the deficits could remain or reappear in another form. As a result, neither the client nor the audited organization will be able to learn quickly (enough), which may prevent the organization from adapting to requirements of the environment in due time and cause it to cease to exist (cf. Feynman 1996, 109–231; Rogers et al. 2003, as an example, where warnings relating to the operational system were overheard and, when astronauts died, finally led National Aeronautics and Space Administration to drop its strategy in setting up a space shuttle program).

Although maintaining an adequate level of the client's comfort is fundamental for the communication of an audit team, it should nevertheless be aware about potentially disastrous effects which may arise by going too far when communicating one-sided illusions of safety. As is indicated above, lack of criticism and feedback can destroy trust in communication processes in- and outside the organization (cf. Power 2004, 5–6; Grote 2011). In such cases, audits lead to results that are counterproductive to the objectives they were designed to achieve. This is an irrevocable fact an audit team could point out in its communication with clients, in case they are not willing to accept an audit finding.

Independence and Need for Social Interaction

While the public wants an independent audit finding, it also expects the audit team to know the inside of the organization and therefore implicitly asks for audit actions, which, in turn, lead to interactions. 'Complete and total independence' is already challenged when client concludes the contract with the audit firm and negotiates the cost of the audit assignment. The number of auditors, their expertise and the time they are permitted for the audit are important prerequisites of an audit and can make a big difference on the audit result. Thus, clients and auditors naturally have an immense influence on the audit (Peemöller 2004; Marten et al. 2001, 156–185).

Responding to the stakeholders' demands without any restrictions would tarnish an audit team's reputation because its independence is an important prerequisite of the audit. When declining to meet a stakeholders' requirement, it will be helpful for the team to refer to the context of the audit and the existential importance of its independence. Putting independence into question implies putting the audit into question. This argument will quickly convince stakeholders that maintaining the auditors' independence is in the best interest of both sides (cf. Simon and Weber 2004, 11 et seqq. regarding counselling).

Objectivity and Dependence on Observers

On the one hand, International audit standards require audit findings to be objective (ISA 2012; Standard 2012). On the other hand, these findings depend on the way the audit is conducted including the interaction of auditors and auditees, the observations of the participating auditors and finally, how they are received by the client (Haferkorn 2010, 35–43). We should remember that in social systems theory 'everything which is said is said by an observer' (von Foerster and Pörksen 2013), existence of objectivity can therefore not be presumed.

To meet the public's and the client's requirement of 'objectivity' by maintaining some neutrality, it has proved helpful for auditors to aim for an early hypothesis on the functioning of the organization before making direct contact with the auditees. (If possible, auditors should use two contradicting hypothesis, cf. Section 'Conflicting Demands on the Audited Organization'.) In the fact dimension of meaning, the independence and neutrality of audit teams thus depend on how carefully they conduct the preparation with regard to the audit contents and on the knowledge they have gained based on professional experience with similar organizations.

General and Expert Knowledge

Not only auditors but also clients need an overarching knowledge about the functioning of the organization and, often enough, also expert knowledge, e.g. an understanding of an IT audit finding. Since a wide and deep understanding cannot be presumed, the explanations provided must be didactically prepared. In order to ensure connectivity, audit teams, which are ideally a mixture of generalists and specialists, should try to explain the audit findings in detail and in the organization's context. A deficiency in an IT-system for instance will certainly have a meaning for the operation of the organization, which then can be linked to a strategic target (cf. Haferkorn 2010, 51 et seqq. for an according audit approach). Generalists and specialists in an audit team should thus work together closely when explaining the audit findings (fact dimension of meaning).

Conflicting Demands on an Audit as a Project

Every project management has conflicting demands and so have audits. Generally speaking, the more time and resources spent on an audit, the higher is its quality. But the audit budget and timeframe are of course restricted. If auditors have sufficient transparency in their work, are ready to explain to stakeholders the important decisions on the audit process and involve them where adequate, they will increase the possibility of obtaining additional resources when necessary.

Paradox of Time

As organizations have to adapt to a changing environment, an audit finding is rarely presented at the right time. It is either communicated too early, and the organization is about to start working on the deficiency anyway, or it is too late because the organization has just finished implementing its organizational structure, processes and IT-systems, and fixing the issue would lead to reorganization and cause resources. Auditors can try to avoid this difficulty by entering into important organizational projects at an early stage and constantly expressing their concerns. Of course, this approach has a downside, too, as not only auditors' resources are tied up, but the auditors' independence and neutrality may also be challenged by becoming involved in the set-up of the organization.

Disagreement on the Facts of an Audit Finding

If auditor and client disagree on an issue, it is helpful to better understand the reason for the dissent in the fact dimension of meaning by trying to distinguish and discuss the following three levels of the audit finding (based on Simon 2006, 72–77 '**drei Ebenen der Wirklichkeitskonstruktion**'):

- The observation of a phenomenon, which causes the dysfunction according to the auditor,
- The explanation of the dysfunction and
- The judgement of the audit finding as 'important' dysfunction or less important dysfunction.

Do audit team and stakeholder agree on the observation of a phenomenon, e.g. the audit team's statement that the organization does not function as it should and that the status quo of the organization is questionable? If not, what are the differences in their observations? The auditors could try to better explain their position, e.g. in explaining the context of the audit finding from different perspectives (IT-auditor, finance auditor, etc.). Widening the view on the phenomenon and commenting on the context may help the stakeholder to better understand the facts and to follow the audit team's further argumentation. The auditor could also try to gain substance by collecting more facts to support their statement (e.g. find historic scenarios causing damage). Additionally, auditors have to think about, for instance in asking further experts to join the audit or in using additional audit techniques.

Do audit team and stakeholder agree on the explanation given for the cause of a future damage, e.g. the lack of control? There are multiple reasons for damage and various reasons why an additional control measure does or does not help to prevent damage (Dowell and Hendershot 1997). What distinguishes auditor's from stakeholder's explanations of the situation? Why has the damage in question not yet occurred or what has changed to make damage more likely now? Do stakeholders and auditors agree on the forecast horizon for probable damage or does the stakeholder think he has plenty of time to remedy the issue? Why do they differ and what makes the difference?

Do auditor and client agree on the final judgement, the risk declaration, e.g. that there is a high potential for a rather high damage or a certain potential for a very huge damage? On which future damage scenarios do the parties involved agree and on which ones do they differ? If the audit team uses historical scenarios and explains situations where similar damage occurred in comparable cases, the client will probably be more ready to accept the issue and follow its recommendations. The auditor could also substantiate its findings by referring to other experts who have adequate expertise and share the auditor's point of view. Their reputation and standing could convince the client that the risk may actually realize.

If auditors want to understand the client's uncertainty, they will have to extend the risk communication and ask questions like the ones described above (social dimension of meaning). To dispel the client's doubts, the audit team can continue the audit process (temporal dimension of meaning) to give more substance to the audit finding by trying to collect more supporting facts and explanations for the issue in question (Puhani 2015 and, as an example for an excellent audit report, see Rogers et al. 2003).

Conflicting Demands on the Audited Organization

An audit team can increase the connectivity of its risk communication to the client if the audit findings are well balanced, i.e. if they show the advantages and disadvantages of the status quo of the audited organization and of the improvement suggested. There are various conflicting demands which organizations have to adjust to (Balck 1996; Weick and Sutcliffe 2001), such as centralization versus decentralization or cost-cutting versus growth. An auditor, who respects these contradicting requirements on an organization, ensures a certain neutrality towards the issue in question (cf. Section 'Objectivity and Dependence on Observers') and helps to avoid discussions with the client in cases where the audit team presents a one-sided audit result and the client elaborates on the disadvantages of the recommendation. This approach is able to reflect organization's ambiguity and uncertainty and maintains the flexibility of thinking of the audit team.

Conclusion

The systemic approach recommends structuring the audit process as a dynamic learning and decision-making process, where each audit step is based on the current knowledge gained in the previous audit steps. The audit team does not search for absolute truth in risk communication, but strives for connectivity to the client, e.g. by emphasizing the background of the audit statement including relevant decisions of the audit process and important assumptions of the audit findings.

The audit team thus deals with the uncertainty of a risk communication by disclosing auditors' blind spots and the conditions under which audit results should be revised. Consequently, the systemic approach enables clients to assess in which context and to what extent the audit team's risk communication can be a basis for their further decisions.

References

Balck, H. (1996). Aufdecken von Strukturbrüchen. In H.-J. Bullinger, H. J. Warnecke, & E. Westkämper (Eds.), *Neue Organisationsformen in Unternehmen* (2nd ed. 2002, pp. 1203–1208). Berlin etc.,: Springer.

Bauer, G. (2015). *Einführung in das systemische Controlling*. Heidelberg: Carl-Auer.

Beattie, V., Fearnley, S., & Brandt, R. (2000). Behind the audit report: A descriptive study of discussions and negotiations between auditors and directors. *International Journal of Auditing, 4,* 177–202.

Collins, J. W. (2010). Mobile phone masts, social rationalities and risk: Negotiating lay perspectives on technological hazards. *Journal of Risk Research, 13*(5), 621–637.

de Shazer, S. (1989). *Wege der erfolgreichen Kurzzeittherapie*. Stuttgart: Klett.

Dowell, A. M., & Hendershot, D. C. (1997). No good deed goes unpunished: Case studies of incidents and potential incidents caused by protective systems. *Process Safety Progress, 16*(3), 132–139.

Feynman, R. P. (1996). „Kümmert Sie, was andere Leute denken?" München, Piper (7th ed. 2005).

Gigerenzer, G., Wegwarth, O., & Feufel, M. (2010). Misleading communication of risk. *BMJ, 341,* c4830. https://doi.org/10.1136/bmj.c4830 (12.10.2010).

Grote, G. (2011). Risk management from an organizational psychology perspective: A decision process for managing uncertainties. *Die Unternehmung, 65*(1), 69–81.

Haferkorn, P. (2010). *Systemische Prüfungen. Systemtheoretische Prüfungstheorie und systemische Prüfungsansätze zur Einschätzung der Lebensfähigkeit von Organisationen*. Heidelberg: Carl-Auer.

Haferkorn, P. (2013). Zugleich ′drinnen und ′draußen. *Zeitschrift Interne Revision* (6/2013, pp. 292–304). Frankfurt a.M.: Erich Schmidt Verlag.

Hänsel, M. (2013). Der Ordnung halber! Grundlagen der systemischen Beratung. In M. Vogel (Ed.), *Organisation außer Ordnung* (pp. 21–38). Göttingen: Vandehoeck und Ruprecht.

Hollands, J. G., & Lipkus, I. M. (1999). The visual communication of risk. *Journal of the National Cancer Institute. Monographs, 1999*(25), 149–163 (Oxford, Oxford Journals).

ISAs 2012: International Standards on Auditing 2012, published by International Federation of Accountants. URL: https://www.ifac.org/auditing-assurance/clarity-center/clarified-standards (23.12.2015).

Ito, T., Matsui, H., Ueda, K., & Yamada, K. (2015). Investigation Report Summary Version of 20 July 2015. Toshiba Corporation. Tokyo, URL: https://www.toshiba.co.jp/about/ir/en/news/20150725_1.pdf (21.01.2016).

Keynes, J. M. (1923). *A tract on monetary reform* (p. 80). London: Macmillan and Co.

Königswieser, R., & Exner, A. (1998). *Systemische Intervention: Architekturen und Designs für Berater und Veränderungsmanager*. Stuttgart: Klett-Cotta.

Königswieser, R., & Hillebrand, M. (2004). *Einführung in die systemische Organisationsberatung*. Heidelberg: Carl-Auer.

Luhmann, N. (1984). *Soziale Systeme*. Frankfurt am Main: Suhrkamp.

Luhmann, N. (1986). The autopoiesis of social systems. In F. Geyer & J. van der Zouwen (Eds.), *Sociocybernetic paradoxes. Observation, control and evolution of self-steering systems* (pp. 172–192). Sage: London.

Luhmann, N. (1990). *Essays on self-reference*. Luhmann's adaptation of autopoiesis to social systems. New York: Columbia University Press.

Luhmann, N. (1991). *Soziologie des Risikos*. Berlin, New York: de Gruyter.

Luhmann, N. (1993). Die Paradoxie der Form. In D. der Baecker (Ed.), *Kalkül der Form* (pp. 197–212). Frankfurt am Main: Suhrkamp.

Luhmann, N. (1995). The paradoxy of observing systems. In *Cultural critique*, 31, The Politics of Systems and Environments, Part II (Autumn, 1995, pp. 37–55). University of Minnesota Press.

Luhmann, N. (2000). *Organisation und Entscheidung*. Wiesbaden: VS Verlag.

Luhmann, N. (2002). *Einführung in die Systemtheorie*. Heidelberg: Carl-Auer.

Maturana, H. R., & Varela, F. J. (1987). *The tree of knowledge: The biological roots of human understanding*. Boston, MA: Shambhala Publications.

Marten, K.-U., Quick, R., & Ruhnke, K. (2001). *Wirtschaftsprüfung* (3rd ed. 2007). Stuttgart: Schäffer-Poeschel.

Peemöller, V. H. (2004). Neuere Konzepte zur Unabhängigkeit des Abschlussprüfers. In G. Förschle & V. H. Peemöller (Eds.), *Wirtschaftsprüfung und Interne Revision* (pp. 758–769). Heidelberg: Verlag Recht und Wirtschaft GmbH.

Pfeffer, T. (2001). *Das » zirkuläre Fragen « als Forschungsmethode zur Luhmannschen Systemtheorie* (2nd ed. 2004). Heidelberg: Carl-Auer.

Power, M. (2004). *The risk management of everything: Rethinking the politics of uncertainty*. London: DEMOS. URL: http://www.demos.co.uk/files/riskmanagementofeverything.pdf (11.10.2015).

Power, M. (2007). *Organized uncertainty* (2nd ed. 2010). Oxford: Oxford University Press.

Power, M. (2011). Smart and dumb questions to ask about risk management. In *Risk watch* (pp. 2–5). Ottawa: Conference board of Canada.

Puhani, S. (2015). *Erfolgreiche Prüfungsprozesse in der Internen Revision. Konzepte, Kommunikation, Konfliktmanagement*. Berlin: Erich Schmidt.

Rogers, W. P., Armstrong, N. A., Acheson, D. C., et al. (2003). Report of the presidential commission on the space shuttle challenger accident. Washington, D. C. (U.S. Government Printing Office). URL: http://www.caib.nasa.gov/news/report/defaulkt.html (13.02.2009).

Roussy, M. (2012). Comment apprécier la compétence d'un auditeur interne? L'opinion des membres du comité d'audit, *Revue d'analyse comparée en administration publique, 18*(3), 33–51. URL: http://id.erudit.org/iderudit/1013774ar.

Selvini Palazzoli, M. Boscolo, L., Cecchin, G., & Prata, G. (1977). *Paradoxon und Gegenparadoxon*. Stuttgart: Klett.

Simon, F. B. (2006). *Einführung in Systemtheorie und Konstruktivismus*. Heidelberg: Carl-Auer.

Simon, F. B. (2007). Paradoxiemanagement– Genie und Wahnsinn der Organisation. *Revue für postheroisches Management, 1*(2007), 68–87.

Simon, F. B. (2014). *Einführung in die (System-)Theorie der Beratung*. Heidelberg: Carl-Auer.

Simon, F. B., & Weber, G. (2004). *Vom Navigieren beim Driften*. Heidelberg: Carl-Auer.

Spencer-Brown, G. (1969). *Laws of form*. Lübeck: Bohmeier Verlag.

Standard 2012. International Standards for the Professional of Internal Auditors 2012, published by The Institute of Internal Auditors, Altamonte Springs. URL: https://na.theiia.org/standards-guidance/Public%20Documents/IPPF%202013%20English.pdf (23.12.2015).

von Foerster, H., & Pörksen, B. (2013). *Wahrheit ist die Erfindung eines Lügners: Gespräche für Skeptiker*. Heidelberg: Carl-Auer.

von Glaserfeld, E. (1995). *Radical constructivism: A way of knowing and learning*. London: Falmer Press.

von Glaserfeld, E. (1996). *Radikaler Konstruktivismus, Ideen, Ergebnisse, Probleme*. Frankfurt a. M.: Suhrkamp.

Weakland, J., Fisch, R., Watzlawick, P., & Bodin, A. (1974). Brief therapy: Focused problem resolution. *Family Process, 13,* 141–168.

Weick, K. E., & Sutcliffe, K. M. (2001). *Managing the unexpected*. San Francisco, CA: Jossey-Bass.

Societal Risk Communication—Towards Smart Risk Governance and Safety Management

Corinne Bieder

Abstract Risk communication has long been thought and conceptualized as based on a centralized model where experts were detaining knowledge and explaining risks to lay persons. Today's risk communication reality is much more complex. It involves a variety of actors, each of them having multiple interests. Safety is one of them, among many others, but is also understood in different ways. However, acknowledging this complexity allows for building upon all risk communication actors' respective inputs to build the overall risk and stake picture and be potentially an active contributor in relation to safety. Eventually, it leads to proposing a smart and open approach to risk governance and safety management.

Keywords Risk governance · Safety management · Risk communication
Complexity

Risk communication is now being considered as a part of safety management. But to what extent does it really influence the decisions and actions taken to manage safety? Conversely, how does safety management influence risk communication principles?

Risk communication has long been considered by institutions and high-risk organizations a controlled and centralized process where knowledge was detained by them and disseminated to the rest of the world to explain and justify decisions they would make on their own.

However, times have changed and so has risk communication. Communication means, channels, pace, actors, forums, expectations and inclusion are among the elements that evolved dramatically over the past decade. Can these recent and future risk communication expectations and practices actually contribute to risk governance and safety management practices? If yes, under what conditions?

In order to answer these questions, it is worth reviewing the traditional risk communication model to identify its pitfalls or weaknesses and analysing how risk

C. Bieder (✉)
ENAC (French Civil Aviation University), Toulouse, France
e-mail: corinne.bieder@enac.fr

M. Bourrier and C. Bieder (eds.), *Risk Communication for the Future*, SpringerBriefs in Safety Management, https://doi.org/10.1007/978-3-319-74098-0_11

communication works today in practice. It will allow to propose a risk communication approach for the future, both realistic in this new era and leading to a renewed and more efficient way to govern risks and manage safety.

Evolution of Risk Communication: A Simplistic Initial Model and Multiple Refinements

Baruch Fischhoff in 1995 (Fischhoff, 1995) proposed an overview of 20 years of risk communication and characterized its evolution through seven developmental stages. It seems that all lessons have not been learned from the past and that almost all developmental stages can still be observed today. Risk communication now takes place in an environment where communication means, pace and practices have changed, but many organizations and institutions still rely on successive refinements of an early 'traditional' risk communication paradigm. Let us further describe and analyse its foundations and evolution to better reach beyond its limits.

The Early 'Traditional' Risk Communication Model: Accredited Experts Watch Over Safety Management

In this model, risk communication is mainly handled and organized (or believed to be) by a prominent actor that is the company/organization/institution (to improve readability, in the rest of the text, we will only use the word organization) operating or supervising the hazardous activity. The organization and its accredited experts represent the only source of valid knowledge and expertise. Risk communication takes place through formal forums organized by the prominent actor and targeted at pre-identified stakeholders. In brief, risk communication is centric, from a central knowledgeable actor (or a very limited number of actors) to specific audiences that are assumed to be risk-ignorant (Fig. 1).

The purpose of such risk communication is officially to debate about the safety risk or convey science on this topic to predefined stakeholders, thus in a sense, to bridge the gap between experts and society (Nishikawa, *this volume*).

Such a model of risk communication relies on a number of implicit assumptions that are worth reviewing:

- There is one and only one Truth on safety risks that is detained by the company experts. Multiple angles or interpretations of safety risks or any reference to uncertainty are seen as malicious attempts to harm the industry's or authority's reputation and destroy the public's trust. They are considered ill-founded statements without any scientific or justified background.
- Formal forums such as official public participation/consultation meetings around hazardous sites (e.g. plants, airports, etc.) involving the prominent actor and

Fig. 1 Centralized and controlled risk communication model

pre-identified stakeholders are the only form of risk communication. There is no other place than the formal forums where safety risks are discussed. Risk communication is exclusively about 'legitimate experts' explaining safety risks to laypersons.

– The dominating concern of risk communication stakeholders is safety management. Whoever takes part in risk communication does it to defend the common interest of managing the safety risks associated with the hazardous activity or situation at stake; there is a convergence of interest among all risk communication stakeholders.
– Risks/Safety is understood with the same meaning and scope by the prominent actor and its audiences. The safety risks considered by all risk communication stakeholders are similar whatever their nature (e.g. individuals vs. companies or institutions). For example, the impacts or consequences envisaged by people living in the neighbourhood of a high-hazard industry plant are the same as the ones considered by the plant managers or the local or national authority. In other words, the understanding of safety risks and the scope considered are 'universal' and are not affected by the different nature of the various stakeholders.

- The audiences targeted by the official risk communication forums listen to, trust and accept what is said by the organization's experts. The public acknowledges that the only valid expertise and judgement on safety are those of the organizations' experts; it relies exclusively on this expertise to get a view on safety.

These assumptions are related to one another and form a consistent framework, where the early 'traditional' risk communication model makes great sense. The overall assumption is that risk communication can be controlled by the prominent actor, not only in terms of messages but also in terms of targets and timing of these messages.

The case of public participation in the debate on industrial risk in France (Kamaté, *this volume*) provides an illustration of the traditional risk communication model. The chapter highlights the formal process for organizing communication from representatives of hazardous industry/local authority towards local residents. It documents how the formal forums involving public participation are publicized in a way that is not so easily or obviously accessible, and organized at times that are not very practical for most people. In other words, everyone is welcome but the conditions make it so difficult to attend that the participation, thus the non-institutional share of voice is limited. To put it more bluntly, everything is organized so as to silence potential dissonant voices. One could interpret this approach as an acknowledgment of the weakness of the assumption that there is a unique scientific truth. Indeed, not leaving room to other viewpoints is a way to artificially make the official experts' truth the only one.

As for the objective of these forums, it is not precisely about safety management in the sense of taking better decisions and actions to manage safety. What industrials/authorities expect thereby is to persuade the public that the decisions they already made on their own are not only the best ones, but are also perceived as collective decisions since the public was involved (even though what they are involved in is not at all a collective decision process but rather an after the fact information process). More than debating with the public about the safety risks of hazardous industrial activities, risk communication is about controlling the public's reaction, both before any safety-critical event occurs but also in the event of an accident. Eventually, the ultimate objective of risk communication, in that case, is to build trust and even further, share responsibility, more than to manage safety.

The weakness of the 'traditional' risk communication model underpinning assumptions is also well exemplified by the healthcare domain, where the risk is not local like in the case of a high-risk facility. In healthcare, there is usually no uphill battle to have access to the risk communication arena, since it is usually a very open one. Nevertheless, risk communication remains one-way and pertains more to public information or public education than to risk communication. Whether the information then actually reaches the intended targets is not always a concern for those who disseminated it. As for the trust placed in the message, the example of the risk communication around A/H1N1 pandemic-influenza vaccination in France in 2009 is eloquent. Convinced that people would trust and follow its recommendation, the French Ministry of Health ordered a massive number of doses that turned out to far exceed demand. A study of the attitudes and behaviours of the general population towards pandemic vaccination highlighted that the public health messages focused on the severity of the risk were “counteracted by daily personal experience which did not confirm the threat, while vaccine safety was a major issue”. “Acceptability was significantly higher among 8.0% of respondents who were formally advised [by their primary care physician] to get vaccinated, and lower among 63.7% respondents who were not advised to get vaccinated” (Schwarzinger et al., 2010, p. 6). The objective of the risk communication initiative by the government was to convince the public to buy into an allegedly safety management measure decided by the government itself without any consultation.

As we have illustrated, the traditional centralized and controlled risk communication model led to some blatant risk communication failures, pointing to a need for greater sophistication and more specifically a qualification of its foundational assumptions.

Listening to the Potential Victims: A First Refinement of the ‘Centralized and Controlled’ Risk Communication Model

In the aftermath of the Fukushima accident, if the initial approach to risk communication from the local authorities towards people affected was to explain the radiation phenomena and mechanisms, its failure led authorities to reassess their approach (Nishikawa, *this volume*). An analysis of the initial experience highlighted that some cultural aspects were not considered in the way it was organized, but also that some of the assumptions listed above proved wrong. First of all, it came out of the feedback from the first risk communication experience that what the affected people were interested in was not to know more about radiation in general (i.e. the science of nuclear reactions or disembodied physical phenomena), but rather about the impact on them and their families of consuming locally grown products. In other words, risks, to them, meant the possibility of being harmed by locally grown products or cattle, whereas for local authorities, risks meant the overall impact of radiation due to the nuclear fallout, compared to natural radiation phenomena. The risks considered by the local residents differ from that considered by the authorities and the industry.

What also came out clearly from this risk communication experience in the vicinity of Fukushima is that the mothers spoke a lot among themselves about the risks (their risks) related to food. Information about the risks associated with consuming local products circulated also through informal channels with a high level of trust in the information, thus contributing to developing people’s risk picture. Not only are there other forms of risk communication than the official sessions organized by the authorities, but also people trust other sources than official experts and ultimately make up their own mind about the risks instead of blindly buying into the official discourse and view on risks. This experience led to adjust the local government's risk communication content to the needs of the affected people and provide them with practical and easily understandable and credible information about the radiation contained in local products and how it compares with other accepted radiation exposure. In this case, risk communication is also about informing the public (the assumption that there are accredited experts vs. laypersons is still prevailing), but this information is meant to help local residents make personal decisions. In that sense, it may be seen as a contribution to safety management, but with a limited understanding of safety. Indeed, information on food radiation helps affected population manage what they perceive as being their safety risks, namely consuming local products.

However, risk communication cannot be considered a pillar or even a contributor to safety management in the widest sense of the word. The disconnect between risk communication and safety management may not be on purpose though. It can be seen as a result of some of the model's assumptions as well. By considering that there is only one interpretation of safety risks (that of the hazardous industry) and that there is only one truth (detained as well by the hazardous industry), involving other parties in risk communication cannot add value to safety management. It may be an information tool, a damage control approach for the industry's reputation, but in no way a useful contribution to safety management.

Is it inevitable, or could risk communication actually contribute to safety management? What would be the conditions to make risk communication a safety management driver? On what grounds should a new model be founded, or how to revisit the underpinning assumptions that prove wrong in reality? To be able to answer these questions, it is worth reviewing and analysing real cases in which risk communication actually made a difference in the way safety was managed.

Crisis of the Foundations of the Centralized and Controlled Risk Communication Model

Beyond the first step of evolution leading to listening to potentially directly affected people, the evolution of risk communication in the broader context of societal evolution severely challenged several foundational assumptions of the centralized and controlled risk communication model, with some significant impact on safety management.

A key societal factor is the crisis of trust in institutions, experts and science, leading to certain defiance towards companies and authorities and their official messages (Millstone and Van Zwanenberg, 2000). The trust relation has become more horizontal. In addition, the evolution of communication means allowed for new and increased exchanges between a wide range of people located everywhere in parallel to official messages. Newcomers get onto the risk communication scene, being considered troublemakers by some, and key safety actors by others, depending on their perspective (Guérard, *this volume*). Some recent cases illustrate how new forms of risk communication did contribute to safety management.

In the case of the Ebola outbreak, listening to local people allowed for better understanding why initial risk communication messages did not work and for adjusting the approach to the local social environment (Bastide, *this volume*). As such, the safety management decisions still made in a centralized way ultimately were better informed. Getting these valuable insights though was not part of the initial risk communication approach but came after a blatant failure of a pure top-down generic communication initiative. It revealed the importance of knowing the local context and understanding individuals' views on risks.

In the Daniel case (Wiig et al., *this volume*), the stubbornness of the journalist led to reopen the case and highlight some hazardous practices and atmosphere in the hospital. By so doing, the investigation went further and came out with some recommendations that ultimately translated into safety measures that were not initially mentioned. In that respect, risk communication actually contributed to the decisions and actions taken to managing safety. Interestingly again, risk communication as it took place, initiated by the journalist, was not part of any formal or planned risk communication by the institution. He was not a 'natural' risk communication stakeholder either. The journalist himself was not directly affected as an individual by the safety hazards he contributed to uncover.

Similarly, the role played by local residents immediately after the start of the Paris attacks in 2015 was key in managing the risk of aggravated consequences, although they were neither part of a risk communication plan nor directly individually affected.

Even in 'peace time', far from any accident and emergency situation, some indirect actors like the media or academic researchers may play a role in the engagement in risk communication and ultimately in risk governance like illustrated in the case of the Risavika, Sola municipality (Baram and Lindoe, *this volume*).

Risk Communication Today: A Complex Reality

Behind the two simple words 'risk communication' hides a complex reality that a risk communication model needs to reflect and build upon to be useful and efficient. With the crisis of the assumptions underpinning a centralized and controlled risk communication model, a new set of assumptions, more realistic need to be developed to serve as bases of a new model.

Nowadays, everyone has access to and gets information from multiple sources of which some are already trusted and others unknown. The information circulating quickly and in different arenas contributes to building an idea about risks (including the hazardous activity's safety risks) in the public's minds, a set of beliefs and doubts, that constitutes not only a starting point but also evolves permanently. In other words, risk communication whether it is formal or not, personal or public, almost never intervenes on a virgin land/territory but rather on a moving basis.

Another key aspect that cannot be denied or ignored is the multiplicity of interests among the various stakeholders. The risks associated with (a) safety hazard (s) are of different natures for different parties and may evolve over time. Resulting individual goals can even be conflicting. This diversity of interests and goals is not related to ignorance or thoughtlessness but rather to the specific context and role of each party. One of the groups of residents in Fukushima involved in the risk communication initiative are mothers above all (Nishikawa, *this volume*), locals in West Africa are strongly anchored in ancestral culture and defiant with respect to European settlers' intentions when it comes to public health for historical reasons (Bastide, *this volume*), small towns in the vicinity of a big municipality remain small towns acknowledging the big gap in resources among other differences (Bergé, *this volume*).

Each risk communication stakeholder has its own goals and interests that make sense with respect to its own context and role or mission. If the risk of an industrial accident can be a common interest to all of them, it is not necessarily the only one or the predominant one. However, each actor through his/her own interests bring a share of the overall picture, some pieces of a distributed knowledge and understanding of a complex reality. Eventually, the global risk picture combines all the stakes and risks perceived by all stakeholders at their own scale, timeline and from their own angle.

Everyone can virtually feel concerned and get involved in risk communication. Whether it is as a direct victim or potential victim or as a citizen or simply a human being, any risk can affect anyone. With the reach and pace of communication using modern means, a huge number of people can be aware of many risk issues and decide to get involved. Formal communication forums are a very limited part of the arenas where risks are discussed.

In the aviation example, self-appointed experts just as extremely knowledgeable aviation fans join the risk discussions, sometimes for a quick participation on a specific topic, sometimes for much deeper and longer debates (Guérard, *this volume*). Likewise, in the Daniel case (Wiig et al., *this volume*), the journalist investigating the case becomes a key actor of risk communication independently from any formal process. Sometimes, anonymous actors have a contribution, sometimes even a very brief one, one-off, like residents in the case of the November 2015 Paris attacks.

The contribution of these many actors may make a difference to safety and safety management. In aviation, by initiating and feeding controversies on some major safety-related aspects, some people who may even not belong to the aviation 'world' have a healthy contribution for they prevent the professional community from drifting into complacency (Guérard, *this volume*). In the Daniel case (Wiig et al., *this volume*), the role of the journalist turns out to be essential in the reopening of the case and ultimately in the safety enhancement measures taken. Likewise, in the case of the Paris attacks, by getting involved in communication, using social media, residents allowed for saving lives.

Fig. 2 Distributed and dynamic risk communication model

Along with this diversity of actors comes a variety of risk communication arenas and alliances, more or less stable or opportunistic, formal or not, using different channels (official forums, spontaneous networks, e.g. journalist and experts in the Daniel case, private circles, e.g. primary care physicians in the case of the H1N1 influenza pandemic, etc.), running at different paces (instantaneous on social media like in the Paris attacks case, at a more planned frequency for formal forums).

Exchanges take place freely with no control body. They involve whoever wants to take part in the discussion (or any other form of exchange). Several 'discussions' involving several sets of actors may take place in parallel, using possibly different means and channels. Risk communication is distributed and dynamic. Topics, actors, communication means evolve with time. In short, there is no dominating actor, not even dominating actors with dominating views remaining unchallenged. Everyone can have a share of voice likely to reach everyone (Fig. 2).

Eventually, an alternative risk communication model for the future needs to start from the following assumptions:

- The interests among the various stakeholders are legitimately diverse (this diversity of interests and goals is related to the specific context and role of each party) and may change over time
- Reality is complex and (risks) must be apprehended from different and complementary viewpoints
- Risk communication actors, alliances and forums/arenas are diverse and evolve with time
- Exchanges take place freely
- The various actors' viewpoints contribute to the overall (risk) picture.

In such framework, risk communication cannot be considered a defensive centralized and controlled tool for industries and authorities where new stakeholders are considered enemies to be controlled and decisions are made upfront by one actor in isolation and then 'justified' or 'sold' to other parties by means of predefined messages in formal forums.

In this alternative perspective, controversy and contradiction are inherent to the complexity of reality. In the audit approach proposed by Haferkorn (*this volume*), 'the audit team does not search for absolute truth in risk communication but strives for connectivity to the client', auditors' blind spots are disclosed. Beyond blind spots, diverging views and controversies are normal and even fruitful. They are an incentive to further push the reflection on safety and how to enhance it. There is no such thing as one Truth and wrong perceptions. There is a complex and dynamic reality that can be apprehended from different and complementary viewpoints that all are valuable. Eventually, understanding the various goals and contexts and being aware of one's own goals and context is necessary to make risk communication constructive.

However, this descriptive perspective on risk communication may not be sufficient to make it a natural contributor to an improved safety management and risk governance.

Can Risk Communication Contribute to a Shift of Safety Management and/or Risk Governance Paradigm?

Historically, risk governance and safety management decisions and actions involved exclusively the ones inducing the risks (as a by-product of other activities) under the scrutiny of governmental authorities that were meant to represent the voice of those likely to bear the potential consequences of the risks, thus of the risk governance and safety management strategies and implementation. The public was not considered directly an actor. It was represented in risk governance by the authorities and not active in safety management.

The crisis of trust in institutions and in accredited experts led to a will of the public to get information from a variety of sources and ultimately get involved directly in decision processes. By having a share of voice and making it accessible to virtually anyone through especially new communication channels and means like social media, some representatives of the public, not necessarily directly affected by the potential consequences, managed to influence risk governance and safety management decisions. In these cases, risk communication contributed to bridge the gap between those who manage the risks and those who bear their potential consequences, thus contributed to the social contract between those parties (Fischhoff 1995).

Accounting for public debates open to all, benefiting from a wider range of information and knowledge (Baumont, *this volume*), combining different perspectives, establishing dialogue (Haferkorn, *this volume*), listening to controversies is certainly a way to complete the picture in all its complexity. As such, it seems a promising way forward to improve risk governance and safety management. However, can this deepening of the democracy of risk governance and safety management by making it more direct be generalized through risk communication? Reviewing the challenges inherent to risk communication in relation to safety may help defining ways forward to make risk communication play a key role in risk governance and safety management.

Challenges Inherent to Risk Communication in Relation to Safety

A Variety of Perspectives on Safety

Although most risk communication actors have safety as a major if not main concern, the meaning they associate with safety varies. Safety is not always understood as a societal stake in the sense of preserving lives or property or the environment. In fact, very few of the risks addressed in risk communication refer to this societal sense of safety. Indeed, the risks most stakeholders are concerned with and want to manage are 'their' risks, that is the ones they perceive as being likely to affect them.

Depending on how far reaching their line of thought is, the risks they may consider range from the ones likely to affect them individually, directly, almost certainly and immediately, to the ones likely to affect them as citizens or human beings directly or indirectly at various time horizons, i.e. the wider societal and even more global impacts. For example, for local residents living close to a hazardous facility, the scope of risks they may consider could range from the loss of their house value to the wider harm to health/lives, property and environment that an industrial accident at this facility could cause. Some may embrace an even wider scope and consider the potential harm caused by any accident related to this kind of industry worldwide. In an emergency situation, the scope considered may be different and focus on immediate consequences on lives.

For an organization, the scope of risks that might be considered ranges from the immediate restrictions of operations thus economic losses to the same wider societal impact of any accident in this field of activity that can be considered by an individual having a global appreciation of safety. At a governmental or regulatory level as well, the scope of risks considered may vary from regional considerations and impacts to more global societal ones reaching beyond national boundaries. In the case of a nuclear power plant, people may engage in risk communication to manage the risks of living next to a nuclear power plant whereas others would do it to contribute to managing nuclear safety in general. The first ones will focus on the risks associated with the presence and operation of this specific facility by the specific management in place. The other ones will address more global and transverse risks such as international regulation or the same risks considered at a wider scale such as sub-contracting and include the risks associated with decommissioning and nuclear waste management. In the aviation industry, the passionate debates around automation is a matter of aviation safety management with a broad perspective of safety management. However, communication involving local residents about the risks associated with a new route overflying a specific area is also about safety management.

Eventually, one may say that all stakeholders engage in risk communication to manage safety, in fact, to manage their view of safety. Risk communication is a way to contribute to their perspective of safety management. However, their view of safety may be far narrower than the implicit scope of 'risk governance' or 'safety management' as generally understood, i.e. the management of the wider scope of risks, wider in the sense of the reach of the impacts, at societal level, all time horizons, and encompassing not only known, known–unknowns risks but also unknown–unknown ones (Taleb, 2007). Indeed, the scope of 'safety management' depends on the unit of analysis and the timeframe considered.

Scope of Safety, Scope of Control

Depending on the reach of impacts considered, the role and control of risk communication stakeholders in safety management varies dramatically. For example, if safety is considered with a very narrow scope by a local resident living next to a hazardous industry facility, one measure to manage his/her safety is to move to a different place. This straightforward 'individual safety' management measure does not have any effect on safety management as soon as safety is considered with a wider scope, especially, it does not reduce the risk of an accident occurring or the severity of its consequences. To make the decision to move to a different place (thereby to manage safety at his/her individual scale), a local resident just needs to be informed about the risks of an accident occurring. Listening to the potentially affected ones and providing them with the information they ask for may be a sufficient risk communication strategy. S/he then has the full control over the safety risk reduction measure (the safety risk being considered here at his/her own level as well). If safety management is understood with a broader scope, e.g. managing the risk of an accident occurring at the facility, the role of a local resident in managing safety is far less predominant. Decisions to reduce the risk of an accident are not in the hands of a local resident.

It is with this societal or even more global scope of safety that a new paradigm is needed to bridge the historical disconnect between safety management as an external stake through its potential consequences likely to harm people, property and/or environment and safety management as an internal activity, i.e. performed by the hazardous industry itself under the scrutiny of authorities either national or international or both. However, aligning risk communication stakeholders' concerns around safety understood as a societal stake requires reaching beyond some difficulties.

Multiple Interests in Tension with One Another

The different views of risks to be managed among risk communication actors lead to a variety of interests at play in risk communication. Among these interests, some are clearly conflicting with others. The reasons for these conflicts can be manifold.

They may be related to the scope of risks considered (e.g. individual vs. societal stakes), for common interest is not the sum of individual ones. The time horizon considered may be another source of conflicting interests including for the same risk communication actor. For example, a company may decide to implement a wide safety awareness and training campaign internally following an accident, whereas a longer term view would have led to other kinds of safety measures including possibly organizational or technological aspects to make its efficiency more sustainable.

Eventually, among the most obvious tension between interests is the conflict between the risks associated with an activity and the benefits associated with this same activity. The attitude around the Chevron facility (Baram and Lindoe, *this volume*) is a perfect illustration of the tension between the socio-economic benefit of having the facility located in this region and the risks associated with the operation of such facility. Likewise, most individuals tend to less and less accept contingencies and risks but are not ready to live without the comfort brought by these same hazardous activities (electric power, cheap food, transport, cf. Bouzon 2001).

These contradictions are no surprise but cannot be overlooked when addressing risk communication as a pillar of improved risk governance and safety management. They are "not the sign of error in complex thinking, but rather that we have reached a deep layer of reality which, because it is deep, cannot be translated in our logic" (Morin, 2005, p. 92).

Complex and Dynamic Exchanges Between Complex and Dynamic Actors

> "It is not simply the human society that is complex, but each atom of the human world."
> (Edgar Morin, 2005, p. 78)

In reality, the interests considered in risk communication not only vary from one actor to another but they may also vary for the same actor in different contexts. Indeed, humans are complex beings (organization or institutions complex bodies). The same individual may sometimes think and act as a local resident considering safety in a rather limited sense (his/her safety risks managed by his/her decisions) and sometimes as a citizen or even a human being with a much broader scope and far-reaching considerations on safety. "The most daily life is a life where each person plays several social roles whether s/he is at home, at work, with friends (…) Each human being has a variety of identities, a variety of personalities in him/herself." (Morin, 2005, pp. 77–78) (Fig. 3).

Fig. 3 Multiple influences and social roles of an individual

Fig. 4 Multiple roles and influences of a hazardous activity company or facility

Fig. 5 Multiple roles of government

Likewise, hazardous industry/activity facilities play many roles, partly conflicting with one another, such as economic actor, employer, competitor, socially responsible, etc. (Fig. 4).

The same applies to the government combining several partly contradictory stakes like citizen protection, environment protection, economic development, foreign affairs, climate change, etc (Fig. 5).

With this in mind, claiming that risk communication is a pillar of risk governance and safety management assumes that risk communication stakeholders only and naturally play the social role of citizens or human beings for individuals, safety responsible for organizations and citizen and environment protection for the government. This assumption either denies the multiplicity of roles of risk communication stakeholders, i.e. oversimplifies the complexity of reality, or considers that these roles naturally align when it comes to risk communication.

Yet, such an alignment is far from being natural. Indeed, whereas people tend to look for certainties (Morin, 2001), safety, especially considered with a broader scope, carries lots of uncertainties (e.g. whether an accident will happen or not, when it will happen if at all, what will be the actual reach of its impact, etc.). Therefore, risks with more direct and certain impacts (e.g. loss of property value or public demonstrations affecting reputation or operations) are more easily and generally considered. Individuals then play the role of local resident more easily than citizen or even human being that rely on a higher level of abstraction. Likewise, organizations are managed through a set of indicators, most often short-term and certain or at least easily quantified in which safety is not always represented or does not necessarily fit, apart from the compliance with regulatory requirements that is easy to assess. The same happens at government level through the multiple roles and stakes managed simultaneously.

To this complexity of risk communication actors, adds the complexity of communication practices increased by new communication means and channels and the dramatic acceleration of pace. Interestingly, in the examples provided by the various previous chapters, the more distant an individual from the potential direct safety consequences, the more likely s/he is to adopt a social role adapted to managing the societal and global views of safety. In the Daniel case, for example, the journalist is neither a direct nor indirect victim nor related in any way to the victim except through their citizens and human beings' status. Likewise, in aviation, the bloggers or other newcomers (e.g. aviation passionate) on the risk communication scene keeping controversies alive on global issues like automation do not express themselves as potential victims directly exposed to possible associated hazards. They contribute to the debate as citizens and human beings. From these examples, it seems that being selfless, free from direct individual stakes (negative risks or positive benefits) related to a hazardous activity or facility, may help contributing to a risk communication focused on risk governance and safety management in a societal sense. To what extent can these observations be generalized? Can the number of selfless sources/actors engaging in risk communication be increased? Under what conditions can risk communication actors have a more selfless contribution to communication around risks? These are questions that still need to be investigated.

Appreciating Safety: The Challenge of Navigating Uncertainty

Eventually, beyond these challenges is another difficulty related to the concepts of risk and safety themselves. Both are closely related to uncertainty, a world most people are not so comfortable with, with no ontological status (Njå, 2017). As such, risks cannot be literally and objectively measured even though they are assessed. They are about the future, whereas loss of property value or financial results, for example, are facts and can easily be measured. "Safety is a dynamic non-event" as stated by Weick and Sutcliffe (2001). This specificity makes it extremely challenging to appreciate the level of safety of an organization or an activity or a region. Safety 'indicators' struggle to find a balance between their realism (reflecting the complexity of what actually takes place in an organization and how it contributes to safety) and easiness to handle (number of accidents—extremely rare events in already safe activities with a stochastic dimension—or incidents—with all the known drawbacks such as the non-reporting risk, etc.).

Several ways forward can be envisaged to partly overcome this challenge of navigating uncertainty. Combining all the knowledge, not only the academic and scientific one held by recognized experts but also the one held by the public, including more practical and situated knowledge and information is a way to reduce part of the uncertainty and better inform any decision. By encouraging the public to participate in radioactivity measurement, the IRSN ultimately has access to a formidable source of data that would not be accessible without involving citizens. However, uncertainty cannot be totally eliminated and talking about risks and safety in terms that everyone is comfortable with remains a challenge.

Towards More Collectively Responsible Risk Governance and Safety Management: A Matter of …

Trade-Offs

Each individual or organization or institution manages, in reality, a combination of risks, safety risks being ones among others, to come up with 'acceptable' trade-offs, 'acceptable' meaning acceptable to them. When it comes to safety though, the impacts of an accident may affect a number of parties and 'acceptable' needs to be discussed. The challenge of risk communication for risk governance in 'peace time' could be summarized in an equation:

$$\begin{array}{c}\text{Multiplicity of}\\ \text{communication actors}\end{array} \times \begin{array}{c}\text{Multiplicity of individual}\\ \text{interests for each of them}\end{array} = \begin{array}{c}\text{Common interest}\\ \text{for something uncertain}\end{array}$$

Stated this way, it seems like an impossible equation, and it may well be. Nevertheless, one can try to tend towards a common interest for something uncertain. It becomes less challenging in emergency situations where most of the uncertainty is removed and interests converge more easily towards saving lives immediately threatened.

More generally, contributing to risk governance and safety management (with a societal view of it) would require for risk communication to come up with options/decisions that would align the citizen and human-being, safety responsibility … views of all and make it an acceptable trade-off to each actor (Fig. 6). Easily said, not so easily done.

By promoting the idea that an organization should be responsible for the consequences of its decisions, the attempt of the Corporate Social Responsibility notion was to make this Socially responsible role of industries and organizations prevail over the others. In that sense, it went into the right direction despite all the shortcomings such statement may include in particular with respect to the multiple uncertainties especially related to the future. However, there is no equivalent at individual level even though similar conflicting interests exist and may lead to overlooking the safety aspects and only contemplate the benefits. The race for the lowest costs possible in many deregulated domains involving hazardous activities such as commercial aviation may ultimately have an impact on decisions related to safety. Even if the impact of an individual decision is significantly more limited than that of a company or an industry, the combination of a number of similar

Fig. 6 A required alignment of views among the various stakeholders

individual decisions may have an important weight (like it has in voting). Therefore, finding a way to give the citizen and human being roles a certain weight over the short-term consumer's one at individual level in risk communication seems an important condition to make risk communication a contributor to enhanced risk governance and safety management. Would an individual social responsibility concept make sense? How could it be implemented?

Distributed and Dynamic Information, Knowledge and Expertise

With the multiple sources of complexity mentioned earlier, governing risks and managing safety are not exact 'sciences'. Therefore, multiplying the sources of information, knowledge, perspectives is key to develop as complete a picture as possible and make it evolve as time goes by and conditions and/or knowledge evolve.

As illustrated in the previous chapters, relying on the public at large allows for having access to unprecedented data both in volume as in the case of personal radioactivity counters (Baumont, *this volume*) and in content, for example, in contextualized qualitative insights as in the Ebola outbreak (Bastide, *this volume*) or the post-Fukushima cases (Nishikawa, *this volume*). In other words, qualifying the notion of expertise and opening it to a wider understanding where several types of expertise in several domains are recognized and valued is a starting point. It allows to reach beyond the 'official' expertise and benefit from the combination of a variety of information, perspectives and expertise needed to apprehend the complexity of actual operations, hazards and the contexts (local, global, etc.) in which they take place.

Thus, the trade-offs and decisions can be contextualized, i.e. account for specificities, and be made flexible enough to be revisited when the context or knowledge evolve, making them eventually more efficient.

In addition, the contextual knowledge and expertise may also enhance the safety of daily operational or practical activities. The role played by local residents in the Paris attacks in 2015 provides an illustration of a crisis situation. But even before any event occurs, the public may play a key role. As an example, a study on medication errors showed that in 11% of the cases where patients were provided with the wrong medication, they detect it themselves and contribute to recovery before any unwanted event (Chenaud, 2011). Eventually, a wider involvement of the public allows for enhancing safety in many ways, from governance to operational practice.

Ownership and Empowerment

Some people consider the challenge of risk communication to be related to the lack of expertise in the technical field to allow for exchanges between the public, government and hazardous industries (Bouzon, 2001). They propose to focus the

Fig. 7 Common decisions being acceptable trade-offs for each stakeholder

effort on popularizing the technical and scientific elements allowing for understanding the hazards. Yet, part of the challenge may be elsewhere. Indeed, as mentioned earlier, people tend to look for certainties. Therefore, the uncertainties inherent to risk and safety make them difficult subject for most people to live with and communicate about. Beyond widening the scope of knowledge, information and expertise accessible to inform decisions, widely involving the public is also a way to give people some control over their fate (thus, to make uncertainty and risk more tolerable, see Sand, 2017) not only in the present but also in the future. Risk communication can indeed be seen not only as a contributor to managing the present but also building the future, the driving question then being: what future do we collectively want more than how to cope with today's risks? (Weick and Sutcliffe, 2015) (Fig. 7).

Conclusion

Risk communication is not naturally exclusively driven towards risk governance and/or safety management, if at all, for many reasons. First, risks and safety as understood by various risk communication actors may vary depending on the scope, time horizon and perspective considered. Therefore, the risks addressed by the ones engaging in risk communication are not necessarily focused on risk governance or safety management in a global sense, i.e. at societal level or beyond.

Second, risk governance and safety management are extremely challenging activities for they take place in a broader context where a number of objectives are competing with one another and refer to uncertain phenomena that are difficult to appreciate. A non-directive and wide risk communication as it partly takes place today in reality beyond formal information forums could become an efficient contributor to risk governance and safety management in many respects. Indeed, it would allow for widening the scope of information, knowledge, expertise both theoretical but also practical, local and cultural, thus better inform decisions and improve practice. In addition, it would give the public some control over their fate by becoming involved in risk governance and safety management rather than just being informed, thereby making risk more tolerable.

Third, individuals such as industrial or governmental actors are complex beings and bodies. They play several social roles depending on the context and their mood and permanently manage several interests partly conflicting with one another, safety being one among many others. Therefore, focusing the exchanges on safety-related matters requires a certain societal and even more global responsibility both individual, corporate and governmental to allow for useful and constructive debates to take place.

Eventually, risk communication as a pillar of enhanced risk governance and safety management is to be seen as a mutual exchange and learning opportunity whereby viewpoints are confronted, enriched and refined and people are given some control over their fate. The objective is to reveal dilemmas and eventually converge towards respectful trade-offs, thus making risk communication a deepening of democracy. Risk communication would then translate into an open co-construction of both the risk picture/safety stakes/overall context and a contributor to risk governance and safety management for the present and for the future. Trade-offs and decisions would be the result of the social negotiation and construction involved by risk communication as a driver of a global societal responsibility at all levels.

Taking the risk communication challenge and opportunities seriously is not obvious and still requires some research and experiments. It involves bringing the stakeholders, all of them, earlier in the risk governance and safety management processes. As a preliminary, it requires an analysis and mapping of all the actors that can contribute to safety, reaching beyond the usual scope. It means identifying the many people who have information, knowledge, ideas and/or are dissatisfied, and incorporating them from the outset in the risk governance and safety management development processes, and even further, in the development of technologies and industrial strategies. It also means acknowledging from the outset the various roles each of them can play.

Some initiatives are already attempting to address parts of the challenges mentioned before but do not combine them all. Addressing simultaneously all the challenges still remains to be explored … Making risk communication evolve towards this key role in risk governance and safety management—and even further—may even require some flexibility to switch from one model to another depending on the situation's requirements. Yet, citizen involvement in societal safety seems a promising way to evolve from an 'annoying people' perspective to a brighter side of wider involvement eventually enhancing safety.

References

Bouzon, A. (2001). Risque et communication dans les organisations contemporaines. *Communication et Organisation*. https://doi.org/10.4000/communicationorganisation.2548.

Chabason, L., Rankovic, & A., Bonnel, A. (2016). *Analyse| De l'expertise à l'expérimentation collective?*

Chenaud, C. (2011). Analyse des événements indésirables graves (EIG) liés au processus médicamenteux et centrés sur le patient à travers le modèle RECUPERARE, miméo, Certificate of Advanced Studies in Living with Risks, Université de Genève.

Fischhoff, B. (1995). Risk perception and communication unplugged: Twenty years of process. *Risk Analysis, 15*(2), 137–145.

Millstone, E., & Van Zwanenberg, P. (2000). A crisis of trust: For science, scientists or for institutions? *Nature Medicine, 6*(12), 1307–1308.

Morin, E. (2001). *La Méthode, 5. L'humanité de l'humanité*. Paris: Points essais.

Morin, E. (2005). *Introduction à la pensée complexe*. Paris: Seuil.

Njå, O., et al. (2017). Uncertainty—Its ontological status and relation to safety. In G. Motet & C. Bieder (Eds.), *The illusion of risk control* (pp. 5–21). Berlin: Springer.

Sand, J. (2017). What can Japan's early modern capital of Edo teach us about risk management? In G. Motet & C. Bieder (Eds.), *The illusion of risk control* (pp. 87–105). Berlin: Springer.

Schwarzinger, M., Flicoteaux, R., Cortarenoda, S., Obadia, Y., & Moatti, J. P. (2010). Low acceptability of A/H1N1 pandemic vaccination in French adult population: Did public health policy fuel public dissonance? *PLoS One, 5*(4), e10199.

Taleb, N. (2007). *The black swan: The impact of the highly improbable*. New York: Random House.

Weick, K. E., & Sutcliffe, K. M. (2001). *Managing the unexpected*. San Francisco, CA: Jossey-Bass.

Weick, K., & Sutcliffe, K. M. (2015). *Managing the unexpected: Sustained performance in a complex world* (3rd ed.). Hoboken: Wiley.

www.ingramcontent.com/pod-product-compliance
Lightning Source LLC
LaVergne TN
LVHW082337200926
848481LV00012B/3376
9781013272981